Transformational HR

Transformational HR

How human resources can create value and impact business strategy

Perry Timms

KoganPage

FOREWORD

PETER CHEESE

As many have said, we live in changeable times, and times of significant uncertainty. Political and social change, economic instabilities and the growing impact of technology and the digital world are affecting us all. The ability to adapt and to be able to take advantage of a changing context in the nature of work, the changing workforce and ways of working have become critical to business philosophy and strategy. At the heart of this is people – how they contribute, how they work together, how they create and innovate, how they are engaged, how we invest in them and how we look after them.

Some might call this business transformation, but it is at the heart of where the human resource (HR) and learning and development professions play a vital and increasingly important role to create a sustainable future of work that is good for business outcomes but also good for people. Good work is a principle the Chartered Institute of Personnel and Development (CIPD) has stood for since its inception just over 100 years ago as the Workers Welfare Association and into its current guise – championing better work and working lives. We've responded to the need for good work as a key element of a flourishing society and it is encouraging to see the debate about the principles of good work emerging more widely into business and even into policy.

Digital technology and ever-faster moving enterprises are giving us all many new challenges and opportunities. We are responding to those and promoting more adaptive practices, and growing the focus and body of knowledge for the profession around evidence, research, science of human behaviour and around the idea of outcomes and principles. There is so much opportunity, and need, for great HR in today's world but we also need to step up, to more confidently engage and challenge organizations and business leaders to improve our understanding of people, driving principles of good work and ethical practice and behaviour.

Which is why I'm delighted to present this foreword to Perry's work around a transformational HR proposition, as he calls it. I think it is very much needed, and Perry and I have collaborated, shared platforms and

PREFACE

The human resources profession

The human resources profession is a professional discipline which, according to governing bodies and institutes helps organizations thrive. In fact, the Chartered Institute of Personnel and Development (CIPD) has set out a very positive picture for this profession:

> HR is about helping an organisation to create value through its people – literally providing human resources. The work of an HR professional will vary depending on the type and size of their organisation, but could include recruiting people, training and developing employees, and helping to decide how staff should be paid and rewarded. There are even roles which focus on employment law and protecting the rights of employees at work. HR professionals will also often deal with legal issues, help to shape the culture of their organisations, and focus on what keeps their colleagues productive and engaged.

> HR gives you the opportunity to work in every sector, from media to engineering and from banks to charities as most businesses need an HR professional to help support their people management. And HR professionals work globally so the world is your oyster!

> So if you're interested in business and enjoy understanding how people work and what motivates them to perform well, a career in HR and people development could be the one for you. (CIPD, 2017)

Sounds great doesn't it? Well, not entirely. For the HR profession I know and have loved and worked within for over 15 years suffers from, what can be best described as, a *reputational deficit*.

An article in *Harvard Business Review* famously offered to share why people hated HR and what HR can do about it (Capelli, 2017). Many leaders will say that they aren't served *that* well by their HR function. Those same leaders though, may well be included in the generic group that the wider population more generally distrust (as much as they distrust politicians, lawyers and estate agents). So I could say 'people in glass houses...' but that won't get us far or change the perception or reputation of HR.

Yet HR does have an issue with its image and is often found shouting into its own *echo chamber* of how they should be given a chance to prove themselves at this fabled 'top table' destination. This is a profession in need of a confidence boost – both internally within its ranks and its reputation externally. It may still be the butt of jokes in Dilbert cartoons, where Catbert the Evil HR Director is, I'm sure, scripted from personal experiences of overbearing and oppressive HR policies.

An inflection point

Yet HR stands at an inflection point in a quite profound way – the ever dawning realization that organizations are made better or otherwise by their own people. Not just process, brand, innovation and capitalization – **their human resources are their *greatest* resources.**

Company value consists of shares, stock, market dominance, product sales and innovation. And yet, a fantastic venture can collapse quickly if the very people who got it there become the oppressed, uninspired 'resources' that HR doesn't seem to care enough about. Never mind toxic leadership, profit-only approaches to ways of working and a blatant disregard for well-being by managers and colleagues alike. HR is seen as letting these people down, of legislating in favour of a small minority of wrong-doers who bring the mood down and the compliance process regimes up. Where poor leadership is seemingly fostered by HR it causes harm to the company and the profession.

There is a realization that it's not *at all* right that a company can know and understand more about its customers and suppliers than it does its own people. And that a company reputation isn't just what it makes/serves/sells but how it does its work. Headlines surrounding poor or unfair working conditions cause as much brand damage as a faulty line of goods or shoddy services.

Bizarrely, those very conditions that tarnish HR's reputation are the very things that may cause its renaissance or even metamorphosis. Organizations that thrive because they are doing right by their own people give HR the greatest chance to do a Phoenix-like rise from the ashes of those oppressors of the human soul. Despite that, we may roll our eyes at every corporate annual report, where it states in a clichéd sense 'people really *are* the company's greatest asset', so therefore, out-of-this-world HR is what could truly create, sustain and enhance success.

The time for HR is now – and it has to be transformed and transformational

'There's never been a better time to be in HR', Peter Cheese, CEO CIPD, has declared on many occasions. Peter's passionate and unashamed promotion of *the time is now* has endeared many people I know to shift their posture and sharpen their attitude from within this oft-beleaguered profession. Whilst such a declaration is met with nodding approval, in many cases, a lack of a shift in how things are done in HR is telling. There is perhaps too much *ordinary* work to do that holds transformation work in abeyance.

Transformational HR though is, in my view, not just a programme of change or a trendy way to label an HR capability initiative. Transformational HR is a *fundamental shift* in how we look at the impact the profession can and should have on the world of work it now operates in. It would be wrong to label everything transformational – some things are more evolutionary – and yet, if what is required feels like a significant upgrade and shift in the way HR is scoped, designed, delivered and measured then it *is* transformational in that context – large or small things can have a transformative effect.

With so many businesses feeling the shifts in new markets, economic uncertainties, the surge of digital technological advancement, sciences, research and socio-political moves, it genuinely feels like there is the need for something of a renaissance in HR. I've called it an 'HR metamorphosis for a transforming world of work'.

Why would I be so confident that this metamorphosis is not only necessary but HR is capable of doing it and therefore practicing and becoming a more transformational HR function? A sense, a vigilant instinct that perhaps never before, has the 'people factor' been seen as such a key differentiator in the world of work. Philosophers, artists, politicians, scientists and innovators are all converging on the point that work – and its future – is all about people and purposeful endeavours. Looking at factors which lead to this conclusion:

It's *people* that really do make an *adventure* into a business *venture*. People who create a solid business, people who delight the very other people businesses and organizations exist for: to solve the problems their customers have – even if that problem is that they don't have the latest smartphone, handbag or pair of jeans.

Work is worth championing

Back to the CIPD and a short pivot they made in 2013 on their mission: 'Championing better work and working lives'. That says it all for an institute whose members are there to look after the people element of business, organizations and workplaces – a conscious move to distance HR from being the masters of prohibiting people processes and to make sure people no longer associate HR as the alchemists of policies and guidance, avoiding further labelling of HR as the risk averse, hammer-yielding professionals who view the entire world as one of nails (and risks). The mission represents an emboldened, business-like, humanity-enhancing aspect of work: 'Championing better work and working lives'.

About this book

This book is talking to every HR and people professional. That list includes:

- every learning pro;
- every organization development practitioner;
- every change manager;
- every communication expert;
- every coach;
- every leadership and management developer;
- every start-up entrepreneur keen to avoid the mistakes of (largely) corporate business HR, they gladly walked away from;
- every line manager and colleague of HR;
- every CEO/CXO who wants to make that line on the annual report that 'people are our greatest asset' *really* mean something; and
- everyone who cares enough about the work we all do, so that others may experience more happiness than hell.

It's time to step into a more transformational mindset, to deliver more transformational activities that lift any business to a new level of human consciousness, to put human beings to work in a liberated way as the truly new technology. It's not digital over human that will power us into the future: it's digital *and* human combined. The sooner we all grasp this opportunity, the sooner we can stop looking to bots to either destroy us or enhance us.

Two words to frame this book

And so before we step into the narrative that sets the context for this book there are two words I'd like to open with and help explain some of the thinking and research that is contained in this book.

The first word is a very business-like word: *proposition*. The word 'proposition' can be defined as:

1 A statement or assertion that expresses a judgement or opinion.

Synonyms: theory, hypothesis, thesis, argument, premise, postulation, theorem, concept, idea, statement.

2 A suggested scheme or plan of action, especially in a business context.

Synonyms: proposal, scheme, plan, project, programme, manifesto, motion, bid, presentation, submission, suggestion, recommendation, approach.

It's the noun version that I want to use for this book. The world of work is full of propositions and challenges to existing propositions. This book will very specifically zoom into a new offering, scheme and transaction that HR needs to offer for the world of work.

The other more obvious word for this book is *transformational*. This is less well defined and is an adjective attached to a range of other nouns like leadership, change and programmes. Yet the two are crucial to this book: we transform, things are transformational, our world is transformed.

So what is the HR proposition we want, need and should transform? What will transformational mindsets and activities do to the proposition we know of as HR? How do you transform a proposition anyway?

This book will look at:

- the journey to the HR of now and how have we come to the HR proposition we currently have;

- reminders for us of the progress we have made in establishing HR as a professional field and what else we might consider to transform how HR operates;

- a series of narratives and case studies which articulate the causes, approaches and opportunities for HR to be more transformational in the way it operates;

- my views as author and practitioner in this space for 15 years, of how I feel a transformational HR function could operate.

The entire premise for this book is the need for transformational HR. A fresh proposition for a more challenging world of work: that *HR metamorphosis for a transforming world of work* I mentioned.

Standing still in business has never really been an option, but running to keep pace is also now a fruitless strategy. Being a multi-disciplined heptathlete appears to be more of the sporting metaphor for HR (and other corporate) professionals of this modern, ever changing, and yes, disruptive era we find ourselves in.

So I would urge you to keep those two words in mind: *proposition and transformational*. As this book sets out to codify the new proposition for HR in order for it to become what we all need: a transformational force for good in people at work, living fulfilling lives with purposeful enterprises doing good for the world.

A higher state of working consciousness is within our grasp if we, the people, can come together to grasp it *together*. We, the people, are the algorithms of the future. We, the people, create the stories of a fiction yet to unfold.

About the rest of this book

In this book we will tell the story of work as a technology, and HR as a profession over the last 50 years, with particular attention to the last 20. Much has happened in those timeframes and this *sprint through the future* proves there is much to come, which underscores the need for a more transformational approach to HR. More specifically we will look at:

- a personal journey of working lives through the recent ages (Chapter 2);

- how the HR profession has arrived to this point in time (Chapter 3);

- what we have in the HR profession and where we can build from (Chapter 4);

- defining transformational HR – what do we mean by it? How can we be transformational? (Chapter 5);

- models that give us shape, clarity and dialogue for past, present and future work (Chapter 6);

- a model specific to HR – the Ulrich model and how it can be transformed (Chapter 7);

- tales of transformation – narratives from people working and aspiring to transform (Chapter 8);

- stories of the future – examples of organizations who have and are transforming work (Chapter 9);
- our playbook – for how HR might transform itself to create a better future of work (Chapter 10);
- strategic HR – strategic-level shifts to have a transformative effect (Chapter 11);
- transformational HR – a new model at play (Chapter 12).

We will explore what has been, and what could be for a profession at the heart of people's working lives: HR. It's perhaps the perfect time in the story of work to show *human resourcefulness* as the calling card of HR. Transformational HR could save us all from mediocre and unfulfilling work so that we, the people, can have work we can be truly proud of, and that makes a difference to all lives on this planet.

References

Capelli, Peter (accessed 20 May 2017) Why we love to hate HR...and what HR can do about it, *Harvard Business Review* [Online] https://hbr.org/2015/07/why-we-love-to-hate-hr-and-what-hr-can-do-about-it

Chartered Institute of Personnel and Development (CIPD) (accessed 20 May 2017) About HR & L&D, *CIPD* [Online] www.cipd.co.uk/new-hr-learning-development/about

LIST OF FIGURES

LIST OF TABLES

ABOUT THE AUTHOR

A chartered CIPD member, facilitator and coach, Perry has led technology-driven business change for over 25 years as a corporate head of learning, talent and OD. Perry runs his own enterprise – PTHR – aiming to transform learning and work *one conversation at a time*. Described by CIPD CEO Peter Cheese as 'The HR Futurist' Perry's energy, passion and insight around new forms of people and organization development and the future of work are his trademarks.

Perry is an international, CPD accredited and TEDx speaker on HR, technology and the future of work. Perry has delivered keynote speeches across the UK and in the USA, South Africa, the Netherlands, Poland, Romania, Slovenia, Italy, Hungary, France and Ireland.

Perry authored the e-book *HR 2025* and writes for a range of online HR and work publications and journals. In 2015, he was asked to join IBM's 'Future of Work' programme and in 2017 Perry became a part of HR software vendor Profinda's 'Workforce of the Future' community. In 2016 Perry became the world's only WorldBlu® Certified Freedom at Work consultant and coach – helping organizations be more democratic and inclusive.

Perry is a social HR Practitioner, voted a top 10 blogger in international and UK magazines. Perry is adviser to the CIPD on social media and HR – he built the institute's first MOOC 'Working digitally: social media and HR' and was a guide for the CIPD/MiX HR Hackathon.

Perry was executive consultant to 2015 HRD of the Year, Karen Beaven (River Island), and is a fellow of the *RSA* and a visiting fellow at Sheffield Hallam University.

Perry's past and present clients include Macmillan, P&G, Shelter, Sky, Toyota, Kuwait Energy, Competo, Ashridge Executive Education, Costa Cruises, Anglian Water, the NHS, Leeds City Council, ACCA and Ampelmann. Perry also leads a global community of practitioners acting as a virtual organization – the iPractice – with over 130 networked professionals from the US, South Africa, Europe and Australasia.

A tenacious reader, enthused networker and voracious learner, Perry describes himself as a 'lifeaholic' determined to 'change the world of work; one conversation at a time'.

ACKNOWLEDGEMENTS

I have been blessed in my work and life to come across inspiring and helpful people. It feels only fitting to recognize their part in my story.

Firstly, and not surprisingly, my parents, **Rita and Terry Timms**. Time after time, what they felt was right in the world centred on giving me the best chances in life. You could easily say 'that's what Mums and Dads do', yet I know I wouldn't be the person I am, with the things I have done, without the support, love and belief shown by my Mum and Dad. Thank you for being the inspiration for the journey of life and for all you gave that I can never show how truly grateful I am – I couldn't have been transformed in life were it not for you.

Secondly, and equally not surprisingly, my wife. Everyone knows her as Mrs T. **Teresa**, we've been with each other since we were 17 years old and as we head to the final stages of being 40-somethings, we are still there for each other and go through life's ups and downs, smiles and frowns. No-one could ever put up with my obsessions with Northern Soul music, Northampton Town or work like you have. It's so easy to forget that we are only what we are because of the love, backing and efforts of others. We're in the game of life together and we've made our life together a loving, strong and supportive one. I'm personally transformed because of you.

Thirdly, one of those turning point leaders in life, **Helen Dudley**. I am in HR because of your belief in me and your support to me as a mentor, friend and director. You helped me in a professional transformation that I will never forget.

Continuing with HR leaders that have inspired me – **Dianne Hughes**, as a director, as a leader, as someone who I felt proud to work with, you were like no other before nor since. I am sorry I let you down when things got tricky. I learned a lot about myself at that point in time and I went through a further professional and personal transformation.

And so it is with **Siobhan Sheridan**. As a friend, mentor, sage and believer I'm truly blessed by your life intersecting with mine. You helped me with a philosophical and spiritual transformation, and how I look at the world was changed forever by your presence in it. **Lisa Gill** you are still my work soul mate and always will be.

Transforming the world is what **Traci Fenton** is all about. You have transformed what I believe the world of work could be and should be – your work is astounding and the people you've drawn to you are amazing. You truly are transformative and I am so honoured to be working with you and all that you have created with WorldBlu.

And to my HR futures collaborator-in-chief, **Peter Cheese**. It's been a marvellous few years working and plotting together and I hope we have a few more to come where we see much of what we both dream of, comes to be.

And to Damiana Casile, Laura Smrekar, Gaylin Jee, Eugenia Dabu, Crystal Castillo, Tonja Blatnik, Christen Bavero, Carrie Brandes, Catalina Contoloru, Ana Marica, Roxana Mocanu, Karin Tenelius, Emma Burrell, Karen Beaven, Trish McFarlane, Gareth Jones, Conor Moss, Magnus Lindkvist, Barbara Thompson, Katharine Nice, Tina Novak Kac, Marta Machalska, Miranda Ash, Tom Nixon, Jon Husband, Matic Vosnjak, Louise Ash, Mervyn Dinnen, Simon Lancaster, Robert Ordever, Pete Russian, Martin Baker, Neil Usher, Lesley Giles, Debbie Carter, Gill White, Andy Swann, Dean Royles, Richard Westney, Erik Korsvik Østergaard, Andrei Dinu, Gareth Bullen, Bill Harrop, Rob Neil, Alan English, Anne Marie Rattray, Trevor Gibson, David d'Souza, Garry Ridge, Alexandra Enke, Reka Ujj, Jaana Nyfjord, Freyja Lockwood, Petra Novak, Ryan Cheyne, John McGurk, Paul Beesley, Steve Bridger, Cyrus Cooper, Cris Beswick, Luis Suarez, Andy Lancaster, Meg Peppin, Emily Garsin, Anna Shields, Meghan Keeley, Rachael Millar, Jo Swinson, Rachel McKay, Khurshed Dehnugara, Teresa Wilkins, Ian Pettigrew, Penny Haslam, Gemma Dale, Tiffany Kelly, Belinda Gannaway, Lisa Minogue-White, Elvira Kalmar, Dunia Reverter, Sara Duxbury, Joshua Vial, Steve Browne, Tim Scott, Tom Paisley, Preya Gopie, June Meehan, David James, Rowena Bach, Simon Heath, Matthew Ash, Anna Jones, Julie Towers, David Hayden, Claire Genkai Breeze, Jemma O'Reilly, Sue Evans, Andy Campbell, Dominic Cushnan, Kev Wyke, Karen Lewis, Mark Cotton, Pim de Moree, Joost Minaar, Jo Stephenson, Rob Jones, Donald Taylor, Dawn Wilde, Tania Atallah, Phil Willcox, Kate Griffiths-Lambeth, Angela Newman, Frank Douglas, Mariska Van Ijzerloo, Jo Cook, Sukhvinder Pabial, Stephanie Davies, Amanda Munday, Janine Lane, Amanda Sterling, Mat Davies, Adelaida Manolescu, Lorna Forrest, Angela O'Connor, Peter Wanless, Chloe Sowter, Saratha Shan, Linda Holbeche, Tash Pieterse, Euan Semple, Steve Toft, Helen Amery, Helen Rivero, Barry Flack, Katrina Collier, Judy Lundy, Michelle Parry-Slater, Flora Marriott, Mike Collins, Julie Griggs, Tamar Hughes, Angela Atkins, Roxana Craciun, Carina Sebastiao, Giles O'Halloran, Ciprian Arhire, Luke Thomas,

Jayne Harrison, Jason Yeomanson, Bob Wagner, Carl Erik Herlitz, Bruno Rouffaer, Ed Wesley, Diana Prodanciuc, Amanda Arrowsmith, Anna Evans, Flick Hardingham, Sarah Morgan, Christine Bamford, Rohit Talwar, Steve Wheeler, George Murga, Richard Martin, Paul Taylor-Pitt, Simon Gibson, Steve Dineen, Adam Stanbury, Matthew Syed, Travis Thomas, Paul Mudd, Henry Stewart, Mark Hendy, James Mayes, Heidi Kharbhih, Julie Bishop, Katie Marlow, Hassanah Rudd, Lisa Sarjeant, Kate Scammell-Anderson, Nick Isles, Professor David James, Gary Hamel, Paul Bennett, Lee Bryant, Myles Runham, Helen Bevan, Nathan Donaldson, Annette Jensen, Doug Kirkpatrick, Linda Barnes, Emma Price, Stephen Moir, Ger Driesen, Gerry Griffin, John Engle, Paul Green Jnr, Don Tapscott, Asia Zolnierz, Janessa Gans Wilder, Keren Elezari, Nathalie Nahai, Aaron Dignan, Stelio Verzara, Porteur Keane, Ricardo Semler, Deb Oxley, Amy Armstrong, Sam Chaltain, Paul Tolchinsky, Martyn Newman, Sabrina Bouraoui, Frederic Laloux, Matthew Gonnering, Michael Tuteur and Jos de Blok.

Inspiring, supportive, transformers – every one of you.

PART ONE
Context

Our ever changing world

Where's the hype and the hope?

Introduction

In this chapter we will codify the world as we see it and the world we may be headed towards. It is important for us that we have a grounded and yet philosophical context to frame the reasons why this book is so important, not just for the HR profession, but for all people in work now, about to be in work and who want to work. There is, as it seems with all modern forms of media, an awful lot to wade through. SINTEF – a Norwegian research institute – calculated that in 2013, 90 per cent of the world's stored and accessible information was created in the last two years (SINTEF, 2017). A common issue we hear is information overload, yet as the esteemed communication expert Clay Shirky said, 'it's a filtering issue' (O'Reilly, 2017). So this chapter is a filtered view on the world that's coming – potentially – and gives us a frame to base the rest of the book on and answer the question 'why transformational HR and why now?'.

How will this chapter transform my thinking?

- This chapter provides a sharp hype-free summary of the transforming world and world of work we're headed towards.

- It will bring thoughts together on the macro trends that are already challenging our present orthodoxies and will challenge on an ever-increasing scale.

- It will set the scene for the future world of work that HR will be operating in.

Complexity is our new norm

This book will not fix its sights on the term VUCA (a Volatile, Uncertain, Complex, Ambiguous world) and be the realization we should come to accept: that the world is more complex beyond this overused four-letter acronym. In fact, maybe nature is trying to tell us that our pursuit of control or simplification of the world is a futile act, and that complexity should be embraced and viewed as a challenging inevitable. We should view complexity in the world of work from the perspective of the *white water canoeist* rather than the *dam builder*.

The world of work does feel like it's getting more complex, pacy, divergent and difficult to keep a focused view on – we face an array of paradoxes, contradictions and challenges to conventional thinking. New disruptions from left-field thinking entrepreneurial types are challenging what we thought of as work. Scientific breakthroughs and serendipitous discoveries are shifting what we know about our bodies and our minds. Research and data-led realizations and trend mapping are giving us both a sense of prediction and a sense of bewilderment. Maybe it's because we're getting more information through our connectedness, that it feels more complex. Or maybe because the data points of the world have exponentially multiplied, we *are* more complex.

More means complex

I think it's the latter – the world is more complex. We've made it so. Twenty-five years ago there were 95 million air passengers from UK Airports, in 2005 that became 227 million and in 2015 the number was 251 million and rising (Civil Aviation Authority, 2017). We've now got around a billion apps in various formats to choose from for our mobile devices. Twenty years ago we may have had about 30 programmes we'd want to buy on CD-ROM and load on our desktop PCs.

I know these examples are more about volume (and that doesn't necessarily equate to complexity), but take that world of applications/programmes in software. When we bought boxed up software it was probably something like a customer relationship management database on a CD-ROM. It was coded, tested, released and sold in boxes. It was normally a programme that had minimal interface to other things – this may have linked to your hotmail for example. Now of course, we're in the cloud and it's *software as a service*.

We have an idea to build an app – our thinking goes like this:

- What platform is it built for?
- What design methodology shall we deploy? There's a range of those Kanban, Scrum, Agile, etc.
- What's the User Experience (UX)?
- Are we using a freemium to premium model or going for a straight subscription base?
- What Application Programme Interfaces (APIs) do we need to hardcode in from the get go?
- With the Software as a Service (SaaS) approach, do we create a user community for fixes and enhancements or do we let some people code their own improvements? If so, what's the security protocol we'd need to adopt for an open-source coding environment?

I've deliberately used the jargon I understand is used in the technology development world. Yet this was not the language of that industry used 15 or 20 years ago. Now there is not a user manual or a documented approach in sight. Instead, developers and designers can literally go into overdrive on listing the needs now compared to 20 years ago. It was the process and data management, outputs and not much else. As agile, scrum and other methodologies have improved how well we code and produce software, so the demands have become more complex and been met.

Work as a technology

It feels like work is an old technological platform trying to run a host of new dynamic apps. We're seeing crashes. We're seeing slow downs where there should be boosted productivity and performance. We're seeing *blue screen of death data dumps* when we just can't take it anymore and our own mental RAM gives way.

Computing power has literally become the world's business force. Take a look at the most valuable companies and four out of the top five are technology companies. The pharma and banking companies still hold some of the coveted top 10 in the Fortune 500 but, the technology companies are coming (Gandel, 2017). The fastest rising (in value and revenue) are all coming from the silicon brigade and no longer the oil or sales brigade.

Regardless of whether you believe in 'unicorns' – start-ups valued at over $1 billion – the smarter money appears to be flooding towards technology ventures and less to traditional industries. So the world is more complex *and* digital and we'd just better get used to it and it's unlikely any of us will be able to simplify it or stop the rise of digital anytime soon.

Whether it's algorithmic news, fake news or real news, we're all seeing a web-like mess of interconnectedness. The financial meltdown of 2007/2008 was a little like previous downturns but its impact was wider, as the markets were all now so interconnected. Joshua Cooper Ramo's outstanding work in the book *The Seventh Sense* gives us a network-related view on this new world we're in (Ramo, 2016). Instant news, 'infobesity', as coined by Magnus Lindkvist, and a post-truth world where expertise and facts are eschewed and we find ourselves in a whole new public relations and reputational ball game.

I could dominate these pages with accounts on the world but for brevity, below is a quick spin into our complex world as it impacts on our working lives.

Technological breakthroughs

Artificial intelligence, automation, robotics and autonomous vehicles; 3-D and 4-D printing, ubiquitous connectivity, e-commerce and e-transactions; machine learning, virtual reality and augmented reality; nano-technology, bio-medical technology and cyber and unmanned warfare machines; blockchain and crypto-currencies. I'm doing these outrageously advanced technologies a gross disservice by simply listing them and, yet again, this book could become overtaken by these factors alone. In a transformational HR sense, digital technologies in itself is a transformation topic all of its own. This book will not set out what that is, yet it is recognized just how much digital technology will influence business and HR transformation in the coming years.

Socio-political changes

Displaced people, economic migration, movement of people for work and a shifting need to import talent to arrest declining birth rates, presents a paradoxical challenge to those who feel their lives aren't improving as a result of this – market forces are letting them down. This has given rise to xenophobia, prejudice and more far-right mentalities being shared and conscripted to. That people feel so rejected by a socio-political system impacts work and lower skilled and lower paid work may come even more under threat with robotics and migration, therefore people are lashing out at the political model that is failing to provide them with a standard of living. Most importantly the political system appears to be robbing people of hope.

Trickle-down, neo-liberalism is failing to talk to those who it was supposed to benefit the most and work has a huge part to play in managing the impact of this reaction. Where people can earn a secure living, with meaningful work that sits alongside decent education, justice and health care, a community thrives. Fiscally independent, educationally enriched, safe and well – fundamental human needs and some might say, rights. Work has had major impacts on lives in this way, forming communities around coal mining, steel or manufacturing – these communities have been torn apart when the labour force disappears. People's sense of not only financial value but their esteem in the world suffers and is often irreparably damaged.

The biggest issues we are likely to face over health in the 21st century are obesity and mental illness. Yes, cancers and other diseases are still big spectres on our health horizon, but we're literally convenience-food-eating and stressed-out-worrying ourselves into earlier demise.

Economic shifts

Power to the east – China and India particularly – and a rising middle-class in areas that were previously malignant for capitalist growth. This has seen traditional world economic powerhouses struggle with debt, deficits and failed fiscal policies. Pensions crises and failing state reforms to working opportunities see the rise of gig working, and a race to the bottom in the case of depressed wage growth and a growing wealth inequality.

It's not just shifts as in geographies but in commodities that people want to invest in. What money is there to actually invest? Reading everything from Raj Sisodia to Thomas Picketty and Paul Mason will show you there's real challenges to the capitalist, largely Americanized way of business and world economics. The value of what we value changes and capital isn't considered the only form of value anymore.

Ageing and overpopulation

To offset some declining birth rates in the western world we are still seeing an increasing population as we're all living longer. Famously, Aubrey De Grey predicts someone alive reading this book will live to be 200 years old and that death is a disease we can arrest through advances in biotechnology to counter the effects of ageing (De Grey, 2005). The 100-year life is a real thing that we are grappling with now, as we realize our pensions policies were crafted in an age where people lived into their late 50s and now work until their mid-70s. Is there enough land, food, water and air to breathe in the world of 2030 and 2050? Colonizing Mars doesn't seem quite as hokey as it once did.

Education and new skills

We are still surprisingly traditional in our approach to schools and higher education. With lectures and study programmes built for the industrial era, the model has received many challenges – most notably from Sir Ken Robinson. Indeed, the World Economic Forum has given us some indication of what the skills of the future look like – and many of them don't appear to exist in school curricula (World Economic Forum, 2017). It's traditionally the workplace that gives these skills a boost but by then, are we missing out on people becoming active members of the working population, because we've denied them these skills in favour of more traditional academic disciplines? It looks like there's room for more of this on the school timetable:

Table 1.1   World Economic Forum: the 10 skills you will need for the future

Complex problem solving	Critical thinking
Creativity	People management
Coordinating with others	Emotional intelligence
Judgement and decision making	Service orientation
Negotiation	Cognitive flexibility

SOURCE https://www.weforum.org/agenda/2016/01/the-10-skills-you-need-to-thrive-in-the-fourth-industrial-revolution/, Alex Gray (2016)

These and more will be needed alongside living the digital lives we now have and crucially the differences in the way we behave towards each other online – not to mention the cyber security and protection to keep us, and the things we value, safe.

Approaches to life

We really could be in a post-materialistic world. Where things we would normally own become a service we merely rent, lease or consume for no cost. This could mean everything from the transport we take, to the digital devices we use and even the clothing we wear. Not to mention that this will all become connected so the data we create through our usage will inform and channel the goods and services we have most when we need them. We could be in an abundant and entirely different model of consumption which leads to questions about economics. That some people are even talking about Universal Basic Income is an entirely radical shift from the traditional acquisition of wealth and stuff to live by. Small housing, tiny living and the slow movements are coming into our lives as antidotes to hyper-stressed, pointless ways of crafting a living. Never underestimate the power of a movement that restores humanity, care and productive behaviours, simply because it revokes the ingrained disciplines our previous generation were used to. People over profit? Care over capital? Inclusivity over exploitation? It could be our way in the near future of work and life.

The Fourth Industrial Revolution

It is a bold and even courageous claim by forecasters, analysts and leaders that we are in the midst of a tectonic shift in our industry model and therefore life model. Klaus Schwab and the World Economic Forum are proclaiming that this is as big a shift as we saw in the 1800s and then previously through the Age of Enlightenment (Schwab, 2017).

Yuval Noah Harari, in his book *Sapiens: A Brief History of Humankind*, did much the same and the 'lost' art of anthropology becomes *en vogue* once more (Harari, 2015). We are a sentient species with a pattern from history and aspirations for the future and once you decode the tribalism and understand our most destructive tendencies, you can also see our most advanced civility and creativity.

We most likely are in the middle of the eye of the storm. And when you are, it's easy to deny, dismiss or decry this as hyperbole. It's also – history tells us this – when those denial-based challengers are ironically acting as proof that we *are* in the midst of huge changes. For deniers and naysayers, sceptics and antagonists are normally there out of fear. And of course some high form of intellect based on old mathematics and computation, and a genuine rubbishing of experts who are simply calling out patterns and trends because they're there and telling us something.

So we ignore the call that we are in the middle of a quantum shift at our peril. Yet we can retain critical thinking and avoid panicked rejections or over-exuberant alliances, as we explore and learn our way into a genuinely new shift that affects all our lives.

Environmental concerns and consumption of planetary resources

Again, deniers aplenty to the damage and destruction being caused on natural resources and our wildlife and ecosystems. Yet, we see polar ice caps melting, higher average temperatures year-on-year and convulsive weather system mutations. Yes, the earth has a history of shifting climates but this appears to be undeniably fast, and causal trail is pretty clearly pointing to our engineering.

That so many scientific figures and now business leaders are caring about the world we live on is telling. Corporate Social Responsibility was an attempt to get carbon use on the boardroom agenda and use reputation capital to force some reductions and compliance.

We now know that it can be more economical to build and use your own wind turbine. That waste is the war we should all be raging on, and that this planet cannot repair itself at the rate we are using its natural resources. With a forecasted 10 billion people on the planet as imminent, we really need to think about water, greenhouse gases and create a surge in use of clean, green and renewable energies.

Will solar power drive us to zero cost for energy use? *Possibly.*

Are Governments reliable enough to steer this agenda? *Probably not.*

Business has a huge responsibility to ethically treat the planet, the people of the world and the consumers of its goods/services and not just service the markets and shareholders.

A decade is a long time in HR or anywhere

If I were to write this book even 10 years ago, we'd likely be talking of the power of the internet to speed up transactions and maybe not much else. We knew about planetary concerns then but saw no way to decouple ourselves from use of fossil fuels. We didn't even know much about any structures for businesses other than the traditional scaled hierarchy. Now we have thousands of variations of business model, business structure and ways of working. It's a world where the sun never sets and globalization is more prominently the model than ever before.

So many things have changed and taken a foothold that we have a term for this rise – the exponential curve. Salim Ismail and others put a strong case together based on Singularity University's own research and study of Ray Kurzweil's Law of Accelerating Returns that it has become the new norm. Quite literally, the world's businesses all want to be Usain Bolt.

Conclusion

Returning to HR for a second, HR's current proposition was built for (at best) mid-1990s businesses and has done very little to reshape itself entirely since then. Sure there are outliers and challengers (and they will feature in this book) yet the basic model of HR is a servant to the organization around the people in its employ. HR involves:

- codifying human endeavour into job descriptions;
- building reward structures based on some from of secret algorithm;
- recruitment and hiring to get the best person possible who fits the description despite being subject to biases;
- development and career progression that can favour extrovert over expert; and
- exits and *right-sizing* routines.

It's perhaps time for an ideological revolution in the way we look after people that will begin to matter to organizational sustainable success. It's time for the 'human' in 'human resources' to really mean something.

Three key transformational HR takeaways and reflective questions to consider:

1 In appreciating how interconnected the world is, we can see how everything has an impact on the world of work.

Q: What are the trends that may transform the nature of your work?

2 Where we found new things to think about in this opening chapter, there is a sense of activated interest towards those trends and factors.

Q: What has this chapter made you want to know more about and identify where to find a rich source of insight?

3 We can appreciate there are unknown elements yet to come to light, yet we can see that certain skills are going to be more useful to us in the future.

Q: What are the skills you now feel are of increased need for you and those you work with?

References

Civil Aviation Authority (accessed 20 May 2017) [Online] https://www.caa.co.uk/Data-and-analysis/UK-aviation-market/Airports/

De Grey, Aubrey (accessed 20 May 2017) A Roadmap to End Aging, *TED* [Online] https://www.ted.com/talks/aubrey_de_grey_says_we_can_avoid_aging

Gandel, Stephen (accessed 20 May 2017) These are the 10 most valuable companies in the fortune 500, *Fortune* [Online] http://fortune.com/2016/02/04/most-valuable-companies-fortune-500-apple/

Harari, YN (2015) *Sapiens: A brief history of humankind*, Vintage, London.

Lindkvist, Magnus (accessed 20 May 2017) 'Magnus Lindkvist on the trends that matter', Lloyds Banking Group, 01/02 [Online] https://resources.lloydsbank.com/insight/gameplan/magnus-lindkvist-on-the-trends-that-matter/

Kurzweil, Ray (accessed 5 July 2017) 'The law of accelerating returns', Kurzweil.net [Online] http://www.kurzweilai.net/the-law-of-accelerating-returns/

O'Reilly Media (accessed 20 May 2017) 'Web 2.0 Expo NY: Clay Shirky (shirky.com) It's not information overload. It's filter failure' [Conference Video]. [Online] www.youtube.com/watch?v=LabqeJEOQyI

Ramo, JC (2016) *The seventh sense: Power, fortune, and survival in the age of networks*, Little Brown Company, London

Schwab, Klaus (accessed 20 May 2017) 'The Fourth Industrial Revolution: what it means, how to respond', World Economic Forum, 14/01 [Online] https://www.weforum.org/agenda/2016/01/the-fourth-industrial-revolution-what-it-means-and-how-to-respond/

SINTEF (accessed 20 May 2017) 'Big Data, for better or worse: 90% of world's data generated over last two years', *Science Daily*, 22/05 [Online] www.sciencedaily.com/releases/2013/05/130522085217.htm

World Economic Forum (accessed 20 May 2017) 'These are the 10 skills you'll need in the workplace by 2020' [Online] https://www.youtube.com/watch?v=ssH70sK07AI&feature=youtu.be

Today's work   02

How have we got to this?

Introduction

In this chapter we look back just as we've teased you by looking ahead – and that is a deliberate and very conscious thing. We are where we are and for some of us, looking back at our (perhaps painful) journey to the HR of now might not make exciting reading. Yet it is vital that we uncover and unravel just how we have come to this. Before we transform HR, we should, arguably, look at the 'ghost of HR past' and perhaps we can look to exorcize the ghost of the HR past that may seriously hamper our transformational HR future.

How will this chapter transform my thinking?

- This chapter will remind us of the journey to the HR of now in order to not repeat the same mistakes and overcome the shortcomings we have experienced to date.
- It will allow us to put distance between the failings of our past endeavours by understanding what this leads us to in the future.
- It will help us honest about our past to help us unlearn and relearn what could become our new signature strengths.

A short journey into the past

The world of work has changed a lot over the last 30 or so years. I've been in the workforce since 1985 – a pretty sobering thought. When I joined the workplace, there were no computers on desks, no mobile phone distractions and pens and paper ruled the office. It is, in the grand scheme of things, a blink of an eye, and yet so much has changed and not all for the better.

As this chapter was conceived, in an earlier draft, I had a very academic and almost dry version of how we got to where we are now. Here is the confessional – I then realized, many of us know this already, it's featured in a lot of other books and talks about our world of work so I'd like to use this chapter to tell a story about two generations of work: mine and my parent's generation if you will. To some people, this covers grandparents, parents and themselves but anyway, roughly two generational swipes of the historical timeline (from my perspective) as told through the lives of a small town family from the United Kingdom.

Work as it was

Our story starts in 1959. June was one of 10 children, the oldest female in a family where the father figure had left leaving only her mother, Frances, to look after the youngsters. June had therefore become an assistant Mum.

Brackley was their home, a small town in Northamptonshire, a nice town, where people knew each other and where every Monday–Friday a few buses took a lot of people into the centre of Northampton to work in the shoe factories there. Northampton was famous as the shoe making town for the UK and beyond. The British Boot & Shoe Corporation (BBSC) was the nationalized industry that brought together a range of shoe makers and formed a large production line of footwear quite literally worn by the many millions of people up and down the country. That Northampton's football league team is nicknamed *the Cobblers* is a further tribute to the town's shoemaking story.

It was at the BBSC factory in Northampton that June met Roly. Roly was a jack-the-lad from another part of the county (Raunds) and he too was shipped in by a different bus each day.

Roly spotted June across the factory floor and made a beeline for her. He knew her birthday was coming up and she was having a party so he invited himself and said he would buy her a nice bracelet as a gift. He didn't, but came to the party anyway. June and Roly started to date (or court as it was probably known in the 1950s) and soon, June and Roly would catch the same bus to Brackley together where she would get home, cook tea for her brothers and sisters still at home (seven of them) and Roly became a part of the family.

Shoe making – that nationalized industry under the British Boot & Shoe Corporation banner – was typical of Britain of the post-war, NHS established state. Many industries – coal, cars, water, electricity, gas, rail, health, education, steel and shoes – were nationalized. Everything was British *something* and it was a model where the running costs came from taxation and the profits from those corporations went into the government coffers. Things were notoriously under-invested in but nonetheless many millions of people in the UK worked in some shape or form for the nation. It wasn't communism but it certainly wasn't free markets like we see today.

A new beginning

June and Roly eventually got married and moved to Northampton. A small flat on the Kettering Road was their starter home and they had less of a commute to work now and could even walk to the factory.

Roly's work at the factory ended when he started his amateur boxing career again. He needed something with more labour involved and whilst he liked the static environment of being a 'clicker' (a highly skilled aspect of shoemaking), he wanted something more physically exerting. After a short stint as an odd-jobber with a local bathroom fitments merchant (found through his working men's club contacts), he then worked for Logans as a contractor working for British Gas in pipelines and gas mains: leakages, new installations and the like. A big yellow lorry was now his mode of transport and a role with diesel, tar and oil stains and smells every time he returned home became the new norm. How June got his work clothes clean via a twin-tub washer is anyone's guess – this was all pre-tumble dryer norms.

June still worked at BBSC in the centre of Northampton, making ladies shoes. The factory was a five floor building. Smocks and aprons were the work attire and the household was never short of rejected pairs of shoes which couldn't be sold but had only minor defects so were OK for workers to use.

By this time, Matthew had been born and was a studious, nine-year-old boy. Having to sometimes go and meet his Mum at the factory, he was used to fending for himself to get to school with friends and to both his parents working to make ends meet. Those ends included a nice council-rented home, decent clothes and a family holiday once a year to Hopton-On-Sea or Weston-Super-Mare. Caravans were a fun retreat for two weeks of the year with cousins and family around. Roly's work lorry came in handy for lifts to and from football games for his middle school, so Matty had some good friends who occasionally joined him in the lorry's cab to get a lift home.

June's sister became a senior forelady at the factory and this was the first time anyone Matty knew wore a white coat instead of a blue or green smock. June's sister was signing off time sheets, moving the work around and generally having some responsibility for decisions – management.

Power struggles – the workers united

During this period, several events occurred which had an impact on work. Strikes by energy sector workers left many power stations unable to stay working and power cuts were regular. Candles at home, heating by coal fires, kettles boiled on gas stoves – not quite the blitz that June and Roly endured from afar but still, weirdly adventurous. Industrial disputes seemed to be a daily occurrence and Matty didn't really understand why. It seemed the workers had a beef with the government and this strange word – conciliation – kept cropping up in news reports.

British Leyland seemed the worst afflicted. Always on strike at the Allegro and Princess factories, it seemed to single handedly give Ford and Vauxhall an advantage.

The 1970s were blighted by this and the price of oil seemed to unfathomably spike causing crises and the famous 'Winter of Discontent' appeared to be the final straw when council binmen went on strike and refuse piles built up across the country. It seemed that enough was enough and in 1979 the hapless Labour Government were ousted by Margaret Thatcher's Conservative Government.

Changing economies

June and Roly had *always* voted Labour and so this was an interesting period in many ways for not only them personally, but the entire country.

Privatization is probably the biggest sweeping change brought under the Thatcherism agenda. Those nationalized industries were broken up and sold off, including rail, energy and certainly shoes. The British Gas contractual arrangements with Logans saw Roly transfer over to the new Pipedyne Construction Ltd. The word redundancy though, became *much* more prevalent in this decade than at any time before. Some people Roly worked with weren't offered roles in the new company. Even BBSC was handing out redundancies as the new American-backed Fortuna company took over the shoe factories. British Rail was broken up and a plethora of train companies awarded contracts to run the trains up and down Britain's railways.

And then the miner's strikes. Arthur Scargill's adversarial standoffs and his almost Lenin-like speeches seemed beyond Matty's comprehension – why the coal mines were being shut down and people being 'laid off' (another regular and new term) wasn't something Matty understood. It didn't sound good though. This all came to a head with rolling disputes, flying pickets, battles with the police and a kind of industrial relations war was quite literally on our hands. Thatcher won of course, and many communities still bear the scars and the hurt and the despondency of those days.

Northampton (and Matty's parents) hadn't been truly affected by any of this and then, due to failing health (arthritis), June was encouraged to stop using her hands to machine shoes. June activated her own network – the former personnel manager of the factory was working at the large supermarket chain in the town and June went to work on the night shift, looking after the health and beauty aisles.

June consulted and took advice from a pensions expert on moving her BBSC pension – something she highly regarded from almost 30 years of service. She moved to a private provider of pensions and this proved to be a terrific decision. The British Boot & Shoe Corporation's overseas owners were allegedly asset stripping the workplace pensions to keep the company afloat and this all came to a head when the factories were shut, people were laid off and then told they'd lost their pensions. Court battles and worse happened as we saw another example of conflict on a wide scale between worker and workplace. The shoe industry – like the coal industry and many others – disappeared almost overnight. Cheap imports were to blame. That and poor management practices and clearly company governance.

The knowledge economy

By now, Matty had left school after sixth form and decided the shoe industry and gas pipeline industry weren't really for him (indeed a two-week work experience stint on the gas pipelines proved to be a deal breaker in Matty using his head not his hands). He worked at the Government Valuation Office as a civil servant. He joined at the lowest level – a clerical assistant but endowed with enthusiasm, drive and a decent amount of intellect he started to shine.

June was now in retail support, Roly in energy and Matty in the Civil Service. Many of Matty's school mates were working at Barclaycard (a big presence in Northampton), Nationwide Anglia Building Society (another big presence), Avon Cosmetics, estate agents, in teaching, in insurance and more. Not many of Matty's school friends were able to work in the now defunct shoe industry and more of his friends found themselves in shirts and skirts in offices in towns and cities. One or two joined the fire service and the police force.

Roly carried on working at various contractors to the gas industry as more of this infrastructure and supply was sold off to become more 'competitive' and market-force led. He retired with a small cash handshake and took June on a cruise.

June had retired long before that. Arthritic pain got the better of her. She loved the job in the store but it had to go on an early retirement basis. June's protected pension still serves her to this day but many of her former friends and relatives had to start all over again in a range of different industries. Her brother Roy still works in the shoe industry for a luxury Italian owned brand – he's the last survivor of those nationalized days.

The winds of technological change

Matty rose to a junior management position in the Valuation Office. He eventually transferred to a larger department (The Land Registry) and worked on information technology projects converting paper records to computerized records. He remembers his first occasion with personal computers from his sixth form – 1984 – and a computer room at the school became something of intrigue to him. Sure Matty had played Space Invaders and Asteroids but he wasn't at all a computer geek. He learned a little basic coding but he wasn't that taken by it. Computers in the workplace in 1990/91? A totally different feeling.

Matty worked on several small and large scale projects involving national initiatives and he quickly became adept at training and helping others get to grips with technology. He became a trainer through some coaching from an external consultant and wrote user guides, built courses and became a sought after resource on many computerization initiatives.

By now, Matty had a whole new group of work friends and some were independent contractors – how brave and bold to run yourself as a tiny business amongst all these huge companies and government organizations. Matty shuddered at the thought of being a hired hand. How dangerous and tricky must that be if no-one wants to hire you? Daniel was one who taught him a lot and seemed to do well on it with clients all over the UK and a nice Vauxhall Calibra on his drive.

Working in government at this time was considered to be a good if not slightly parochial way of earning a living. Civil servants didn't earn as much as their private sector counterparts and often came under fire for being jobsworth and not efficient. Efficiency drives were the order of the day and much of this was where computerization came in to reduce the headcount and make for more efficient processes.

Matty was trained in PRINCE2 at this time – a hugely popular project management methodology. He spent many an hour on WordPerfect 5.1 crafting manuals, guides, overviews, product definitions, project documents and business cases. So good at WordPerfect did he become that his IT colleagues urged him to take the test to see if he could become an analyst programmer. Matty passed and he was taken into a project coding role. He hated it, he wasn't built for this. So he stuck it out for a while but was relieved when he got to lead a massive records centralization project for payments from local offices.

It was the first project in government that featured an all-new thing by the John Major Government of the day – a Private Finance Initiative (PFI) contract with a tech provider SFD. Some of his friends transferred over to the winner of the PFI competition and he found himself working in an entirely different bureaucracy where money for services became an entirely new element to working together. 'Ooh that change is going to cost you' became a daily conversation. Loads more contractors seemed to come and go and this new form of fluidity became a norm. Elaine, his boss, hadn't moved over to them and was now 'contract managing' her former colleagues. It was really different she told him. All of a sudden bureaucracy became rife.

Matty worked on this project and through some great support, brought the project in on time and under budget so something went well. Matty later went on to lead the national implementation of this and office managed the new centralized unit. It was tough and he had to put in long hours and applied leadership, but he turned it into a real success. Success that meant Matty was moved into a London-centred national programme roll for the entire England and Wales Land Registry. Matty became a fully fledged project worker. Roles that no-one really knew what they were (Stakeholder Manager?) and work that was massive at times and intricate at others. New language with this role included 'business models', 'technological disruption' and 'process re-engineering'. Brown paper on office walls and post-it notes became a regular thing, and events, summits and speaking at conferences became part of Matty's world.

Boom and bust economics

The dot com boom was over and the recession hit with a massive budget cut – all of a sudden, Matty's work was pulled, literally overnight. Sure he was moved into other areas and some people did take the 'R' package (redundancy) and some were shipped over the HM Revenue and Customs and the Department for Work and Pensions. Matty stuck with it but there were leadership changes and all wasn't good. Luckily, the Department had invested in management and leadership development and Matty had bene-fited from much of this. He had approached and become mentored by the Director of HR and Learning. At one mentoring session, he was sharing his disillusionment with the current ways of working and being led and the mentor offered a way out – a job in her division (HR). Matty leapt at the chance.

Project and team leadership and running the learning and development patch for the South East of England and being part of a progressive HR programme of change, Matty became pretty enamoured by this world and went on his own personal learning rampage picking up a range of new disciplines like coaching, neuro-linguistic programming and business part-nering skills. He was in a really sweet spot. Matty quickly joined forces with colleagues to create new performance management routines and introduced some more progressive leadership development.

It was this that came to the attention of a senior HR manager who had been and gone from the department but was now working in a research institute in the not-for-profit sector. When he head-hunted Matty to lead his new workforce development function it felt like professional cred-ibility in HR had been achieved. Taking on massive change, building new talent development programmes and working with the CIPD on a research programme all led to Matty getting to talk at conferences, to help other connected organizations and to become known as a different kind of practitioner. Like many people in 2008, the great recession had an impact and this previously pioneering institute contracted. It wasn't so innovative anymore and didn't seem to regard Matty's abilities in that way. Matty became disillusioned and by taking on too much work from others and being over-involved in projects of all types he lost his mojo, made mistakes and resigned.

Enterprise and entrepreneurial ways

Matty then joined that freelancer world he'd first come across some 20 years before. Armed with a good network and equipped with a decent reputation, he set about making his own way. Matty has now taken on international clients, is a reputable organization development practitioner and coach, and is known for his new thinking in changing company approaches to the ways of working. Matty is now committed to his new venture and remains focused to making his mark in the world through being a freelancer with strong views on his profession and the world of work. Matty has seen how much the world has shifted and how unpredictable and volatile it is for **all** people in work – mergers, failures and 'right-sizing' programmes have made all work vulnerable and there's probably more fear in the world of work than previously known.

So if there's not even security in large organizations or supposedly safe companies, then being on your own, nimble and adaptable may be the new way. No state-owned factories, no government agencies. Whether it's choice or necessity, being in self-employ is a growing model and might just be the way the majority of us will be. Matty is happy with his lot, fluctuating income and all. June and Roly still have no real idea what it is he does but are proud of their son's exploits still.

Conclusions

So, an everyday fable of two generations of workers – from Britain of the 1960s through to the present day. What does this fable tell us though? Let's just do a quick decode:

1 **Educational attainment has increased**. More people going to and coming out from university with degrees. In June and Roly's era, only the most privileged went on to get a degree. Many people in the 1960s and 1970s were working in manual labour type roles in production lines and factories – not much need for degrees.

   In Matty's era it was more commonplace but still not for the majority of his friends. More knowledge work was emerging through the 1970s and into the 1980s and Matty was a part of this shift. Yet into the 1990s and 2000s it proliferated even further. Is this enough for the future and a world where transformational HR has become a shaper of the working proposition of the future? 'No' is the simplistic and rather sad response. We're better educated, but it feels like it needs a shift to be a really powering force in the world we now see Matty operating in.

2 **Factories are no longer the predominant working environment**. OK, Elon Musk is building some in the US and there's still big car plants all over the world but increasingly a lot of the jobs in these places are now robot arms and machines. The bottom must've slowly fallen out of the smock and apron world (except for the ones in coffee shops sported by hip Baristas). I've heard some offices referred to as 'white collar factories' which gives me a sense of less dirty 'dark satanic mills'. Offices are the ubiquitous working space but of course, they are also being challenged now by co-working spaces and coffee shops. We will look at HR's role in transformational workplace design at a later juncture in this book,

but clearly what we call a workplace now is a range of things other than factories or shop floors.

3 **Employers are mostly for profit.** We've seen the sell offs of nationalized industries in the UK as a good thing for market competitiveness to drive up standards and service levels. And costs and profit-making, subsidized incentivizing. In June and Roly's era, a **lot** of people worked for the State. In Matty's era this was in decline at the start of his working life and has become a smaller percentage year-on-year. Matty is now an example of what will probably be the dominant force – freelancers. They will be for profit (not many freelancers are registered not for profit) yet they will rarely do more than make ends meet. Many freelancers plough all their revenue (and even go into debt with financiers either of the banking or venture capital variety) and will be non-profit for years. Therefore the majority of employers will be for-profit, followed by nationalized or governmental then not-for-profit and then the freelancing 'get by' sector specializing in 'just enough' economics.

4 **Pensions are a challenge.** In June and Roly's age, if you were lucky you got a workplace pension; then in Matty's era, it was a given for employers to offer it and now is a compulsory UK piece of legislation. In an attempt to minimize the crippling burden on state funds – where the modelling was for more people to die younger, now we're all living longer. The predicted life of leisure was built on the premise that we'd have more time on our hands and be independently financed by our set aside investments. These have either been raided by failing corporates, devalued by failing markets or ignored by people desperate to use all the money they have immediately.

5 **Development at work raises the bar.** We've seen through Matty's story how, because he was invested in by his governmental and not-for-profit experiences, his level of capability rose and he became a viable market in himself because of this increased and enhanced knowledge and ability. What we also see is that at times of hardship, this gets immediately culled and costs justified to the point of bureaucratic debarment of the very thing that might get you back up to a costs/income ratio of positives. June and Roly were given enough training to do what they did proficiently. As we move into more automated routines for the mechanical aspects of work and therefore to more complex tasks and problems to be solved by us humans over the robots, then we HAVE to see development as a necessary not a tolerated existence.

6 Career progression helps align personal esteem and achievement with company commitment and success. June and Roly never experienced any career progression of sorts although Roly's success in moving to 'clicker' proved there was a pathway even in the factory world. June's sister as a forelady meant she had progressed into a management role and felt like she'd accomplished something which then was wedded to increases in accountability and power. In Matty's world, this saw him rise to levels of management in the Civil Service and in the HR industry. Now, in his free-lance role, he's responsible only for himself whilst helping clients by using his networks and knowledge accrued. As more companies hollow out their middle (a resourcing strand deemed unnecessarily large and expensive), this route may be denied to others and indeed the entire pathway system might be negated by flatter and more agile company structures. Career progression was a somewhat visible success feature yet also was the only choice for many people. Choices have now changed and expertise, adaptability and portability are utilized in different ways other than upwards, linear progress.

7 Organizational design and change became a regular thing. In June and Roly's era, the design of a company was probably the same when they started to when they left. It was hierarchical and with a standardized approach to research; finance; operational and HR. Now the predominant appears to be the fluid, adaptive state. So we're much less likely to see ourselves at the lower rungs of organization design and more as part of interconnected but responsible nodes in a network.

So how did we get to this?

Well the industrial model begot the factory model and then this was then disavowed in favour of the creative/knowledge/work model. We got to this through the de-nationalization agenda and to and market forces economy model. Which is a really trite way of short circuiting a **huge** amount of socio-political change. The Cold War ended, Germany reunited, Communism pretty much evaporated, and the oil and gas dependency created wealth from the Arab world. A rebuilt Japan became (temporarily) a dominant world market force and then not so much again. The United States largely rode this storm to still be the number one economy in the world and China rose as an economic superpower to challenge the US's dominance.

But how did we get to here?

The brief timeline (around June and Roly's start in working life) goes somewhat like this:

1959 – the personnel model (a personnel function and manager to oversee the hiring of new labour and conformity with newly crafted employment rights) was the guiding force for people matters. Placing advertising in job centres and newspapers, preparing interview panels and papers, working on employment contracts, and the payroll and pensions function became essential components of the personnel team. June and Roly were hired in this way and their eventual exits were also handled by this team.

1970s–1980s – During the 1970s and into the 1980s there is no doubt how prominent the industrial relations factor became in both handling and resolving disputes, and knowing the law and rules for dismissal and punitive measures. Employment law really shaped the 1970s and 1980s. Until the Thatcher era which effectively broke the power base of the Unions and brought more market force mentality to the workplace. By this time, the US models of performance management, performance related pay, a range of benefits and a highly competitive strain to work as a performance enhancer were becoming dominant. Ironically the successful Japanese working model adopted a lot more uniformity and hierarchical reverence whilst treating workers in an equal manner. Famous physical workouts (pre-manufacturing shift) were seen as radical ways to energize people to outperform. Training and development were beginning to feature beyond mere compliance measures and into the realms of managing and understanding people. When Matty entered the workplace it was already an established practice that personnel handled 'those people matters'.

The 1990s – During the 1990s a more sophisticated human resource management model had come through. With more people development and more sophisticated techniques to get more from people – let alone the advent of more information technology gave us an expanded range of considerations. Psychometric testing and assessment were beginning to be normalized and the qualities of leadership really started to proliferate in journals and development programmes. The odd recession/crash didn't really help but the continued privatization of the service world gave way to more profit-chasing edge. Matty found himself now being part of recruitment panels, was a health awareness officer and then eventually found himself as a fully fledged part of that function as a training professional.

The new millennium – Through to the 2000s and personnel really was dead. HR was ubiquitous and the HR business partner role and three-legged stool of University of Michigan's Professor Dave Ulrich had taken hold of virtually all HR functions in the western world. More on this in later chapters but there was an attempt to get HR's function from administration and servicing things like payroll and learning to being a much more progressive function and resource in itself. Change management became an industry and an almost constant restructuring role, HR found itself in more designing and calibrating exercises at organizational level. Mergers and acquisitions became even more prominent as did redundancies and complexities around employment law, fairness legislation and equality of opportunity. Employee engagement became a thing and an indexed number, and all sorts of 'awesome place to work' accolades found themselves at the awards ceremonies up and down Park Lane hotel ballrooms.

Where do we go next?

We find ourselves now, in 2017, with a range of different models and a business that compared to 1959 when June and Roly entered the workforce, is barely recognizable.

The next chapter will talk us through the more detailed version of this situation we find ourselves in and illuminate a range of choices taken by the world of work, organizations and leaders, and the HR profession itself which has either given it a place of eye-rolling discord or a role of significance and prominence in building a thriving organization as a workplace of repute and effectiveness. It's more fascinating than most people would give it credit for and yet there still remains so many unfulfilled potential gains and promises to make that could give the world of work a huge uplift in many people's lives. At a time when precisely what work looks like in the near future is perhaps more unclear than ever before. Which is really why we need to look at the *habits HR has formed* and which ones are going to see it push on into that future. And transform itself and the organizations it works with. Transformation really isn't a nice to have around this unclear proposition for work. It's essential.

Three key transformational HR takeaways and reflective questions to consider:

1 We have seen a huge shift in the nature of the work we do and the way in which people are engaged in their work. It may help people understand the here and now more if you can tell this story.

   Q: What is the heritage of the place you work or the story that got you to where you are?

2 A sense of the journey travelled lays a strong cultural foundation for the future.

   Q: What challenges have you/HR and the organization had that shows your past resilience and adaptability which may be needed in the future?

3 Instinctively, we conform to what's around us and we assimilate (sometimes bad) habits and rituals.

   Q: What habits have you, HR and the organization formed that are taken for granted and will no longer serve you as well in the future?

The story of the human resource profession

A problem child of the post-industrial era?

Introduction

When you work in a professional discipline, recognized by a chartered status, with specialist qualifications and known the world over, you'd think it'd be pretty safe that you'd have automatic professional regard and respect. Not if you work in HR unfortunately – it is one of the single-most criticized roles in the workplace today. With not just HR non-believers at play, there are some downright venomous attacks on the profession – ironically, some of it from within its own ranks. So it's not at all a profession you could say is thought of as business critical. More likely it is *criticized* by the business it operates within. Why is this so? And what can be done about it?

> **How will this chapter transform my thinking?**
>
> - It will help form clearer views on the complexity of challenges and opportunities for 21st-century human resource management (HRM) which may benefit from a transformational approach.
>
> - It will give a deeper appreciation of what has trapped HR in a mindset and mode of operating which is not serving it or the organization well enough ethical, attitudinally and procedurally.
>
> - It will consider the concept of organizational disabilities and the removal of interference to identify what can be done to transform and bring more progressive ways of working that create smarter ways to deliver the best design and development for people and the organization.

The human factor

In Chapter 2 we took a brief look into the shifts over the last 50+ years of the world of work and the personnel function that became HR, and left you with an overview of the changes in the focus of the people profession.

Of course, people having responsibility for the human factor in organizations is nothing new. From recruiting military personnel to overseeing the deployment of domestic support to the gentry, someone has had the role of being 'Chief People Officer'.

There's really no need to review the *entire* history of the profession – that's been done elsewhere and doesn't really take us forward. This can be found on the CIPD website in a revealing look back over 100+ years of the CIPD's existence at https://www.cipd.co.uk/about/who-we-are/history. Instead, I'd like to zoom into the way HR has crafted itself over the last 10–15 years that I've been operating within the profession.

So before we get into what *transformational HR* is – and therefore how to be transformational and do more transformation – we should look at the current position and elements of HR.

Do the basics well

I've heard this a lot. I still hear it coming from conferences, chats with new HR teams and those looking to establish some form of credibility amongst their corporate colleagues. By basics, it largely boils down to paying people accurately and on time and hiring people well and in response to the needs of leaders demanding to have the best people delivering their parts of the business: recruiting and paying people. A conversation on the priority for HR might go something like this:

> **HR Director or Chief Human Resources Officer (HRD/CHRO)** – 'OK – so we're good then. We're starting HR from scratch here. So let's get focused on the best ways to find the right people through our new hiring methods and the systems that will ensure they get paid accurately and on time'.

> **Business Leader** – 'Sure and not just that. We need support in those cases where people break our rules. And they may even fight us to a tribunal'.

> **CHRO** – 'OK so that's recruiting and paying people; **and** employment law and tribunal defending. Great so we'll...'.

Business Leader – 'Of course, we need to train people well. Induction, technical skills, governance and compliance, health & safety, risk management, lone working, diversity and equality. Selling skills, customer service. Oh and management'.

CHRO – 'OK so recruiting, paying people, employment law/tribunals, training so we'll build...'.

Business Leader – 'And of course there's the Unions and Staff representative councils. We need someone to stakeholder manage those. And respond and keep things on a positive footing'.

CHRO – 'OK so recruiting, paying people, employment law/tribunals, training, employee relations; so...'.

Business Leader – 'And then culture. That's **so** important these days. And leadership development and succession planning. And the need for diversity at the top. And our employer brand out there...'.

I'll stop there as you get the picture. I'm sure there are equally as demanding a conversation with the CFO, CTO or CMO but surely not as vast, often polarizing conversations as these between business leaders and HR professionals. It gives us a paradox, where everything becomes a top priority.

The paradox of pluralized priority

I'm not using this element (multiple priorities) to say that other aspects of the corporate world aren't similarly afflicted with a lack of prioritizing. Yet, priorities do become a bit of a misnomer. If something is a priority it is intended to be singular: *the* most important thing. A list of priorities sees a range of things – sometimes everything – where there is clearly no single priority therefore everything is important. Even putting things in priority order is a false practice. For the number one thing is the priority so that needs doing above all else.

In the scenario-based conversation, the *priority* is for HR to react to the most important business need at that time. So the priority for HR is to be responsive, not overwhelm itself with a list of demands. There is a more robust conversation for the HRD to have with the CEO on this fictitious, but recognizable list called 'priorities'.

If the conversation isn't as robust about focus, it explains why we have HR in the situation it's in. Overburdened, misunderstood, laboured, maligned, underappreciated, overeager – whatever collection of adjectives you can think of from past experiences, it is rare that HR is readily labelled as outstanding, brilliant, unbelievable, adept, creative, covered in glory and this could be because the demands are incessant.

Even in the early parts of this book, we've established that people are the essential *lifeblood* to any organization beyond rhetoric with the proof being huge research piece in 2015 by Development Dimensions International (DDI) of over 13,000 leaders on *what keeps them awake at night* (DDI, 2017). Without great people, an organization is a brand with products and processes. People are also the most unpredictable, variable and challenging of assets.

Acclaimed author and researcher Yuval Noah Harari in the book *Sapiens* talks of 'fictions'. That apart from people, animals, the world itself, everything else is a fiction: nations, money, organizations – all fictions and created by the minds of Homo sapiens. Yet it is those fictions that direct our energy, attention and focus. As he is against factory farming, I am against factory work (not working in a factory but the profiteering, soulless version of work many people find themselves in).

Back to HR's bewildering set of conflicting and overstated priority wish list. Without denying the specialties and significance of any other corporate function, research is research; packaging is packaging; customer service even, is customer service.

HR is a fascinating, challenging aspect with a large, far-reaching range of responsibilities. Perhaps as far reaching as the CEO's responsibilities. Except in these days of profiteering, the CEO is responsible for the financial performance of the organization and that's the ultimate buck-stopping element.

So it's my assertion that HR has **the** most complex, diverse and challenging set of corporate responsibilities – all things – and yet is often the most heavily criticized, underfunded and under-invested aspect of the corporate machine. Sure the salary bill is often the highest outlay for any enterprise but as I said, without people (until the advent of serious robotic capabilities) an organization is nothing but a Harari-like fiction.

To look at an organization is to look at a collection of people; assets; property (intellectual and physical); technologies; machines; partners; products, services, processes, capital, legal frameworks; ethics; networks; clients; potential clients; shareholders; stakeholders and more. HR's role – looking after the people proposition – touches many of those elements. And rightly or wrongly, a lot has been given to HR; taken by HR and as a result it's a **very** complex range of responsibilities.

To say 'HR is people' is true, but is like saying 'politics is all about elections'. It's **way** more than that and showing signs that it is getting ever more complex with challenges like artificial intelligence and automation, data and behavioural science and so on.

The multidisciplinary nature of HR

So HR has many basics, elements or disciplines. It therefore has to cover a range of activities and is often a small team compared to customer facing divisions. Many will say this is rightly so. Of course. HR's direct impact on revenue generation, customer growth and new product development is somewhat distant and hard to prove on a spreadsheet.

Yet it does have an impact. Hiring policies that get the right people in to do the customer facing roles could affect all of those things. Management philosophies and skills that allow good people to go unrewarded and micro-managed will see the best people leave to competitors and lose an edge in the battle for customers.

Most roads lead to people therefore most roads lead to HR. The fabled 'seat at the table' has been so often emphasized as many CHROs/HRDs/People directors are **not** represented at the most senior level. Chief executive; and chief operations officer; finance officer; technical officer; legal counsel; marketing officer, all there. The CHRO/HRD may indeed be found reporting into the CFO (where the people issues may become lost in the forensic analysis of financial performance).

Profit over people might be too strong a way of describing it but of course, money talks. To use Harari's language money is a fiction but one of incredible focus in the world of work.

Complexity and priority 'wrangling'

I mentioned complexity in Chapter 1. In expanding on this initial thinking, and to use a North American cowboy metaphor, wrangling is to round up, herd, or take charge of (livestock). In this metaphor the herding is of complex and conflicting and challenging priorities of HR and people in the workplace. Nothing at all to do with herding people literally (although some companies may operate on a more herded mentality than others but that's a whole different book).

This conundrum (complexity) has somewhat impaired HR's influence in corporate life and forced it to seek out the places of most impact: keeping the company out of court and winning any tribunals that occur; simplifying the people proposition to a yearly staff survey and a data point of engagement; restructuring the company and settling payouts to people no longer deemed necessary to deliver the company's future.

This inability to go beyond the very basics of good people and organization design and development is demonstrating that a *just about* (good enough) mindset is a potentially dangerous place to be and is a fragile state to be in for sustained impact and longevity. If you're just about good enough in recruiting and looking after people, then there's likely to be competitors in your field that are really good at hiring the right people and keeping them in a high performing state.

Organizational disabilities

Where an organization has a *just about* mindset in the way it looks after its people, this puts HR in a difficult position if it *wants* to be transformational for the good of the people and the organization. There are many versions of why good people leave organizations and these can impair the chances of HR being transformational and to good people either not joining you in the first place or giving up on you all too easily. For example:

- poor and ineffective leadership;
- under-resourcing or poorly allocated resources both in a people and capital sense;
- stress, burnout and generally poor well-being measures resulting in overworked people;
- dangerous and poor physical working conditions;
- poor career and development support / prospects;
- under-investment in new technology and new markets;
- micromanagement and oppressive forms of leadership;
- industrial disputes and confrontational staff representation;
- managing change poorly and convulsing from poorly scoped and executed initiative to initiative;
- high turnover or static workforce with little or no fresh thinking;
- inequality and bias shown to people with protected characteristics;
- unethical and illegal dealings and trade;

- survivor guilt on major downsizing exercises;
- culture and friction, for example from mergers and acquisitions;
- pay differentiations between senior executives and customer-facing people;
- low pay, paltry benefits and exploitative conditions of employ.

These are all dangerous elements yet we hear of reports almost every week of some company suffering one or more of these 'crimes against good work'. Organizations are either poorly supported by HR to allow such damaging elements to exist or HR is complicit (perhaps with an unfair brief and poorly defined set of parameters to work with).

So there is an under investment *somewhere* in such situations even if it is in something like too little communication and dialogue (a constant need of almost every company I have ever come across).

All of which feels like some organizations are *getting by* rather than *thriving and striving*. A company in combative mode with its own people and barely tendering to their needs is one which feels instinctively like it is *only just viable* not a at all a *just enterprise*.

This form of 'just' means 'based on or behaving according to what is morally right and fair'. So important is a just organization that a new index has been created by JUST Capital, who provide information and rankings on how large corporations perform on issues of public interest. This sense of just appears to be a topic that HR should be more activated by and towards for the benefit of people and the organizational. Transforming a well performing but unjust organization into one that performs well and is just might be just enough transformation for some companies and gives HR a shot at something truly useful for people and company.

The one priority to rule them all

How then, do we overcome this deficit or as other might call them disabilities? We could start with one simple rule. I'd like to use this book to have a provocative stab at this one basic rule HR and business leaders could focus on in its attempt to overcome any of those people-based deficits. I would therefore urge HR to adopt one key principle: *be the upholders and stewards of a just organization*.

It takes a brave CHRO/HR director to insist on the morality, ethics and legalities of this sort of action yet whose role is it to act as conscience? Who has the humanity of the company to uphold? Who can outlaw practices because they are biased, unfair and borderline illegal? It could therefore be argued that is HR. A moral protectorate and an auditor of ethics.

Such issues are often themselves complex, challenging and there is a threshold to go to and avoid crossing which HR is holding a very thin protective line against. If the HR function can enlist other humane senior leaders to their cause then perhaps such scandals and crimes could be avoided. HR isn't the Sheriff of Nottingham nor is it Robin Hood. HR is the protector of the right, proper and ethical in sometimes ambiguous circumstances.

Organizational justice as a term has been around since the late 1980s. It refers to the perception and the experiences the employee has around the behaviours, decisions and actions that influence their attitudes and behaviours at work. Many people may label this fairness or even dignity at work. It can cover all from day-to-day decisions to executive pay and is a concept based on the exchange of what employees give and what they get back. The psychological contract often fits in this frame – how connected people feel beyond contractual terms and how the relationship between worker and workplace feels. I fear though, that HR has chosen to battle on some less than fruitful grounds that feel more like petty enforcement than organizational justice, such as:

- behaviour at office festive functions;
- allocating car park space privileges; and
- the creation of bureaucratic performance assessment regimes.

These have all served to simply box HR into the administrators of (un)necessary evils. Colleagues have chosen to report offensive smelling food consumed at desks to HR; who in turn produce a policy on eating at desks and conform to Dilbert cartoons and stereotypical bureaucrat approaches.

So a new sensibility comes in the shape of organizational justice as a fairer, more dignified, ethical, humane workplace.

Influencing the most senior decision makers in any organizations is often cited as a top reason HR is not as effective as it could be. This crucial skill is practised well by the most successful HR leaders and there are some critical factors that result in a success-oriented relationship with the CEO or other senior leaders.

We'll look at how later when we look at how you might *repurpose* your HR function from the transactions of now to the transformation of the future and how transforming your HR team will create some necessary space and energy to operate at a more impactful level.

Table 3.1   Influences on the credibility of HR with other business leaders

Credibility	The need to demonstrate an effective grasp of the organization's field of operation; the demands on it as a business and the challenges it faces is one dimension. Together with the leading of an effective HR function that spots the areas of interference and works diligently to support all areas of the business with people management, development and enablement. If HR removes interference as much as possible and creates no further interference, it will be looked on well.
Creativity	The key ingredient to helping a company feel more innovative around its people proposition is to be creative whilst maintaining surety and compliance. Interference removal often needs a creative approach and a leaning towards innovation.
Collaboration	Easy to say but not always easy to do. Serving the interests of your colleagues whilst not overwhelming your HR team is a fine balance. Working collaboratively to share the effort and bring about equitable participation means HR won't be 'done to' people but people are part of HR-related positive and purposeful activities. The more collaborative we are, the less likely there's the interference which may have hampered previous launches, initiatives and new ventures.
Challenge	There's a role to play to ensure the right calls are made and the interests of those impacted by decisions are taken into account. A challenge for the good of all concerned will help deliver the right outcome and not something that creates more interference.
Confidence	Gaining senior leaders confidence and being confidential, along with self-worth, self-awareness and self-determination show confidence as someone who is credible, creative, collaborative and challenging.

The dawn of 'next stage' organizations

To underscore my analysis of this – HR is how it is, because it is trying to be an omnichannel and all things to all elements. I'm as guilty as anyone with an active and vivid interest in all things work. I've wandered off course and into new realms and I've tried to put my arms around more than I was physically capable of doing.

In engineering HR to its current model, we've built a function of well-meaning decent people, desperately seeking validation as a support function known for its adherence to risk-averse protectionism. Allowing others to gain momentum in adventurous, creative and business-enhancing activities. We're seen as the backstop not the pitcher.

And yet we see – time and again – people issues which are on the wrong side of *just* being delivered in corporate life. The financial crisis wasn't caused by banks, it was **people** operating in outrageous ways that caused debt to spiral. Corporate manslaughter was down to neglectful people allowing dangerous practices to prevail. Poorly paid people in retail 'sweat-shops' isn't the result of an algorithm it's people making those calculations and decisions.

HR was culpable in all of these incidents. Through either ineffective arguments against such malpractice or a misguided belief that because the business leaders said it, it had to happen.

One place to start in bringing a more just approach to organizational justice lies in the form of friction. Things that people feel don't help them do a better job and get in the way of creative thinking and applied endeavours.

Stubbornly low productivity, higher than expected turnover, burnout, bureaucracy, micro-management, distrust, even well intended programmes of development can all turn the organizations people on themselves. Create a sense of distrust, of exhausting and soulless jumps from day-to-day. As philosopher Alain de Botton recently said at a conference on talent – 'we didn't used to have to pursue happiness'.

The elimination of interference in people powered performance

Friction can be created in all sorts of ways which when aggregated have a detrimental effect and cause interference: mental and physical.

Don't pay well/on time? Interference. *Don't lead well?* Interference. *Don't provide growth and support to progress in roles?* Interference. *Don't know if you have a future in this company?* Interference.

HRs has a gift of an opportunity to spot **interference** and eliminate it. By showing what that interference results in – lost growth financially, reputationally and operationally – the rest of the boardroom and the company might just sit up and take notice. This doesn't mean spoiling anything that helps people enjoy their work more and therefore be productive for the company and fulfilled as an individual. Yet we introduce forms, rotas, ritu-alistic meetings and other interference creators and brush them off as norms and tolerances.

Ever had to get sign off from someone to spend £30.00 on some refresh-ments? Yet call a meeting and invite too many executives who don't need to be there and kiss goodbye to £3,000 of human productivity without anyone batting an eyelid. Interference of that kind should be in HR's crosshairs.

The abdication of management and personal responsibility

So HR isn't the only one to blame for its label as the 'politically correct enforcers'. The abdication of management in this example and the shift towards reporting rather than discussing behavioural indiscretion have all landed at HR's door.

HR has perhaps rarely said back to the reporter of the incident 'what responsibility have you taken to discuss this with the individual concerned?' They've taken it as a chance to show they can act and acted, merely inculcat-ing the view that the function is there to police people.

Societal shifts towards lacking confrontation or not, within the corpo-rate walls is an ecosystem where we can ALL play a part, and the role of nanny-state operator is never something that appears on corporate value statements or organizational end of year reports. Yet HR gets dragged into such pettiness and often asked to form some kind of arbitrator or concilia-tory role – probably against its will. No other corporate function would be tasked with such issue resolution. You have to feel for HR at times.

HR is *not* there to be an ombudsman yet often is dragged into a regulatory role because of poor management or legitimization of the knowing-doing gap. This gap – so eloquently described by many academics and sociolo-gists – is the distance between **knowing** you should/could do something and the conscious act of **not** doing something.

I'm sure people know that they can, and should, take someone to task over their fish curry at their desk in a busy call centre; or their blatant and unsafe driving methods when delivering for a client, yet they don't do it. Instead they ignore it, report it to management or HR and give someone else the responsibility to close the knowing-doing gap. This has given rise to HR's position as the backstop. The point of escalation and the solver of petty problems that really should be worked out in many other more concil-iatory and direct ways.

Creating more adult-oriented enterprises

It appears that many organizations still operate in a mental model that is akin to a parent–child mode which sometimes put HR in the position of childminder. So what has HR done to address this? Does it – as a function – even recognize this narrative that has given them a less than favourable time?

Yes and no in answer to the latter question. I've been involved in – and seen – many initiatives which are aimed at an HR function more 'business-savvy' about what it does. I've seen conference speaker after conference speaker talk about their journey to success in HR and that seat at the fabled table. I've seen online chats, groups and exchanges which talk about the need for braver HR; for more strategic HR and for a new model to sweep in and reinvent the entire proposition.

Conclusions

Complexity

HR is possibly the most complex area of the business world with a wider range and reach than any other corporate function. Even the basics of the function are probably more varied than most other corporate divisions. We should not forget this and plan for this complexity more actively. How we do that will feature later in the book.

Significance

It really *is* all about the people. Company success or failure is down to people. Decisions made by people, actions not taken by people and so on. That means how people are treated and enabled can make the difference between roaring success and shambolic failure. HR has a key role as steward of this and should have more impact in its advice and deliverables.

Later in the book, we will look at how to create the least interference and resistance where people are concerned to truly be a transformative HR function.

Organizational Justice

Organizations don't have ethics, people do. So HR's role in this space is currently under-represented and needs to make a distinction between the old policing role and more assertive organizational conscience role to ensure people act ethically, responsibly and with moral and legal fortitude.

During the course of transforming HR and/or an organization there will be many challenges to the morality and ethics that bind people with the company's goals. This book will provide thoughts and ideas on how to maintain a moral yet transformative state that quite literally puts people first.

Interference

Doubts, bureaucracy, distrust, duplication you name it, there's a lot of useless things happening in the workplace that prevent us from not only reaching our full potential and boosting productivity, but that actual slow us down, cause us ills and lower productivity.

Attitudes

HR's often criticized yet helpful nature hasn't always provided the best outcomes for either itself or the businesses it works with. What hasn't helped is a slightly lost and apologetic attitude mixed with an insular and protective mindset.

In looking at transformational HR, attitudes are vital. Whilst this book doesn't advocate transformation for the sake of it, it unapologetically calls for more ambitious, daring and challenging ways to deliver the enabling people aspects in modern businesses. Data, analytics, proven methods, experimentation, design thinking; behavioural science all combine to help our attitudes, beliefs and mindset to be influenced, challenged and shaped. This book will look at how we can influence for the better in and out of our own professional ranks.

Three key transformational HR takeaways and reflective questions to consider:

1 Having a deeper understanding of the complexity of HR's mandate means that more transformative thinking is needed in providing the best possible ways of working to even more complex 21st-century people and organizations.

   Q: What opportunities do you see from this audit of circumstances which would immediately realize people and organizational gains and build more trust in the HR function as a transformational force for good?

2 The HR mindset has become a little protective or even apologetic yet it has a hugely responsible moral, ethical and humane role as a protector of justness and organizational justice.

Q: How can you start to build more belief in the power of a more confident HR proposition that will help organizations do better for their own people and sustain success through that trust, belief and enablement?

3 How organizational or institutional disabilities and interference is hindering sustainable success and there are more progressive ways to deliver HR support and development that would help productivity AND fulfilment.

Q: How can you overcome those disabilities and remove interference through HR interventions that show the value HR can add through the power in the organization's people when they are freed up to get on do brilliant work?

Reference

Development Dimensions International (DDI) (accessed 26 May 2017) 'Ready-now leaders: 25 findings to meet tomorrow's business challenges', *Global Leadership Forecast 2014/2015* [Online] www.ddiworld.com/glf2014

What's HR ever done for us?   04

Introduction

In previous chapters we've taken a historical look at how work and HR have arrived to the point we are at right now and the recognizable shape and face of what billions of us experience every day.

We also looked at what was behind some of the chain of events that have created a reputation for HR that is less than complimentary. It is a view I have come across that HR is the cause of much friction and bureaucracy at work. To add balance to the view, there are some well respected HR functions and professions who exemplify great practice and add value.

Many people simply detest the term HR (Human Resources). People will challenge this and say 'I am *not* a human resource I am a person', yet seeing beyond the term, there is much to be grateful to a profession about that often is unseen, unknown and now part and parcel of an everyday working life that is better than 30, 50 and 100 years ago.

How will this chapter transform my thinking?

- It will shift our mindsets from either a victimized or persecuted view of HR and remind ourselves of the benefits HR has delivered – and continues to deliver – in the world of work which we may otherwise take for granted.

- It invites you to consider building on what is already useful, successful and purposeful in your existing HR proposition.

- It will help you to better appreciate the vast range of complex and adaptive systems HR operates with and urge more collaborative, cooperative and co-created ways of moving HRs people and organization design, development and effectiveness work forward – strengthening, iterating on and continually improving what you already have and working more closely with pioneering and successful methods of working such as those adopted by IT professionals.

What has HR ever done for us?

In the famous Monty Python sketch from *The Life of Brian* several cast members are in conversation about what the occupying Romans have they ever done for them. The list becomes rather a long one and it's a true parody of how ungrateful and lacking in recognition we can become. A little like civil liberties. We only realize how much freedom we might have when it's threatened or taken away. So it has been for HR. In the nicest possible way, there's a lot of good things HR has done for the world of work which I think many of us have disregarded, forgotten about and taken for granted.

In my 15 years of working in that professional field, I've been involved in several discussions which have been labelled 'HR-bashing'. I've had CEOs intervene in discussions when other leaders are showing not only a lack of appreciation, but attacking their HR colleagues. I've also had directors tear me to pieces over systemic failure (and to be fair sometimes it was my failure) which have been brutal and hard to take. Not entirely unjustified but brutal nonetheless.

It surprised me – when I entered HR more formally – just how badly behaved some people were to their HR colleagues and how firm and stoic HR had to be when having to challenge more senior colleagues, specialists and other business leaders for what was often illegal, immoral, toxic behaviours and approaches. I have worked with some HR professionals who were literally the David to their corporate Goliath in being outweighed and outranked yet held firm and achieved a just outcome.

I say none of this without good reason. Over 15 years and several thousand connections and hundreds of conversations have accumulated to become my evidence base. We don't need another survey to tell us that most of the time, **it's *not* easy being in HR.**

If only everyone understood HR more

I'll agree that one overarching aspect that hasn't helped HR's cause in pursuit of some recognition is that *HR is not that good at its own PR*. Customer service, marketing, digital and R&D departments – all seem a lot more inclined to promote their own successes and are a lot better at not being hauled over the coals. Indeed it's rare that other parts of the organizational structure have to justify their role, impact or needs as HR appears to have to do. True that some of the shortcomings mentioned around bureaucracy or inflexibility may score against HR. So HR will find it difficult to defend itself let alone promote itself.

I worked in IT programmes during the 1990s. Methodologies for IT design weren't that good in those days. In fact, I would say there was a raft of jokes, rolling of eyes and general disregard for IT colleagues then, much as there is about HR now. Perhaps this says I make the wrong choices about professional pursuits or perhaps I am just bad at timing. Anyway, enough of me. Fast forward to now and the scrum-based, agile methodology, UX-designing IT world, it is almost unrecognizable to the one back then and as I said earlier, powering the world in a quite significant way.

In that 20 years, the IT profession has been transformed. So much so that the CIO/CTO is probably the number one ally to the CEO even ousting the Legal Counsel and the CFO.

So a metamorphosis can occur in the world of work, and IT is proof of that. Was this through others understanding them more? Yes, and also the proverbial *stepping up to the plate* and transforming through imagination, creativity, adaptability, applied thinking, commitment and stamina. Plus of course, technological innovation.

HR is not IT but can learn from it

Of course HR is not IT. HR is dealing with complex, adaptive systems – variable entities that are people, their brilliance and their shortcomings. There is nothing binary about people. So HR is more complex than IT surely?

Yes and no. IT is complex. IT is about a connecting resource for people to solve problems and make things happen. So IT does understand people. Both in its own ranks as engineers, designers and leaders with their unique and ever-adaptive ways of working and its understanding of people – its users.

So whilst HR isn't IT I'm continually frustrated at the lack of crossing of streams. I feel there is so much the IT community can help the HR community with – about the all pervasive nature of technology for sure, yet more about the all-conquering ways IT has created a dynasty and successful enterprise within the world of work and commerce.

Say agile to many HR professionals and they'll say remote working. Say scrum to many HR professionals and they'll think Rugby Union or the tussle over car parking spaces. OK I am perhaps being unkind to many of my fellow professionals but at times it feels like IT is 2017 and HR is 1997.

In order to help you, as readers, activate thinking and doing from this chapter, I will create some ideas, suggestions and nudges to start to create a more transformative mindset in each of the areas that follow. Next is the first one and there will be a summary at the end of this chapter.

> **What do you know about the way IT professionals engage, innovate, design, deliver and lead projects and their work?**
>
> If the answer is 'not much' there exists a whole new world of thinking in how you can conduct yourself in the way you work in HR so you could start to research this immediately.
>
> If the answer is 'a little' you might need to deepen your awareness and assimilation of IT ways of working and leading projects and engage with IT expertise to help strengthen your understanding.
>
> If the answer is 'a lot' you're probably already nodding about this section, and all you may need to do is enlist more of your HR colleagues to help you get more traction in IT ways of working adapted to HR. Be an HR+IT skills practitioner ambassador and advocate.

In IT's favour is the advancement of technology. And yet in HR's favour is the continuing realization that it's the people that *really* matter in an organization. So we may have a transformation on our hands like IT had in the mid-1990s before and then after the *dot com* boom. IT is literally the *killer app* these days in business. Yet IT *and* people as illustrated in Chapter 1 is the perfect, winning combination. It is my assertion that in order to do this perfect fusion of people and technology, HR needs to up its game about technology and the ways IT has had a renaissance. Also in HR's defence, HR might argue that it hasn't had much time or insight to use, to promote its cause; but I'd argue against that. I'd also argue against vanity and arrogant overstating of significance.

HR has not just been reluctant to promote itself because of a lack of time or information, HR has often seen itself as a supremely humble function that *shouldn't* promote itself. It does what it does. It doesn't need fancy metrics and a distinct brand to do what it does. Yet, when budgets are cut, learning often gets a massive hit and HR goes into a sulk and a tailspin. Woe is me. Partly the architect of its own position in the pecking order. When there's a need for a new HR Information System, HR has often found it difficult to get the investment. So the humble nature of HR may backfire when it comes to getting the attention it needs for investment or recognition for its contributions. In the war for attention in corporate life, HR missed the draft let alone ended up on the losing side of the battle.

How do you promote and appropriately showcase the benefits and value that the HR function brings?

A key consideration here is that HR can still be modest and considered about what it does, whilst highlighting its work a little more and gaining appreciation for what it does do well for the people of the organization.

Activate your awareness and appreciation agenda through collaborative and deeper understanding of the impact HR has. Working honestly and collaboratively with your business colleagues.

If there is little impact to demonstrate, that in itself is telling and the HR Strategy may need some recalibration or revision.

If you have a strongly supported HR proposition, use that to gather evidence and create more appropriate belief and participation in HR activities including – for example – the evaluation of learning impact and the high levels of advocacy amongst employees.

How HR can create value and impact business strategy

So, 'what **has** HR ever done for us?' people might **still** say. Some of us at work just haven't seen enough of what HR does to understand it, appreciate it and give it any kudos. What is it that HR talks to the organization about and get the appreciation for? We'll start where most people's interaction with HR starts: at the hiring stage.

1 Employer brand

This is now a very well defined 'thing'. Indeed so much of a thing, it's nearly as valuable as the products/services brand. If you find your organization on the wrong side of a 'sweatshop' or draconian working practices story, it is as damaging as a recalled product or consumer anger.

For some time, employer brand has been a marketing function and followed a more product oriented approach until recently; where more HR teams are now conscious of the need to have a good employment proposition to promote their recruitment activities. Not through some fabled war for talent but for to make good on the pretty substantial investment many organizations expend on recruitment activities.

Outreach, careers websites, careers apps, YouTube videos, blogs and company testimonials form key elements of many employer branding strategies. It's a far cry from *expecting* a volume of applications – now there's differentiation to make; appealing employment propositions to show why the best people should come to work for you and grow a pipeline of star performers.

In recognition of this, many HR awards ceremonies and specific recruitment gongs now feature the best of the employer brand showreels. *Jaguar Land Rover*'s outstanding artistic remote-control cars; the *Swedish Army* with their person in a box and the *Those who can: Teach*, TV adverts have captured attention and shows there's high value at stake with employer branding.

Of course employer branding cannot make something out of nothing. That is, if the culture, working conditions, leadership, career prospects and rewards packages aren't that good, then no amount of employer branding is going to win with overstated or falsified claims. Therefore there is an art in HR putting together a plausible, captivating view of the organization built on things that matter to prospective employees.

If your company has an award-winning, creative and compelling employer brand that's one reason to be proud and appreciative of your HR function. How can you help HR create the best possible employment proposition?

If your culture leaves a lot to be desired and you cannot create the compelling narrative, then demonstrate the lost value this will achieve and use that to look at areas for improvement and how HR might lead a cultural transformation programme.

If your culture is good but you are a best kept secret, HR activities can create more alluring outbound content to appeal to the right candidates and create more interest in you as an employer of repute and choice, potentially cutting down your recruitment costs and delays.

If your culture is strong and you have a great employer brand, you can keep it that way through active utilization of more stories and invite people to learn about your company through culture tours and workshops into 'your way' (which may also lead to revenue generation or charitable contributions).

2 Recruitment and selection

Applicants and candidates are of course the HR equivalent of external customers. For many years, their application experience was often a laborious and badly designed process. Why would HR be bothered about people who may not even set foot across a threshold in the company? Except word gets around. And some of the best people may be put off of a lame duck of a process. Indeed, any representation of a poor process reflects badly on the organization. Much attention has been put into this process and a smoother path to application and clear selection criteria and uploads of CVs means if there ever was a war for talent, the candidates won it...!

The number of places applicants can find vacancies has of course also proliferated. So there's a real marketplace sweep and placement exercise for recruiters and HR professionals.

Recruitment and vacancy management has now become a complex and multi-platform discipline much more effectively stewarded by HR in a more competitive marketplace with many employers now active and searching for distinction and appeal to job seekers.

In an ever challenging recruitment marketplace, HR is having to apply ever increasing creativity, low-friction processes and highly demanding timeframes. Credit where it's due and any appreciation and support will be gratefully received. HR and recruitment experts are doing their best in a competitive arena.

Of course posting vacancy information or instructing agencies or executive search partners is only the beginning of the process. There's sifting and selection processes which are meant to be objective, fair and of course, legal.

Many involved in the selection process need significant guidance and training to make sure they're on the right side of not only the legal boundary but also are applying ethical and moral approaches to recruiting. Not showing any unfair biases to people or prejudicing because of disabilities, age, gender, ethnicity, sexual orientation, religion or any other protected characteristic. That many recruitment decisions are now made within this framework is down to the diligence of HR professionals to make sure panels for recruitment and selection are fairly constructed and representative of the demography of the company, area the company operates in and professional standards that are applied.

Selection is – in itself – a complex situation. To find the right person for the role is often a costly decision to get wrong and many an emerging superstar employee fails to pass certain criteria at interview only to shine elsewhere. Human beings are notoriously hard to measure, predict and assess therefore the recruitment and selection processes are attempting some of the most notoriously difficult and complex situations.

HR has also added a range of psychometric and intelligence tests, scenarios that are similar to the working situations the candidate will find themselves in and scenario-based immersion in assessment centres.

These additional activities have provided more data points with which to make candidate's selection choices and should be recognized for what they are: more rigorous, scientific and contextualized moves towards better selection.

And so the selection process reveals a clear winner and the offer of employment is then to be drawn up. Here again, HR has had to balance the needs of an eager hiring manager keen to get the position filled with the high calibre candidate and making sure there is consistency and due diligence applied. After all there's a range of bureaucratic hurdles to navigate here such as eligibility issues; data for HM Revenue and Customs; past references to check; criminal records checks and more. HR professionals have to be on point with this – it's essential administration to ensure fairness and security at all times for both the candidate and the employer. Much of this eligibility and contractual work is a must and largely, HR is acting firmly, as swiftly as it can and with rigour.

There may be times when hiring managers want to break the budget, want the candidate to start immediately as the work is piling up and want to see all the things done overnight. And HR generally does its best here but it may have to put the handbrake on for a while. This isn't HR being deliberately unenthused or dogmatic. It'd be a lot worse if people were taken on without eligibility checked or an offer made that caused a massive pay revolution in other colleagues. This almost invisible work is where HR spends some of its time. And of course, I'm not advocating here that HR needs medals and plaudits for doing what it has to do but this is where often people's 'what has HR ever done for us' can be a bit harsh.

Respecting HRs administrative, compliance and governance diligence should at least be understood more widely. HR may have to make sure people know what important 'invisible' work is done to protect candidates; the organization and hiring managers whilst also making the recruitment proposition a shining example of a human, fair and effective experience.

If your recruitment experience is cumbersome, slow and overly bureaucratic, this will form a damaging first impression of your organization and could require significant upgrade.

If your recruitment experience is effective there could be ways to make it ever more frictionless and this could be a great point to join forces with marketing minds and technologists from your organization.

If your recruitment experience is 'best in class' you could make more of your methods known through articles, features, conferences and share your learning with partner organizations.

3 Job profiles

When we hire there's normally something called a person spec (specification) or a role profile or a job description. An assembling of the key responsibilities, skills, behavioural competencies, technical competencies, certifications and qualifications, levels of experience or expertise and so on. These are normally designed by HR to existing template. There's often a consistency to them. There's a series of common threads and recognizable traits. They are also some of the dullest documents known to humankind.

Perhaps that is a bit harsh, after all we have to start somewhere in defining the roles and responsibilities for people. We have to have something to benchmark the level of pay and benefits this role attracts and ultimately to use in our recruitment and selection processes. It is the human equivalent of the technical data of a smartphone. Yet we often purchase a smartphone on anything BUT the technical specification. We like the look, the feel, the screen size and the operation of the applications within it. Some will dive into the memory capability and the storage space but these are normally once we've been lured by it's look and feel.

They serve a necessary purpose these job profiles. They're the technical schematic to jobs that people do with their heart and soul and head fully engaged. Often though, these profiles appear to be cast in stone. Aren't regularly reviewed, can be deemed inflexible to reasonable adjustments made for alternative working patterns or specific needs of individuals with disabilities and kept in step with the changing demands of the working world.

> **Wherever possible the process of job profile construct should be an open, transparent and inclusive process allowing for adaptation and flexibility. HR, leaders and job holders all have the responsibility to keep these as living documents that capture the key elements of jobs.**
>
> If your job design process is a cut-and-paste exercise largely conducted 'behind closed doors' and made up of pick-and-mix options, you may be suffering from under-utilization of people's talents and some unnecessary interference in pay and reward psychological impact on people.
>
> If you have a more open and co-created approach to job design, you could enhance this with continued focus on making sure there are adaptive and iterative ways they can stay sharp once drafted and used.
>
> If you already operate a more progressive and dynamic approach to job design – such as self-built job roles and adaptive profiles – this is newsworthy and adventurous and the HR press and CIPD would be keen to know more about this approach and the impact it's having.

4 Rewards and benefits

We mostly go to work to earn money. In a capitalist economic world, that's the way we've built our society. Of course there's volunteers and other models for work but largely, there's a financial incentive to get a job, perform well, advance, save for our older years when work is less desirable and we invest in support through those years in life via our previous gainful employ.

HR has this *huge* responsibility here. And of course, pay is never quite right. Most people would say that more money would make them happier – even though that's rarely proven as an absolutely *definitive* cause and effect. Many people have an idea of how much they're worth based on the salaries offered for roles they feel capable of doing. Others have a more outlandish view on their worth and many of us settle for what appears to be a decent living wage.

Indeed the living wage and minimum wage legislature of recent years has put a societal frame around wages to discourage unscrupulous organizations from constantly driving down wages and forcing the lowest paid workers into tax credit situations burdening the state even further. Free market economic forces are at play with much of what we term salaries and increasingly, this is defined through comparison benchmarking activities. HR and specialist organizations often collaborate in assessing the value of a role and a pay range calculated and some secret sciences (pay/value algorithms).

These are based on data and research of comparative value based on technical expertise, scarcity of expertise, decision making, budget and resource responsibility, years of experience brought to the role and more. Of course pay and benefits are a huge aspect of most organizations operating costs and there is constant scrutiny on the paybill. Any need for savings needed will inevitably force a keen eye on spend in salaries.

In heavily unionized environments of course, pay has been a major cause of negotiations and disputes. So market forces, combine with company austerity aspirations mixed with representations from unions for members, has made the remuneration world, a combative, volatile arena. And of course we've seen an upsurge in a more benefits-rich employment proposition as a competitive advantage. In the past, company perks like a car and healthcare were then taxed by governments who saw a reduction in actual tax revenue from this as creative accounting to cessate. That said, paid sick leave, discount schemes, loyalty membership cards, gym subscriptions, parental leave and childcare vouchers, cycle schemes, healthcare subscriptions, free food and drink onsite, clothing allowances, technology devices, legal services, transport loans, development support and more. Indeed, there is now an entire benefits industry to allow busy HR teams to buy in packages and now platforms and apps for their people.

And of course pensions. There's an enormous amount of concern and research in this field with state and business finances unable to support us as we live longer post employment. Hence the raising of the retirement age and the increased concerns around state funded pensions with auto enrolment schemes now the law for UK employers.

On the whole, industrial disputes are fewer and less linked to pay and more job threats, automation, extending hours and pensions so you could say this is a combination of two forces; a more compensated workforce more generally and legislation around unions which has tipped the balance of power away from their favour.

Not as much an invisible task – pay in particular is far too emotive a subject for it to be invisible – but an often thankless and tiring task. Pay and benefits is developing into a specialist field within HR and the creation of an industry proves how much we have commoditized the job offer and how complex and specialized a task this is for HR.

If your pay proposition is a finely tuned process and you are retaining people and you appear to be ethical, fair and at market rates for the work people do, then you can still augment pay. There are a large range of no-cost (to the employer) or low-cost benefit add-ons from the growing benefits providers and platforms ranging from charitable deductions pre-tax to retail and lifestyle discounts.

If you have a more progressive and dynamic pay offer – which includes open book accounting options or transparent pay open to the entire organization, then this is considered next stage practice and whilst a sensitive and tricky area to manage, has enabled a shift towards more inclusive ways to build a pay and benefits structure.

5 Well-being

One 'benefit' – or realization – is that levels of stress, overwork and anxiety are on the increase. So even if people are earning well and have a range of benefits, they may be doing more complex, challenging and demanding work. With punishing schedules, long hours, toxic leaders, competitive colleagues, demanding clients and more. Mental ill health is being described as the likely cause of premature demise in the 21st century.

In response to this, HR has taken the lead on the well-being of people – a relatively recent addition to the HR portfolio. Coming as a more positive look at people and their health, sickness absence was a cause of much concern in the 1980s and 1990s. As paid sick leave was considered more a 'benefit' it was felt there may be some abuse of the provision and so return to work conversations and sickness absence monitoring was introduced. Dismissal or medical retirement were consequences of people no longer fit enough to do the work or absences so frequent they impaired performance and people were capability managed. None of this felt particularly humane but was introduced to ensure there was fairness across those who weren't using sick absence as some form of entitlement.

Moving beyond this management of absence, there was a compelling shift in thinking to more of a preventative and whole-person approach than a punitive absentee approach. Morally this all felt, and still feels, right. Instead of people feeling *more* stressed about sickness they were unfortunate to be genetically predisposed to, or a victim of; this well-being approach took more of a caring and supportive approach and allowed those in breach of the moral and ethical code of paid sick leave to still be identified and given options and choices to help themselves.

As with all modern workplace phenomena this too has created an industry. Advisers, consultants, apps, packages. From mindfulness sessions to Indian Head Massages in the staff rest room. This is though, an ever important aspect of what's previously been neglected. It's no longer all about a macho survival of the fittest but an acknowledgement that when we're not well in any way – particularly stress – we're not only risking our very being, but we're likely to be less effective at work.

Research into our physiology – and indeed our psychology – has proven just how much we're in need of breaks; movement; kinetic and cardiovascular activity in order to get our brain going. That the brain works best when the electric impulses are firing and that glucose helps our brain rev a little higher means we need to eat well; think more about our energy levels and manage our rhythm.

> **Well-being has to be recognized as a fundamental shift towards a more humane workplace. This is more than an HR initiative – it looks at how important our health is in performing well for the organization, in developing ourselves and in sustaining organizational success into the future. HR should be supported through well-being initiatives but also in more humane and considered ways of leading, working and supporting each other.**
>
> However trendy well-being might seem, it is attracting attention because our health really does matter beyond our performance but of course, it can help or hinder our performance. Consider what people really value and include all your people in what well-being is, what it means to people and how you could activate it sensibly. A company that stands for the well-being of its people, is a company likely to be successful in all other ways.

6 Employee engagement

A title that often courts some controversy in the HR world. How engaged people are in their work and for their organization. What started as a staff satisfaction survey (an offshoot of the value of data received from customer satisfaction surveys) these became vogue in the 1990s and introduced the concept that if a company found where energy and enthusiasm was abound, yet where friction and frustration was also found, any corrective action could result in more productive people and indeed, help those people feel more fulfilled by their work. A not entirely philanthropic gesture but nonetheless considered a win–win for person and organization. HR felt the absolute right place to own the administration, involvement, analysis and reporting of this as an initiative and involve all staff through a surveying mechanism. Of course there were (and still are) many organizations where ignorance is bliss and so not everyone jumped on the bandwagon and secured services from survey companies. The early movers in this space who provided services were those used to polls and citizen / consumer surveys. They also had the data analysts and reporting mechanisms so the natural leaders were the Gallups and MORIs of this world.

Of course we can all collect information but the *right* information? By asking the right questions and by using the right context and conditions impacted on the accuracy and therefore usefulness of the data and insight derived from the survey.

Yet, up until this worker voice and influence was restricted only to the Union representation if there was one. For the first time, many people had their chance to let people in the leadership positions in their organization know what really impacted upon them. This had to celebrated for that alone. Leaders now had many more data points with which to assess the impact of their leaders, the recent restructure or acquisition, the pay freeze, etc.

Anonymity and an ability to speak up was a key feature of this process. It was considered that some matters may put people in an uncomfortable position. Through an algorithmic approach an index score was often derived which enabled companies to benchmark against others and find out how engaged their people were and perhaps how much more productivity could be attained if people were more engaged.

Many shades of success have happened as a result of the rise and rise of employee engagement:

- Boards were made more aware of how employees felt. Bizarrely, up until this point, companies knew more about their customers than they did their own people.

- Leaders were given a sense that any shortcomings in their leadership ability could come through in a low engagement score and related comments.

- Matters of poor management right up to outright bullying could be anonymously reported on the surveys.

- Ideas for improvement were either given or clear through the survey analysis.

- Scatter maps, bar graphs, radar and pie charts all came from the data and many versions could be produced: divisional; team; country; level of experience and grades.

- People felt they could have a say on the things that mattered to them.
- The results were communicated company wide so all could see.

There were downsides to this – invariably down to poor execution or an already challenging culture:

- Leaders became fixated on the numbers and simply targeted an increase without really knowing what they meant / gave people.
- Company inactivity to respond to key issues was met with scorn and felt to be a real let-down. It meant people lost faith in the usefulness of the exercise.
- Fancy charts were great but free text narrative was often under-utilized and even ignored. Many people gave up and just ticked boxes and ratings making it a purely numerical process.
- Inertia and apathy set in and no matter what incentives were created to complete the survey, low completion rates diluted the value of the exercise.
- Poorly designed surveys often invited over 100 questions and people lost interest in completing this much information. A range of apathetic average responses was doing nobody any good.
- Some felt the industry that grew around this was simply another scheme to capitalize on a faddist thinking in HR.

There was more to come. For the UK Government itself (though many people credit David Cameron it was in fact Lord Mandelson then Secretary of State for Business, Innovation and Skills) commissioned a report by former ICI senior executive David MacLeod and former advisor and union activist Nita Clarke authored *Engaging for Success* (Macleod and Clarke, 2009). For the first time, people talked about how important it was that *all* people were listened to, involved, considered, included and had influence in the affairs of companies and organizations they worked for. This was engagement. The products of this more open relationship were considered to be greater profitability, lower attrition and absenteeism and a new phrase 'discretionary effort'.

Research reports, features, conferences – all of a sudden this became a headline intervention. David Cameron did – two years later in 2011 – launch a task force to investigate further employee engagement. This task force still exists and is made up of some large organizations' HR directors/ CHROs alongside consultants, academics and professional associations.

Whilst this represents a very UK-centric appeal, Gallup in the US is responsible for a worldwide-quoted statistic that only a third of people can report they are engaged in their work (from both 2013 and 2015 survey analysis).

What this says is that 66 per cent of people at work *aren't* engaged in what they do and/or who they do it for. Images of a trance like existence for many hours a day as people somewhat depressingly step into their work-place and only become engaged in life again when they leave the building and head home. This somewhat *Tim Burton-movie* view of the world, clearly this shows a long way to go before many people can talk of fulfilment and joy from their work. You may wish to recall that mental ill-health epidemic I mentioned earlier in this book as a potentially harmful outcome for the millions of people reporting as not engaged.

It is a conundrum HR is being asked to solve often, unfairly, in isolation. HR alone cannot fix employee engagement deficiencies any more than facilities management can reduce the company's energy budget through long-life bulbs. The entire population of the company is there to resolve employee engagement issues: Through attitudes at the highest level to expectations of operational staff; to recognition given by managers at support levels.

Employee engagement has suffered through being overly number-chasing; non-responsive and HR's initiative. It's not – it's everyone's initiative. Give HR some help and join in with what's truly needed to help people feel as enabled as much as they need to be; and included as much as they want to be.

If you are yet to embark on *any* form of data gathering or dialogue capturing with your people, then it's never too late to listen and take action on what really matters to your people. You don't *have* to do a survey and get a number to base your engagement activity around. Consider how you can create the dialogue and capture the information by inviting your people to help you design what would be most effective.

Many companies are now using internal social media to capture the essence of what causes friction and flow for their people. There needs to be attention paid to the comments people make, but an open and flowing sense of dialogue may seem like unmanageable chaos. Yet, a once-a-year tick box exercise may equally be misleading and not that revealing of things that matter day-in, day-out for your people.

Initiatives such as listening sessions where leaders invite people to enter into conversations about anything at all to do with the organization may seem like very brave and time consuming processes, yet they bring leaders and their people together in dialogue for a better understanding than any simple data exercise can give.

7 Performance management

If I could pick two more maligned and eye-rolling topics it'd be employee engagement and performance management. So you could say that we're getting to the most knotty elements in the HR tree of life. Performance management certainly is that.

Let's be clear what we mean by this of course: appraisals, career development conversations, performance reviews, and all manner of chats with line managers fall into this camp. As does ratings and assessments, performance related pay, promotability reviews and even forced distribution curves.

It hit home to me how despised this whole process was in making tea one nondescript afternoon in 2011. Two IT colleagues making a drink in the kitchen areas and one said to the other 'I've got my performance appraisal in 10 minutes. I hate this time of year and I hate having this conversation'. Being a seriously committed HR professional I interjected and asked why. Here's the list of what was causing such hatred.

Table 4.1 Performance management friction

I wait six months to be told what I did was any good or otherwise. If there's errors, they'll get raised. And I'll be invited to propose what I do about them when I can barely remember what caused the errors in the first place.	I get told what my assessment rating is and that this is something I should be building on to achieve a higher rating next year. I don't even know how this is worked out.
I get invited to discuss my ambition in a one and three-year timeframe. I rarely know what I'll be up to next week so this is very difficult for me. I don't lack ambition but I don't want to be a manager and that seems to always be the conclusion. I feel like I'm not valued because I don't want to be a manager.	I have these five objectives and they get a little walk through and then straight into examples. I don't really have that many examples I can remember – I just do what I do and do it pretty well it seems. These five things on the form don't bear much resemblance to what I do so they seem pretty pointless.
I have been cancelled twice and so it clearly isn't that important, nor am I come to think of it.	I get asked to then record the actions and work on those for the next six months and that's it.

I'm sure if you're reading this with lots of nods, you've either heard this story or you've experienced this yourself. It's not what I think the performance management process was conceived to do but it's perhaps how it's been designed and implemented that's caused such a negative and even repulsive reaction. There is a lot wrong with it, I can't deny that. Relevance being the main culprit. Regularity being the other. The main problem I see with performance management is *ownership*.

People point at HR and say 'you inflict this process on us, so it's your fault it's not good enough'. Yet it really is a management tool. Not an HR tool. Before there was widespread adoption of performance management the *only* time you were invited in to talk with your manager was if it was bad news. I'm not sure this stigma still applies but the way they have been conceived their psychological impact is not one of safety or inspiration. More one of punishment or mechanistic compliance.

However, many HR professionals are now taking the torch to performance review processes and banishing them to some bad practice Room 101. Instead, check-ins; career conversations and even removing ratings and assessments. Unless performance is noticeably and regularly below par, only then will there be a more formal approach to give fair and measured targets and progress reviews.

Why HR – which doesn't own the process as I said – is able to start the process of abolition is because of what performance management data has been used for. So whilst HR doesn't own the performance management process, it owns some of the processes that have come to depend on the outputs of performance management. Performance related pay and associated increments being possibly the biggest one. Capturing learning and development activities; looking at the spread of performance management assessment ratings; compliance with the policy for equality and diversity – ensuring everyone is given a fair, accurate and open performance review conversation whether they're full or part-time; remote or local.

It is perhaps a more elegant way of describing HR's ownership of performance management as that of the ethics, philosophy and most of the data-related outputs than to entirely abdicate HR from this process.

So as a business tool, it's owned by the organization. More particularly the leaders and managers as a tool to clarify people's roles and responsibilities; their priority focus; their behavioural expectations and give definition to the criteria which measures success at an individual level in accordance with the necessary success at team, divisional and organizational level (as applicable to scale).

And yet to me, this still feels too 'done to' and won't overcome the dread and reticence, the irrelevance and waste felt by my IT colleague – who is merely a representation of millions of people who share that view.

So in my view, ultimate ownership for the process, compliance, benefits, relevance, inspiration is with the person whose job is subject to the performance management.

Whilst it is accepted that this may take a level of personal and organizational maturity not currently part of the performance management protocol, this principle of ownership will see the job holder:

- seek out an understanding of what their job is all about if they are new to it. This will be with experienced colleagues; the previous role holder or the manager with ultimate responsibility for the person and the role;

- develop an early understanding of the priority element of the role and gradually build up further activities; behavioural elements; links to other's work; processes and tools needed; growth elements within the role; space to innovate; and ultimately, success criteria;

- build a regular flow of feedback as they deem it necessary. Creating a more conversational, useful dialogue with line managers, colleagues and others. This will help the individual get better by understanding their strengths and development areas and be more open to giving and receiving feedback to others to create more harmony and open exchanges. Some of HR's problems where they have to 'arbitrate' between colleagues is down to people not being comfortable giving other people feedback;

- not be surprised by late in the day criticism, grading of performance and be unaware of things that they thought were to standard. The yearly (or half-yearly) ritual of the performance review isn't as helpful as it's intended to be. Too long is left between reviews and people find them frustrating and irrelevant;

- boost their own confidence and engagement with their work. Regular feedback; ownership of instigating shorter and more regular conversations about performance is likely to give people a greater sense of their achievements, their relevance to the overall success of what they're part of and the connection to a high-performing culture;

- escalate to others if their manager is not providing feedback, is inappropriate or handling their responsibility poorly or if they feel they are being victimized or even bullied.

> **Performance management is not HR's tool, it's *our* tool for all people at work. HR's key role is to make sure people are skilled, confident and capable of leading the process around their own role and that the entire process is ethical, inclusive and inspiring.**
>
> Start with people owning the process of their own performance management process/appraisal reviews not managers doing it to people. They will need some assurances, skills and an approach that means they get managers's time.
>
> Develop the feedback protocol that it is immediate, regular, is forward looking with a degree of reflection on learning moments and key points of challenge. Managers support and guidance in the process will help out of duty of care for their team members.
>
> Create multi-dimensional aspects to performance management where people at all grades naturally help, feedback and improve others.
>
> Ensure career conversations are a part of your approach to understand ambition to progress upwardly, across or strengthen capability in the core role.

8 Diversity and inclusivity

Working people in the 21st century may find it hard to believe that as little as 10–15 years ago, law, policies and training activity was at the forefront of helping us be more aware, tolerant, adaptable and even forceful about the rich diversity that is the human race.

It took time, but the phrase 'protected characteristics' came into parlance in business to describe people. It represents a series of diversities including:

- gender;
- ethnicity;
- ability;
- sexual orientation;
- age; and
- faith.

HR has had a lot to do in this area to ensure use of language, biases, behaviours, processes, adaptations and opportunities have been adjusted to take protected characteristics of people to the top of the list of considerations at an organizational level.

Has this been a roaring success for HR and the world of work? I can recall heated sessions (especially around faith) I have also seen first hand supremely well handled discussions on adjustments and total failures to recognize the needs of a person and a catalogue of disasters that made people feel second-rate. Generally speaking, this is a never ending area of constant attention and activity. As we become an older population, age becomes a more noticeable feature and as the world opens up to migrating workers, faith, ethnicity all become a more profoundly relevant focus.

HR has – by and large – handled this aspect of our working lives with care, diligence and compassion. I've seen many a sensitively handled representation by a strong HR professional over an inconsiderate colleague or manager. I've seen people hold firm in the face of taking measures against unacceptable behaviours and attitudes. I've been part of HR-sanctioned networks of support that have increased awareness, insight and activism to make good on legislative implementation without the need for prosecution.

As we continue to face socio-political unrest and many see a rise in nationalism, populism and far-right narratives, the workplace as a place of sanctuary for difference has perhaps never had as much meaning as it does right now. We live in uncertain times but the workplace has more certainty about it now than ever.

HR holds together many cultural aspects of organizational and working life and representing, supporting and advising in situations of difference should not be under-estimated or undervalued.

We all have a responsibility to support the work of understanding and working with differences and it is a given that diversity of workforce, and therefore diversity of thought becomes an innovation advantage.

---

9 Culture and values

HR's role as 'cultural architect' has been mentioned to me many times by learned practitioners and academics. It's like HR is some form of designer of spiritual boundaries that allows an organization to develop an identity. Yet, HR isn't the cultural shaman some people seem to think it is. It does though, have to be both an active participant in the culture and be able to define it and suggest human intervention that would improve it.

In-depth analysis of what makes and improves a company's culture is a series of books all by itself. Suffice it say for this summary and keeping in the 'What's HR ever done for us?' theme, culture is a key element for HR to be tuned into and influential about because culture is made up of all the interactions of people in the company.

Long hours working majority = long hours culture. Toxic powerful people = toxic culture.

Culture quite literally is the combination of all those things. A little history, heritage and habits; and a lot of active, behavioural and beliefs-based projection.

Senior leaders have an awful lot to do with the culture. The most senior leader really does act like a conductor of culture that becomes the company way. Famous transformational leaders like Ricardo Semler, Herb Kelleher and Anita Roddick all shaped a culture on their beliefs, principles and behaviours. What I **have** seen is either denial of this by senior leaders or the feeling that a culture change programme can fix a dysfunctional culture.

HR is often then 'gifted' this opportunity. With culture being like a constellation of past and present beliefs; behaviours and approaches this is difficult thing to engineer. It's like asking a sporting crowd to only gently applaud. Once someone sings, it spreads. Once outraged at a referee's decision, it spreads.

So HR's role in culture is a mixture of stealth-like adjustments (through behaviours and values the company stands for), direct interventions (training courses, coaching programmes) and ways of working (self-managed teams, project orientation, agile development teams).

Change programmes are often where HR might shoot itself in the foot a little – promising a culture change – but as Mark Fields (former Ford Executive) once shared that Peter Drucker supposedly said to him 'Culture eats strategy for breakfast'; similarly, that oft-utilized HR tactic of restructuring fails to amend the culture except to bring in a culture of uncertainty that you could restructured out at any time. Culture is now so important many job-seekers say they want to know what the culture is like. Many corporate failings aren't down to the lack of governance processes they are down to the culture of ignoring them. Perhaps HR *should* become the cultural *shaman*? Whether this is an opportunity or a poisoned chalice, culture is not disappearing from the key differentiators of successful organizations.

HR as a key stakeholder and steward of organizational culture has a tough job.

Whilst it would be wrong to think it's all down to them, HR needs support, activism and positive influencers to join their pursuit of a thriving, humanitarian, productive culture that acts like a beacon for new employees and customers whilst maintaining a magnet for those people who make it a successful and fulfilling place to work.

Culture has become so important that (as mentioned in employer branding and recruitment earlier on) it is as much a critical attraction and retention factor as pay so it would be wise for organizations to regularly ask the question of themselves 'who are we?' and HR can help them define and utilize that in a positive sense.

10 Change and organization development

The quote from Heraclitus 'the only constant is change' never seemed more apt than in the 21st century. We've seen change programmes for years yet there's a different scale and feel to the change we now see in the world of work.

HR appears to be a much more active proponent in organizational change programmes. The recognition that people are impacted upon by change in not just a formal, transactional way but in a deeply psychological way has given HR a more prominent part to play in change programmes. Indeed, most change programmes are looking toward a future shape, flow and direction that will have a huge impact on people. Some positively, others not so but there's a human element to change that falls right into HR's lap – the psychology of change; the impact of active support and active resistance to change.

So many change programmes purport to fail. And whilst there are numbers that appear to support this, it is less about failure per se and more about not delivering all that the change was set up to do. Change legend John Kotter wrote in *Harvard Business Review* in 1995 that change programmes were hampered by eight main errors (Kotter, 2017):

- not establishing a great enough sense of urgency;
- not creating a powerful enough guiding coalition;
- lacking a vision;
- under-communicating the vision by a factor of 10;

- not removing obstacles to the new vision;
- not systematically planning for and creating short-term wins;
- declaring victory too soon;
- not anchoring changes in the corporation's culture.

Most of these have a human factor. For example the lack of urgency means people would be continuing to operate and behave as they do now; with a low powered coalition and lacking vision, there was no compelling energy for people to desire the change and with few short-term wins and low levels of communication people probably couldn't hear or sense the change anyway.

So the human factor is vital in change. All of those 'fail factors' aren't tending to processes or technology – they're about bringing understanding and energy, connectedness and belief to human beings.

And *change's* more academic–practitioner bedfellow, organization development (OD), has a similar reaction from people. Planned, systematic approach to improving organizational effectiveness – one that aligns strategy, people and processes. When most organizations talk about change programmes there's often OD operating under another name. HR is often involved in change but not always leading it. And its OD fraternity is normally well-positioned to either design, deliver and drive much of the change.

OD is a key discipline within HR and the utilization of great theory and practice in that field could help make change programmes more effective and involve and engage people more widely and actively across the organization.

A mature organization will have an OD mindset throughout. With design, development and effectiveness as key areas for focus. Senior Leaders are sometimes devoid of this skill and discipline and so OD professionals from within HR or Change teams can, and should, help lift the level of proficiency at all levels. To more successfully navigate change, adapt, take a systemic view of factors influencing the organization's performance and of the psychology of people involved in that complex system.

OD is a undervalued and underutilized discipline and an OD mindset is deficient in all but the most successful and lasting organizations.

11 Learning and talent development

Training has been a mainstay of most personnel and HR functions for as long as I can remember in the workplace. Not, of course, the only ones doing learning and development related activity but certainly the major programmes and development activities that feature in classrooms and off-site locations, plus, of course online or e-learning has been the domain of the L&D team.

It is fair to say that some form of recognition and even a separatist movement have long waged an internal battle of recognition in HR for the learning professionals. Some divisions have created their own training functions, some HR teams have almost entirely outsourced L&D to external partners and consulting firms and the recognition within HR has been a sensitive and often passionate one.

We, thankfully, appear to be in a better, more harmonious place where there is not as much visible outpouring of discord that HR doesn't understand L&D and such divisive terms. Credit to the work of Peter Cheese, Gill White and Andy Lancaster at the CIPD for bringing more focus to L&D in the UK HR arena. Elsewhere, with the Learning and Performance Institute, ATD (in the US) and Institute of Training and Occupational Learning (ITOL) we have much more focus on the professionalism and accreditation of learning practitioners in the workplace.

L&D is a key driver of HR's influence on the workplace through skills, behaviours and better performance across the workforce from joining through to specialist skills.

A mature organization will have a highly functioning L&D approach where there is a strongly active method for people to get the learning they need, when and how they need it. A variety of methods and models exist for how to deliver L&D with the now (almost) ubiquitous 70/20/10 model being the dominant shape of corporate and workplace learning.

Learning is changing and the way people adapt to new content streams through digital channels and their active networks of mentors, coaches and experiences means this area is constantly shifting, being challenged and having to adapt itself whilst servicing the needs of demanding professionals in the workplace.

Conclusions

HR has done a lot of good that is now taken for granted in many walks of working life. We are more just, inclusive and fairer about our ways of working. Much more can be done and HR has been as guilty of any corporate function in not always hitting all the necessary targets yet in these 11 areas we have a much more powerful outcome in a range of ways that are helpful to both organization and human being working for that organization.

Business colleagues: to be critical of HR is often unfair and doesn't always help things move forward. Help by understanding more about the challenges HR faces, about the approaches HR uses and lend more support.

HR practitioners: spending a little time and effort bringing more of your business colleagues into our world might just create more of those guiding coalitions to bring about lasting change and positive impact to organizations.

There's a lot to feel proud of being part of an HR team that holds up organizational justice and creates the best possible conditions for people to thrive in their work. People and work are complex systems in operation and a myriad of factors impacting on our working lives. Just keeping up with that means somewhat radical approaches are needed; fresh thinking; applied sciences.

It isn't easy being in HR. And after all, what's the business ever done for us?

Three key transformational HR takeaways and reflective questions to consider:

1 In looking at shifting our mindsets to being a more effectively recognized function, HR professionals should remind themselves of the reliable, powerful work they do and ensure this is understood by business and operational colleagues.

   Q: How can you open up more productive dialogue with colleagues so they not only better understand HR, but be more active in shaping how the work of HR is delivered, shaped and recognized?

2 Where we are already performing well, ensure this is widely felt by the HR team and their colleagues across the organization.

Q: Using tools such as the Appreciative Inquiry method (as one example) what could you do to interrogate where HR is performing well and use this strength to inform progression in areas in need of improvement?

3 With corporate functions such as marketing (data analytics and consumer science); finance (forecasting and modelling) and particularly IT (customer-centricity and rapid development methodologies) our colleagues have much to share with HR that would improve the way it operates and delivers a more effective HR proposition.

Q: What could you do to bring more of the adaptive practices of IT and others into HR to improve the way HR scopes, designs, delivers and evaluates what and how it does?

References

Kotter, John P (accessed May 2017) Leading change: why transformation efforts fail, *Harvard Business Review* [Online] https://hbr.org/1995/05/leading-change-why-transformation-efforts-fail-2

MacLeod, D and Clarke, N (2009) *Engaging for success: enhancing performance through employee engagement*, BIS, London

PART TWO
Models

What is transformational HR? 05

Introduction

In this chapter we look to explore how we can define transformational HR. Until now, the term will have been subject to a wide range of individual interpretations. This book sets out to provide a definition as a *foundation-level principle* which can be adapted and contextualized.

With 'transformation' being such a crucial word to many of us impacted by the shifts coming towards us set out in Chapter 1, we could lose ourselves in a debate on the term, rather than action to transform for good. This debate on terminology has distracted many of us in HR and beyond from action, so this chapter describes as much as possible about what we *mean* when we use the term transformational HR.

How will this chapter transform my thinking?

- It will give a definition for transformational HR and provide more depth to ensure the term is used wisely.

- It introduces a new model which defines the component parts of a transformational HR mindset and mode of operating.

- It will explore transformational leadership and the concept of transformational quotient (TQ).

Defining transformation

Transformation is such a big word that sources give us a number of categories and subcategories to allow for context. It is, therefore, a word subject to misuse, overuse and confusion. We will hear executive boards, HR practitioners and politicians talk about a transformation when, in reality, it is anything but that. Adaptation, improvement, re-alignment and even rescue could really be what people mean. So we have to be clearer about what we mean by transformation in an HR context.

To define business transformation, esteemed change and business teacher and author John Kotter has produced this: 'Business transformation is about making fundamental changes in how business is conducted in order to help cope with a shift in market environment' (Kotter, 2017). In looking at little more forensically at Kotter's definition, 'fundamental changes' is a key statement – right at the core of something. Defining principles that are re-defined and significantly altered – not some window-dressed alternative but a shift at the very epicentre of the state of being, knowing and doing.

Two small words also stick out for me as important in the way we interpret Kotter's definition of business transformation: *how* (business is conducted) and *cope* (with a shift in market environment).

I confess that I really struggle with the word 'cope' in a transformational context. Cope feels like a somewhat *victim-oriented* word to use. When I hear this word, it conjures images in my mind of a bruised brand, breathless and struggling but somehow picking itself up off the floor – but for how long? Adapt is maybe a more elegant way to describe cope. Capitalize on? That feels a little too – well, capitalist.

I sense and believe transformation is not just about coping and is more about energetically and actively *joining in* with that shift in the forces of change. Be that the market environment or otherwise – being part of the transformative effects that are being experienced. All of this is set in a business and world of work sense of course.

Or even better than joining in, *leading a shift* and create the forces of change (be that in a market environment or otherwise). Now *that* feels more like transformative to me.

What is your definition of transformation?

We can all get swept up in transformation being something done to the world and businesses by high-ranking officials and leaders or by clever products that change our lives. Yet we probably all have transformed something about ourselves at some point in our lives; even if that felt as normal as being a parent or moving jobs. If it transformed us even a little, it was transformational.

In Chapter 2 for example, June's decision to move her pension out of the state-owned company transformed her future because it wasn't then raided and used, it was instead what's keeping her going right now.

CEO Satya Nadella said about Microsoft recently 'we need a culture that allows you to constantly renew yourself' (Redmond, 2017). Where you read 'renew', also read 'transform'. For that was a transformational thing to say about Microsoft where product (Windows) was king. Renew yourself, transform yourself.

Instead of this book being all about receiving my opinions and experiences as the author, I'd like to invite you to briefly break from being a reader to consider this definition for a little longer. On a piece of paper, at your favourite device's keyboard or spoken into a recording device, please record some thoughts, notes and images around what is you:

- being transformative about yourself;
- being transformational about your life;
- transforming your social environment;
- being transformational at work;
- being transformational in your professional sphere;
- transforming your future.

You could find yourself looking at activities, aspirations and ambitions that looked a little like coping but I am guessing much of it looked like you being more in *control*.

Control is, oddly, a word I am not used to using and one where I have a normal reaction of rejection. In my rejection context, it is about others controlling others (or me). In this instance I mean it in being in control of you and your influence on the world. And I don't mean control in an entire market sense either – although at times, many businesses *have* done that. They have been so dominant that they virtually controlled almost every element of that market: Google with internet search; Boeing with commercial airplanes – both transformed their market and how we live and work.

This book's definition of transformational HR

Transformational – in itself – is often defined by what it is that is *being transformed*. You transform something today and tomorrow and further on, it will be a normative state therefore, no longer transformational. It can therefore be difficult to define without that subject.

Like the fabled *Escherian Stairwell*, transformation is a story that continues endlessly, so any definition of transformational, has to be of the open-loop variety rather than closed. And therein lies a tension. For some of us, the lack of a destination may be frustrating. You have to head somewhere, to stop, to achieve that end goal or arrival. For others, the journey *is* the destination and as long as you're on a journey, the never-ending nature of it is the point of it all. Arrival is a stop along the way and the destination is always emerging as the route unfolds before us.

So, in defining our *Escherian Stairwell* that is transformational HR, I'd first like to *hack* Mr Kotter's definition of business transformation and insert the word control (and lose the word cope in the process).

Control in this context is about the changes you are making. Coping does not feel like a strong enough intent or method for making your transformation successful.

So the definition of transformation for this book and for the HR profession:

> Transformational HR is leading and delivering fundamental changes in how people and the organization work and conducts its business; in order to control its aspirations, intentions and influence in an ever shifting world of work.

So I've kept most of Kotter's spirit in this message and added *aspiration, intention* and *influence* for a reason. It's not 'to grab market share' it is more that a superbly well-defined and believed in intention, aspiration and influence will deliver the right market share, business outcomes and impact on society and the world, whilst being good for the people in the organization and that the organization serves.

A Transformative Purpose

Aspiration gives us – what is being described in many circles (particularly with those organizations experiencing huge growth) – a *massive transformative purpose (MTP)*. This is well described in Salim Ismail et al. *Exponential Organizations* work out of Singularity University (Ismail, Van Geest and Malone, 2016).

Daniel H. Pink, in his seminal Drive work about the truth behind what motivates us, talked about companies that have a transcendent purpose as ones who truly ignite the spirit in their people (Pink, 2009). Where it goes beyond the profiteering, brand reliant norms we've seen from some of the corporate giants of the past and now.

A purpose that is transformative is, by nature, a high plains reason for being. Peter Drucker said 'the reason a business exists is to create more customers'. I guess that's as simple as it gets. No matter your company size, with more customers, you'll do well. With less customers, you'll go out of existence, eventually. Your purpose serves customers and more customers serves your purpose. So any purpose which gives compelling reasons to have more customers is surely going to be the winning exposition of the reason customers will want *you*. Any organization that can galvanize such support, belief and dedication from its people, will likely see that transferred outwardly into customers.

Researchers who go to that *extra* depth to get the best insight into customer need, because they believe in the company's product aspirations, will no doubt strike a chord with customers because of that depth. Marketers who believe *so* much in the company vision, will act more creatively in how they represent the key messaging about the product and service, giving it more allure and likely success in gaining more market share through more customers. And so on.

Transformational approaches to a purpose aren't *always* necessary you might say. And you might be right. If a company has transformed a market place (say the electric vehicle with Tesla) why should it persist with a transformative purpose? It's already served it's purpose – to transform. Yet let's think this through: a transformational purpose may indeed get you there, but will it keep you there?

Once you've conquered a market or created a new market, the transformation may not be that *significant* anymore but in order to keep the 'more customers' mantra, you will need to watch for competition, keep abreast of regulation, understand customers now growing demands. We will cover more of this in the models we explore in Chapter 6. Customers themselves can be, and invariably are these days, transformational in how they want to lead their lives.

Transformation as usual

So once transformed, keep transforming? Very much so, yes.

I am suggesting there are **scales** of transformation. A complete and utter transformation which is high-risk but high-yield when successful. And then there's continued transformation. Transformation as usual. Whilst this may appear to be adaptation, iteration or improvement, some element of transformative thinking is necessary in order to not stagnate, calcify and perhaps even crash. Transforming something means it will never be the same again.

Nokia was a transformational organization that I studied in the early 2000s. What a market share Nokia once had in mobile phone handsets. And yet in 2007 with Mr Jobs's iconic iPhone, and the reluctance Nokia demonstrated to move beyond their Symbian operating system and the eventual buy-out by Microsoft, proved there wasn't *enough* transformational thought in Nokia's camp. That's an overly simplistic telling of a highly complex story, however it – and Motorola and BlackBerry in telecoms alone – proves transformational mindsets are needed. Transformation of differing scales is a key feature of people and organizations that thrive.

If we look at the music world and some of the most enduring artists, many had profoundly transformational shifts in their style, image, genre and in collaborations: Stevie Wonder, Madonna, Prince, The Beatles, David Bowie. Of course many other artists stuck to a winning formula and instead of being transformational, they held a philosophy that endured – Springsteen, Cohen, Dylan to name but three. And yet they had already transformed to create their place in the market and were lucky enough to be in tune with their audience to keep their niche. So they transformed growth into loyalty. These artists are rarer than we might think as the music world is littered with 'has-beens' who failed to transform in the first place and then failed to keep transforming as the 'market' dictated.

Such is the Apple story. Many people will *never* desert Apple – yet more people lately are taking to criticism of the lack of transformation the enterprise is showing, so they will lose some market share and probably already are. Yet Springsteen-like loyalty will keep people attached to this brand and its products partly because they had *already* transformed a key part of their market. They may not need to do such seismic transformations as the iMac, iPod, iTunes, iPhone, iPad again, and yet they could find themselves outtransformed and a gradual decline in kudos and customer share will not be seen as a good thing by anyone working for Apple or investing in Apple.

Even in Apple's case, if their purpose is still transformational, it should see them through any blips in blinding innovation-led products and some disdain from a fickle market. Google seem to be doing pretty well with their massive transformative purpose, as are Amazon, so whilst they may not be always out-innovating everyone else, they are sticking to their transformative purpose. There is clue for all aspiring long-haul success stories unfolding right before our eyes.

Business transformation and its relationship with HR

It is my experience that HR is *not normally* renowned for its transformational qualities. It may even be actively *discouraged* from it by the organizational leadership it is operating with. At times of transformation, HR's role is often to provide stability, certainty and rigour at times of madness. Or flex like crazy as rapid growth means all sorts of shortcuts might be needed in hiring, compensation systems and learning.

So whilst all around the organization, people are frenetic and pressured, HR's role is often to hold a strong core of governance and applied administration to the otherwise chaotic mayhem. Rapid recruitment, swift training, super-quick processing of contracts and payroll systems. Get the people in; get them ready and give them their most fundamental dues.

So is that transformational HR? No that's responsive HR in my view. It's *good* HR if it helps a transformational business to scale and capitalize on a successful launch or product switch.

Transformational HR then is more about the taking of an already transformational organizational to be *even more* transformative. From other people's experiences (so not directly researched by me) Spotify, Netflix and AirBnB's approaches to HR *are* transformational. They aren't just tendering a fast-growth machine. The HR functions there are adding to the transformational impact of the company with even more progressive thinking/acting HR. I haven't chosen to cover those in this book as there are extensive stories and articles on these companies out there already.

There are a number of factors which contribute to a company's transformative effect and increasingly that is also in its employer brand and people proposition. I've used the word 'proposition' deliberately here. It's the offer that HR has to the working world and specifically to people who don't work for this transformational company. A transformational approach to invite people to come and work there. OK some of the company's external, consumer/customer brand is at work here but still, there's a need to have not only a transformational product or service but have transformationally-minded people operating within it, for it and to make it even *more* transformational.

There are some legends and folklore of amazing company cultures – wherever you sit on the progressive darlings of tech, retail or start-ups spectrum – which have become a marketing lure of their own:

- *Valve's* employee handbook;
- *Zappo's* hiring and happiness philosophy;
- *Virgin's* unlimited vacation policy in some areas of its business;
- *Morning Star's* contracting between people in different functions;
- *Semco's* disregard for any formality;
- *Buurtzorg's* lack of managers or a bloated corporate HQ;
- *AirBnB's* approach and practice of employee experience and not HR;
- *Netflix's* culture deck and their take on performance management;
- *WD-40s'* tribes and learning moments;
- *NextJump's* learning partners not managers;
- *Google's* approach to objectives and key responsibilities plus their Google X/20% time for experiments;
- *Atlassian's* 24 hours of 'work on what you want';
- *Matt Black Systems's* self-organized ways of working;
- *Barry-Wehmiller's* philosophy that all employees are like a member of the family.

And of course there's more. Whilst we do have a lot of technology companies in this list, we also see nursing, engineering and agriculture so this isn't just for the coders and designers.

HR may not even be visible in some of these companies. They may not have an HR director or function. People 'stuff' still goes on – of course. We need payment for our work; we need development to get better and we need dialogue with others in order to keep the company honest to its purpose. In many of these examples, rather than a parenting HR function, we see a more adult–adult relationship develop and a maturity between teams, people and their managers (if indeed, they have a manager).

So have these companies been so transformative they've negated the need for HR? In title, and role specifics, many have. And this is serving as both a warning and a beacon of hope.

If – and let's use one example here Buurtzorg, the homecare nursing enterprise in the Netherlands – with a declaration that you don't need a formal HR function, you engineer your organization in a different way. This means we see nurses and other healthcare professionals stepping up to be coaches, situational leaders, recruiters and project managers. Buurtzorg's philosophy is so strong that this is about empowered teams of 12 nurses who don't need much formal administration.

The sciences that support transformational HR

If you're wanting to do HR in an alternative organizational setting, you'll need to be at least aware of a range of people-related sciences that will come into play still. It is such sciences that I believe will give an HR proposition a competitive advantage and a transformational quality to *keep* relevance and add value whether it's called HR or not.

Table 5.1   Transformational HR: a new T-model for HR

Psychology	We'll need to understand much more deeply how people think; act and are motivated beyond the myths and stereotypes perpetuated by popular media. And not just people, organizational psychology too – treating the organization as a thing with an identity and personality traits.
Behavioural science and behavioural economics	Where people really do come alive and the science of how to move people to a more cooperative state for good, we may need to nudge them with incentives.
Sociology	Complex societal structures need to be deeply understood in order to appreciate the dynamics of communities and how people interoperate in social environments including how we design our physical work spaces and gathering environments.
Anthropology	How people have adapted and where our most primal responses and needs are factors in how we behave, work and operate. If we knew more about anthropology I'm sure we'd never have designed work cubicle farms.
Philosophy	It is vital we mix deep thought and more philosophical ways to define who we are as human beings, why we exist and what frames our ways of behaving towards each other as we get more connectivity but less connected to people and things.
Neuroscience	And whilst many think we already do operate with an increased sense of neurology, there is already an awful lot of questionable content to wade through before the most useful elements of this are truly understood and are useful.
Linguistics	Use of the most authentic and powerful language isn't as obvious as it sounds. Our use of metaphors – for example — can either amplify or nullify how we feel about a topic or proposal. Storytelling features within this – or in more business-like language – a strategic narrative.

(continued)

Table 5.1 (Continued)

Agility	An overused word but in this instance is the almost ubiquitous act of developing a sprint-based, iterative design methodology to work and a flexible and fluid approach to working. Project management of this nature appears to be delivering the better result-oriented and rapid approaches needed for a fast-changing world.
Design	Design in all manners but particularly along the design of the organization, the teams and the people within it and supporting it. Business modelling is one art of design as is the discipline within organization development. Too often this is done via an organization chart and like some form of schematic-induced magic, the rest follows. It's more complicated than that. Design thinking, systems thinking, complex adaptive systems are powerful approaches to an something I feel is not always well deployed by HR or indeed, desired by 'the business'.
Innovation	Understanding how innovation happens, is harnessed and leveraged and is best deployed, is ever more critical for HR maybe even over the many other corporate functions. R&D, digital, design, engineering have had to operate with innovation as a constant to achieve competitive advantage or ensure survival. HR's time has come to innovate else there will be bots, automation and enabled people to do the work HR has traditionally delivered. This won't just be innovate to create a new dependency, this will need to be innovation to build added value from a previous 'cost only' division.
The science of learning	More than the professional field of learning and development. This is about deeper understanding and deployment of developing human skills and behaviours applying a pedagogical style and a range of other factors that we know how best to make learning mission-critical and that it sticks with us. The *black box* approach of learning through failure is also becoming a critical element in learning to move away from purely teaching or coaching styles.
The science of performance	How do you create the most compelling, responsive and purposeful environment that allows people to achieve beyond even their own understanding of performance? Knowing the mix of stimulus, incentives, consequences and energy sources is a critical skill for HR in assembling its design and process toolkit for people at work. Flow – the sense of people having enough skill and enough pressing need to perform well – is something HR professionals would do well to understand and deploy better.

(continued)

Table 5.1 *(Continued)*

Metrics, data and analytical skills	Over the last three to five years this has been a regular feature for HR – know your data more. In response to increasingly challenging decisions to take, data about our people is more valuable than ever and a rudimentary demographic nature to our data isn't as helpful as a richer, deeper set of data.
Modelling and scenario-making	In looking at future shifts, the ability to model – on a mental and physical, structural sense – is ever more critical to play through situations rather than simply guess at impacts and unintended consequences. Scenarios are one way of helping make decisions with more data points and the ability to try out situations before inflicting it upon people in real life.
Creativity and art	Expressing things in alternative forms to corporate board reports and slide decks is becoming more needed as we realize how human beings respond to varying ways of presenting issues, challenges and situations. It appears to be an increasingly held view that HR is science (of humans at work) *and* art (of expressing humanity at work).
Good governance and ethics	This isn't so much a skill per se as a combination of process; attitude; strength of conviction; courage; activism; reflection and persuasion. In order to steward the most senior leaders and others to act in an ethical, moral and responsible way takes guts.
Self-awareness and social intelligence	And without the awareness of self, the belief in one's own ability and true strengths, without the realization of impact on others and in social situations would negate a huge amount of influence and data gathering about human beings operating in a work environment.
Networking	HR's role as a connector and creator of connectedness is more in need as we realize how much power there is in networked ways of working and leading.
Sense-making	Spirituality and meaning – not necessarily of a religious denomination – but the deeply powerful sense of existing to do something and that work is an extension of that something. Sense making isn't about an indoctrination, cult-like views on the workplace or brain-washed compliance, it's about a massive urge and sense of meaning inside someone that happens to line up to their work.

It's a rather large bucket list. And on top of all this are the traditional HR skills which are largely a technical set around recruitment and selection; learning and development; employment law; mediation, discipline and grievance, well-being, diversity and inclusion; pay and benefits; coaching and consulting.

A new 'T-shaped' transformational HR practitioner

The sciences and alternative approaches are why I think HR is on the verge of a new model for those people who work within the people and organization design, development and performance worlds – a T-shaped model like this:

Unlike most T-shaped models, where the deep, vertical is one specialist area amongst a range of generalist skills, this T has a *really* thick vertical. This isn't about one deep skill. It also doesn't mean you have to practice or be skilled in all of the areas in the vertical. They are though, a rich field that is potentially being under-utilized in HR, organization development and change.

This model could be called an iceberg with lots of hidden elements however there should be nothing hidden about psychology or behavioural science. This is more of a *hack* of a professional standards map (so could sit alongside things like the CIPD Profession Map) and is not an attempt to recreate that, but complement it. Indeed, the thicker vertical elements in this T-shaped model I am also demonstrating the move from transactional, conventional HR practice, *in harmony with* transformational, progressive HR application.

It would be difficult to have transformational HR practice without a solid transactional foundation. And similarly, once transformation is underway, the transactional elements will be changed and possibly transform themselves.

Figure 5.1   The T-shaped HR Model

| PRACTICES
What the rest of the professional world sees | Recruitment and selection: pay and benefits: diversity and inclusion: employment law: mediation: well-being: discipline and grievance: learning and development; organisation design; coaching and consulting: culture and values |

| SCIENCES AND DISCIPLINES
What HR professionals are practicing and are skilled in – to drive more progressive versions of the surface-level practices | Psychology: sociology: anthropology: philosophy: behavioural science and behavioural economics: neuroscience: linguistics: agility: design: innovation learning: performance: metrics: data analytics: modelling and scenario-making; governance and ethics: self-awareness and social intelligence: creativity and art: sensemaking: networking |

Transformational quotient (TQ)

Rather than transformational HR being something that we all shift to, transformational HR will be something that is either an ongoing 'special tactics squad' within a larger HR team or a transitional project-oriented activism assembled and disassembled in smaller HR teams. Freelance consultants can, of course, specialize in transformation and be like hired-help to boost an HR team's transformational quotient (TQ). Indeed, we could look at TQ in HR as we do emotional intelligence (or EQ) in us all. We don't dial down our intellectual quotient (IQ) in favour of EQ – they exist alongside each other and situationally, we flex one more at the right time.

TQ is therefore a combination of those factors in the thick vertical of the T-HR model and could form a series of flexibly defined activities according to the transformation that's needed. It would be wrong and perhaps even dangerous to try and label three, five or seven key aspects of transformational HR and instead provide a broad frame of skills, attitudes and behaviours that help bring transformational HR to life. Transformational HR is therefore a little like having a super-hero alter ego in HR. Someone who by day, is a payroll administrator, but by night is a people-enabling hacker and innovator. In any given day, you may find yourself involved in a petty dispute over car-parking privileges and then involved in a massive transformative forum designing an entirely new strategy for corporate social responsibility.

Transactional HR does not switch off waiting for transformational HR to finish and nor does transformational HR need transactional HR to totally pause whilst it does its thing.

Instead, this is very much in line with R. Buckminster Fuller's famous quote, 'You never change things by fighting the existing reality. To change something, build a new model that makes the existing model obsolete'.

Assessing your TQ

If you are an aware practitioner, you will already have found the CIPD profession map to assess your skills across much of the horizontal of the T-HR model. The map is broad enough that you can also use it to assess your proficiency in some of the vertical thick stem of the 'T'.

In looking at how you might further your TQ, a short process of self-analysis and some feedback from others may reveal *how* transformational your current level of skills is using this grid:

Table 5.2   Self-assessment for transformational HR skills and preferences

Area	Narrative and Questions	T-HR Discipline
Knowing *self*	The very essence of understanding starts with you knowing *who you are*. What brings you to life and how do you feel about your self-worth?	Psychology Self awareness Science of learning Creativity and artistry
Knowing *others*	How do you show warmth? Relatedness? Empathy? In this, we are looking to be the exemplar of relationships. Connected, considerate and considered about how you create links with people and for what purpose.	Sociology Networking Science of learning Behavioural science Behavioural economics Linguistics
Know *skills*	What do you have as skills and capabilities? What skills do others have? How can you best use and deploy yours and other's skills? Analytical know-how is needed here mixed with an instinct and a sense of what people themselves may not even be aware of – their impact and brilliance.	Creativity and artistry Mastery Governance and ethics Science of performance Science of learning
Know *systems*	Using design *and* sensing skills, understanding the world that you and others are operating in. We create systems and systems shape us – this is a vital skill in understanding how to combat hidden forces preventing transformation and in harnessing energies towards a transformation.	Anthropology Modelling and scenarios Sense making Performance Science of learning Innovation Design thinking
Know *need*	The critical thinking needed to truly get what others want of you and your work. There will be times that what is being asked of you is a possibly misguided understanding of need and there are times when absolutely the other person is spot-on with their requirement. A high self-worth, knowing practitioner will know what questions to ask to get this right and a critical thinking mind is vital in getting to the truth of a need.	Analysis Critical thinking Sense making Science of performance Modelling and scenarios

(continued)

Table 5.2   *(Continued)*

Area	Narrative and Questions	T-HR Discipline
Know *energy*	It is so important to not only get the data right but the energy that will help transform in you, others and impact on the systems aspects of the world around us. Social intelligence is possibly the nearest discipline that guides us with this. Some of the energy clues are in the mood, the visual cues and the tone being used by people.	Psychology Sociology Analysis Neuroscience Creativity and artistry

Operationalizing transformational HR

So I think this is where transformational HR sits. In the *adjacent space* not in the middle of HR's core activities.

Clearly, where something like recruitment and selection is radically over-hauled through a transformational project or programme, then we're in a new norm situation. However, instead of trying to rebuild the *entire* recruitment and selection process, transformational HR activism can be run as a parallel stream.

Company X wants to transform its graduate scheme and transform its workforce demographic by employing more people without degree qualifications but that show hugely entrepreneurial potential. Note that the scale to which they want to overhaul or change their current approach will denote whether it's transformational or whether it's merely a continuous improvement exercise.

In this scenario it's transformational. The company wants to transform how it attracts a wider set of candidates to better represent a certain demographic, and to attract candidates not based on traditional academic qualifications but a range of other skills and attitudes. They want to increase their level of game-changing and entrepreneurial mindset whilst at the same time, not *just* appealing to young graduates but innovators and those less suited to degree study programmes who want to kick-start their careers.

Whilst this isn't transformational for the *entire* company at once, the shift needed not only benefits from being labelled transformational – i.e. the need to be very different from current practice – it also feels like it could transform a key part of the company's workforce and bring much needed diversity to a range of functions/teams.

Transformational HR in action

In this scenario, the three people in the recruitment team all have some input but they all agree that Jo spends 50 per cent of his time on this project with Carrie from the OD team. Jo and Carrie enlist three volunteers from marketing, ops and the programme office who all spend 10–15 per cent of their time on the project. They do their day job and the transformational programme and (because this is an illustration!) they deliver a superbly well planned pilot/test with the IT team which is then quickly replicated across the entire company. And they all worked happily ever after.

Another example could be the HR Director and Head of IT Security are concerned about the amount of technology compliance the people in the company have to manage without formal guidance and awareness. So they engage an external consultant, ask for volunteers – three from HR and three from IT – to work part of their week on the project and deliver a transformational programme of knowledge, skill and capabilities to help *all* their people better manage their data and understand the ethical use of their information both in and out of the company.

This external expertise and internal boost to capability brings about a transformation in the way HR provides protection for people and the company on data and use of information by suppliers, vendors, partners and technology providers and wins awards for the ethical use of digital tools and becomes a key element in the company's reputation as an employer with a modern, people-centric outlook. The company's value in the market improves, their order book for products and services grows and the company offers HR related digital ethics consulting support as a new business venture in this area in partnership with the external consultant.

OK this is fictional but is based on experiences I've seen in the world of work. Nonetheless, there's a lot of transformative elements in both stories. Does it pass my earlier test via the description I gave for transformational HR?:

> Transformational HR is leading and delivering fundamental changes in how people and the organization work and conducts its business; in order to control its aspirations, intentions and influence in an ever shifting world of work.

Yes, HR led and delivered a fundamental change (demographic shifts in hiring and ethical and protective use of data in a digital environment – even creating a spin-out business venture) and controlled its aspirations through inclusive, properly managed transformational projects with key energy and expertise from their own people and external partners in meeting their company needs in an ever shifting world of work. They were in control of these transformational elements not simply coping with the changing world around them.

So the teams assembled for these illustrative ventures all enhanced their TQ during the exercises and will probably apply a lot more of their transformative mindset and skills to their everyday activities from now on.

Embedding a culture of transformation in HR

When people have been involved in transformational HR activities, HR will never likely be the same again. So by engaging in transformational activities, HR is seen as more transformational and will be more transformational. It's a self-fulfilling prophecy. Does this mean that transformational HR becomes the norm?

In a way, it does. In a way the restlessness that HR finds itself in once it has been involved in transformational activities may see an increase in HR-instigated transformation that the company values and uses to spark it into acquisition, new product lines, enhanced service propositions, expansion or even consolidation and focus in one key area.

There are, of course, a range of circumstances where transformational HR activity is then suppressed and overtaken by business survival. An aggressive take-over may mean the incoming acquirer wants consistency not transformation and so channels HR's energy towards more compliance of the newer, larger more complex business it is now part of. There can be a range of reasons why transformational HR is no longer *de rigeur* and is actively discouraged. This can create some negative tension and HR transformers may find themselves at odds with this new forced choice option, and move on to find more transformative organizations to work their magic within.

Nothing lasts forever is the saying that springs to mind and so it goes with 'peak' transformation. When there is no need to do anything other than super-administer the organization, then all those skills in the thicker part of the T-HR model become under-utilized even unhelpful so this provides a mismatch of aspiration and reality that cannot be sustained once discovered.

Now that such skill, energy and aptitude has been identified, TQ is quite literally a genie out of the bottle. There is no putting it back. It's not like we are desperate to transform everything we come across, however, there doesn't appear to be a shortage of business and people challenges that some form of transformative approach won't help. I suspect the work of transformational HR will *never* be done. Which I hope is good news for all of us except the Belbin *completer-finishers* amongst us.

So vast are the challenges – many of which were highlighted in the earlier chapters – that we need at least a minor form of transformational HR approach to all of those new issues we're facing in the world of work, and shifting expectations and needs from people at work be they leaders, entrepreneurs or role holders. In essence the transformational HR professional is a practitioner; a people scientist, a solutions engineer, a systems architect, a creative designer and an activist in using people and organizational psychology.

Leading transformation

I mentioned leadership earlier and return to this now. HR as a function can become a transformational function and have its people become more skilled and adept at transformational activities (increase their TQ).

HR needs help to be transformational though. Much of that comes from leaders at all levels – not just situational or positional leaders. Leaders in this definition are people with energy and attitude towards transformational activities who others will follow.

In most organizational structures, there is a hierarchy and the leaders at the top of the pyramid are perhaps most critical for transformational activity to be either instigated, led or sanctioned by them.

If we have a little more clarity on what transformational HR is, what is transformational leadership?

Of course much of it is the same and comes back the definition:

> Transformational HR is leading and delivering fundamental changes in how people and the organization work and conducts its business; in order to control its aspirations, intentions and influence in an ever shifting world of work.

So part of transformational leadership is to work with and/or support the transformational HR activity. Indeed, a transformational leader is probably one who has given a mandate to HR to be transformational or indeed in response to an HR-instigated transformation programme, work with the HR team and help them be as transformational as possible to achieve maximum people and business benefit. Just because a leader is part of a transformation programme does not make them transformational by association. They may be involved in the programme to audit, sanction, scrutinize or sign-off transformation. That's procedural and process-oriented leadership. A truly transformational leader is someone who is urging on the people in the organization to go beyond their current operating confines; who can express a desire to transform the nature of the business and its way of working; to inspire people to innovate and creatively apply themselves to their work and the future of the company. Transformational leadership is a mixture of opportunity identification, spirit galvanizing, activism alignment and problem solving. It's the future and now, it's the head, heart and guts of the pursuit of the possible.

Transforming through futurology

Some of the ways to demonstrate transformational leadership is in taking on the role of a futurologist. Whilst this may seem just another 'not real job' it's a very real thing.

Magnus Lindkvist is one of the premiere trend spotters in the world. He may even proclaim to *not* be a futurologist or futurist and yet it's his work that has given me the strongest definition of what we mean when say futurology. In his book *When the Future Begins* (Lindkvist, 2014), Magnus calls out four key traits needed to practice futurology:

- **Be the analyst.** There's a lot of answers in data and particularly in the analysis of data. Trends, increases in, shifts and the like give us patterns that we can use as part of a process to help us predict. Indeed, predictive analytics is one attempt to give us as much certainty about future predictions as we can get. And it isn't just numerical and graph-type data, ethnographic studies; social habits and use of time give us an indication of what the future might be when we can see patterns and trends in information.

- **Be the historian.** Answers to future sometimes lie in the past. I love it when Magnus describes today as the future of the past. I use the example of benevolent employers in the past like Rowntree and Cadbury – ironically confectionary makers but this is not about the product – it's about the way they treated their workers. Housing, education, health – all were provided as part of a package of working for the 'family'. Of course, this was before the advent of full-on market-forces led capitalism and when the agenda switched to manufacturing and lean process engineering to minimize errors and delays. Now we see a rise of benevolent employers attracting headlines; free fruit; flexible working terms; leave allowances for a range of family and caring responsibilities and educational support are giving us a new sense of the benevolent employer – and it becoming something people appear to want their employer to be more like. History repeating itself? Partly, yes. So looking back helps us look forward.

- **Use scenarios.** Earlier on, I mentioned modelling and scenario planning. In this instance, in order to try and make a prediction about the future, a scenario is created and played out or walked through. Complex issues, may need more than a documented description in order to assess the impact and either a physical or mental model would help to then role the scenario forward. I saw this in action in Bucharest, where two people with NGO Volunteer experience were constructing a scenario for a group of learners interested in going to help overseas aid. The scenario was a virtual walk-through (akin to role player games) using only conversation, flip charts and notes. It predicted a way that those new to NGO volunteer work could get themselves started safely and productively in a virtualized scenario ahead of a real experience. Predicting the future or even altering it can be conducted in this scenario-led manner.

- **Understand asymmetry.** The existence of multiple futures alongside each other sounds like a massive conceptual leap but if all you've ever done is work on a ranch in Patagonia and then suddenly get taken to the Gigafactory of Tesla, you might think you'd time-travelled, so different was everything. Of course you know you're not in the future except you probably are! Some people's working methods and ways of operating are the new norms and therefore are the future to those who haven't progressed to that way of working yet. Looking up and out and researching those who are experimenting and delivering more progressive ways will give you an indication of the future to come for many more of us.

Analyst, historian, modeller, asymmetrist are four very useful elements of transformational leadership with that keen eye on the future.

Conclusions

The transformational leader (and transformational HR professional) will likely be demonstrating these futurologist attributes and be a visionary storyteller alongside. Someone who can describe that better future, who is opportunity vigilant and ethically sensed will be seen by many as a transformational leader. Of course alongside this the transformational leader will also have to be able to deliver on this vision and that's the key element of transformation – not just the conceptualization but the activation and operationalizing of the vision.

This crucial element comes next: from how we get transformational to how we do transformational HR. In later chapters, we'll look at some places that are giving us the operational models and methods to do transformation.

Three key transformational HR takeaways and reflective questions to consider:

1 In understanding what *is* and what *isn't* transformational HR, a definition helps us decide whether this is continuing improvement or a larger, more fundamental shift.

   Q: What is the definition of your transformation and what is the transformational HR definition for your organization/client(s)?

2 Where we feel, sense and know that a shift is transformational, we should activate more of the TQ in our T-HR model and look more deeply at the people and organizational sciences we might need to utilize to truly transform.

   Q: Where do you see your greatest need and opportunity to enhance your TQ and what will that give your organization/client(s)?

3 Leading transformation of any sort – and particularly HR – requires us to be clear not just on our intent but how we will control and activate others towards that transformation.

   Q: What processes and methods will you need to activate in order to be controlled with your transformation and lead with applied efforts and confidence?

References

Ismail, Salim, Van Geest, Yuri and Malone, Michael (2014) *Exponential Organisations,* Diversion Books, New York

Kotter, John P (accessed 17 May 2017) 'Leading change: why transformation efforts fail', *Harvard Business Review* [Online] https://hbr.org/1995/05/leading-change-why-transformation-efforts-fail-2

Lindkvist, Magnus (2014), When the Future Begins, LID Publishing, London.

Pink, Daniel (2009) *Drive: The surprising truth about what motivates us,* Riverhead Books, New York

Redmond (accessed 20 May 2017) 'What Satya Nadella did at Microsoft', *The Economist,* 16/03 [Online] www.economist.com/news/business/21718916-worlds-biggest-software-firm-has-transformed-its-culture-better-getting-cloud

Transformational 06
HR

The models

Introduction

In Chapter 5 we looked at a definition for transformational HR (T-HR) and at the risk of over repetition, I defined it based on John Kotter's business transformation frame thus:

> Transformational HR is leading and delivering fundamental changes in how people and the organization conducts its business in order to control its aspirations, intentions and influence in an ever shifting world of work.

A profession that is one of the most model-led I know, HR has often been accused of being a little obsessed with the models more than the effective utilization of them. Yet models serve a defining and helpful purpose in helping us deal with the complex adaptive systems we call organizations and the work they do.

How will this chapter transform my thinking?

- This chapter explores a small number of powerful models used in the business world which will help take a transformational approach to the work of HR.

- It will look in more detail at the model of disruptive innovation and separate fad from forceful application and ensure we are not swept up in hyped-up thinking around disruptive HR.

- It will look at the value proposition of HR through the utilization of the Business Model Canvas and the Value Proposition Canvas – two widely used tools in the dynamic world of business and organizational success.

Whilst there are a range of technical and academic factors that will contribute to delivering to that definition of transformational HR, models are something the business world has embraced and fixated upon with a high degree of verve. Indeed, such is the pace and variety of modern businesses, those models which did appear to be the ubiquitous cornerstones of business are themselves being usurped, hacked and challenged by an array of new models. In reviewing only a few we can see just how challenged once revered thinking now is. We'll start with an old favourite.

Michael Porter's five forces

When this model was conceived Wall Street still ruled the finance world and would soon come to the silver screen and you could feel the testosterone and combative spirit in the world of work. Businesses ruthlessly took each other on and challenged each other to make better products and deliver profit and gain for shareholders and the markets. There is no doubt that of its day, this model was a mindset shift for many business leaders.

Where once serving local markets with patriarchal, family businesses reigned supreme, the new norm was built by aggressive, scorecard-led corporations buying up competitors, ruling the supply chain and feeding ever-demanding consumers. War-like metaphors of threats and power were causing entrenched, loyal foot-soldiers to fight cost wars in a battle for commerce and returns.

Figure 6.1   Porter's five forces

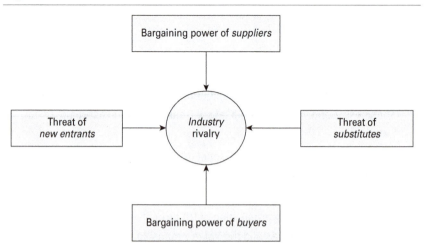

SOURCE Adapted from *Harvard Business Review* 'How competitive forces shape strategy', Michael E. Porter, March 1979 (Porter, 2017)

Flattened costs + increased sales = profits multiplied. Greed quite literally was, good, when it came to creating competitive advantage.

The bargaining power of *suppliers,* together with bargaining powers of *buyers* are added to by two threats – *new entrants* and product *substitutes.* With the centre force of *industry rivalry*, it was, and still is, a very product oriented model and view of the world. Of course in 1979 – when the work was first published – the world was very much still in a production-led, industrial model and much of what we know now of empowered consumers; supply chain, outsourcing and more has radically changed.

So in transformational parlance, does Porter's model have any relevance?

Bargaining power of suppliers – 21st-century style relations

There is a different challenge in supplier relationships in the 21st century in that this is very much a global game even more than it was in the 1980s. With the advent of the web, supplier relationships can even be forged at the click of a purchasing website link. Costs are still ever increasingly being driven down and whilst it is recognized how much the supply chain is probably more fragmented than it was in 1979, there is an increasing need to have suppliers as part of an ecosystem that can affect brand, reputation, compliance and stock value. Choose a terrible supplier (in any dimension of working systems, products or exploitative practices) and it damages *your* brand. I think Porter would concede it's a more complex relationship now than it was in 1979.

Bargaining power of buyers – consumers won the price war

How much has the consumer relationship changed since the advent of five forces thinking? When it was TV or mass-media advertising only, we had to believe what the makers told us. Now with reviews and products being endorsed by anything from bloggers to social media sites that tactic is blown apart. Consumer relationships have changed drastically to the point where consumer advocacy is the new gold in marketing. Which is the reason that many brands will demonstrate rewards and recognition of pro-brand posts on Instagram, Facebook and Twitter and we're encouraged to post product reviews on Amazon, Alibaba and others.

Them and us? More like 'all in it together'

So I'd view that those two elements of the five forces have gone into over-drive and are very much at play when business success is being plotted. They are of course relevant but this has significantly pivoted towards connected, loud voices of consumers and more transparent scrutiny of supply chain by everyone.

New entrants and substitute products

What then of the new entrants and the substitutes? In many ways, some of Porter's work was eclipsed by another theory that Harvard Business School shared with us all – disruptive innovation. Before we have a look into Professor Clayton Christensen's work let's continue to look at this element 1979 *vs* now.

New entrants

As with consumers, new entrants *are* a massive part of a whole new dimension in business. Mainly because the competitors in business are no longer the obvious competitors who look like you with perhaps a new branding or slogan. That Apple – as a computer company – saw how they could use a version of the Napster model of MP3 music formats to disrupt the music industry, probably doesn't get the credit it deserves for being disruptive and a 'new' entrant into the music game. Such ventures entering into a market means they're often totally unforeseen and so venture-capital funds all sorts of upstarts with platforms, with a transformative purpose (as mentioned in Chapter 5) and something really good for the customer: more convenience and a premium attached to the customer experience (CX).

CX really has taken over from other phrases in the value chain as the ultimate differentiator. Not just what you sell but how people experience it, in the choice architecture you create before the sell, the ultimate moment of truth when you sell, and the after sell – the use of the product/service and then the recommendation to others that it really was an inspired purchase/experience. Brian Solis's work in this area really is leading the thinking in this space and we will look later at the rise of employee experience (EX).

Product substitutes – the ease of replication

Substitutes was the other of Porter's forces. If anything, brands are still aware of cheaper substitutes but make such a play on the premium of their product this appears less of a success inhibitor than in 1979. We all know you can buy more budget ranges of smartphones and tablet devices, but that doesn't stop people drooling over the established leaders in the market whenever a new version of their product is out. Brand loyalty has been created. Countering much of the substitute market.

Of course it's still a threat to recognize, and product features in the substitute products might just have something. Which is why we now have a bigger smartphone; and we have a tablet with its own stylus and keyboard and we have rear parking sensors on many cars. Nokia didn't have a hugely threatening substitute product for some time (arguably). Until another product (the iPhone) just shifted the market away from them entirely and by the time they tried to catch up, they had lost their market share and brand reputation (Knopper, 2017; Huy, 2017).

Industry rivalry

Arguably this is more intense than ever. Those included in the top 500 of relevant market indexes find themselves there for a lesser period than ever before – either through demise and insolvency or through acquisition. Initial public offerings (IPOs) of startups is now headline news. There's a competition to be the next unicorn (a startup company valued at over $1 billion) and there's a host of acquisitions based on the data you hold, the market you've captured and the innovation you've got and could have.

Developments since Porter's theory have also given us the blue and red ocean theories of Rene Mauborgne and W Chan Kim (2004). Why take on competitors in a red ocean (where the analogy is about blood-spilled in the shark infested waters of your competition) and instead, create a blue ocean strategy – a product, service and proposition where no-one else is. This alternative approach takes rivalry into a different realm – an avoidance tactic built on product/service innovation – the signs were already there that battles aren't the only way to claim a share of a market – creating a new one is an entirely different way of approaching business success.

Summarizing the five forces for a transformational age of HR

Porter's model isn't outmoded *completely* but it feels a little under-sophisticated and perhaps overly simplistic for arguably more complex 21st-century businesses and business models. Does it have use for transformational HR practitioners and teams therefore? A little and here's how.

If CX is supreme, then we are likely to also think about the value in an EX approach to our organization (Richardson, 2010). If we fixate *only* on customers we could imbalance the very thing that will bring us success time and again – our people. We will take a look at EX in our closing chapter on how to bring transformational HR to a practical and applied method but now, we can focus on improving how things *feel* for our colleagues.

Supplier power in HR

For example, supplier power is a critical factor for HR to consider. HR's suppliers are now more prevalent than ever as we enter a world of heightened expectations about what constitutes a core employment benefit and a range of suppliers who can deliver that for us.

Consider your pensions provider; IT platform host; benefits aggregator; childcare provider – they will all have an impact on your EX and therefore will demonstrate how much value is put into people with the chosen partners. Will they ever be transformational? With the right partners and packages, they could be. You could certainly sharpen your innovation quotient with the right partners as some I've seen have done. Penguin Random House and their transformational use of video for pre-selection interviews by for example (Bowyer, 2014) – a classic case of supplier and client in transformational harmony with each other.

'Buyer' power regarding HR

As HR's *buyers* and therefore *customer base* is *all* the people of the organization, and being attuned to their needs hasn't always been seen as a strength. From worker's welfare, through hire and fire, through industrial and employee relations, and into engagement and culture, we are now seeing the advent of a more responsive and accountable HR function over the previously tolerated, bemoaned and often inhuman resourcing function personified by the 'evil' Catbert in the Dilbert cartoon. We covered a lot of this in earlier chapters and yet we do have to see how HR sees its people increasingly as customers.

We are seeing a shift from maligned to aligned. We are seeing a move towards accountability and compatibility. Having the entire organization's people as your customers can create a conflict in many formal and informal ways and yet, HR's role as protector of the ethics of people management and development is the foundation which is now moving into a period of employee enablement, enlightenment and the aforesaid experience. A more progressive view is that people can and do matter, much more than had previously been engineered in organizational systems and design. People can and do make the difference between customer loyalty and customer 'promiscuity' and therefore more should be done to get the best from the people an organization has. Enter HR and it's need to shift from bureaucracy and protector-in-general role to enabler and enhancer of people-powered success.

Concerned about professionalism, impact and value, HR is now a much more customer-oriented function and at what appears to be, just the right time as we shift from Porter's product orientation to a people orientation to business, work and therefore systems.

New entrant and substitute product threats to HR

New entrants and *substitutes* is where HR will need to spend a little more time in the thinking and doing space.

New entrant threats here is, I believe, with those unicorn-type new organizations (think Uber and Deliveroo), new organizational models and new ways of even doing work. The advent of the gig economy, work-as-a-platform and alternative models for working relationships between employer and worker. These are also considered as *substitute products* and could catch organizations out if they're not paying attention.

Employer brand is now a truly leverageable thing and having spent time with HR students proves this to me. When asked where is their ideal organization to work for, many will report back to me that they would like to work for Google, Apple, Virgin, Facebook and there is an awareness amongst those students of things like the UK *Sunday Times Top 100 best companies*.

Employer brand matters to them and will matter to a range of other prospective workers. Many of the same students report their decisions are not to do with salary packages, annual leave or similar but to *culture* and *feel* of the company. When equally successful brands are factored in, replies have been very illuminating 'they may be successful but there's stories about their oppressive working practices or autocratic leadership style'. Brand and culture really matter to prospective employees.

New entrants with great employer brands and stories of people-centred approaches will perhaps attract the very people who will make that story more powerful and likely to succeed. If you vision it, they will come and build it with you.

The rise of *Glassdoor* as a web review of your company, its leaders, its culture and its hiring processes is another 'genie out of the bottle'. Glassdoor may not yield quite so much consumer brand power as *Trip Advisor* or *Yelp*, but you may never know who is deterred from applying to you because of poor reviews of your company or hiring process on Glassdoor.

Industry rivalry – the HR version

To some degree, HR has apparently had very little in the way of rivalries but I'd dispute that. And now more than ever it has rivalries it may not be aware of.

Automation of processing and self-service applications negate the need for HR administrative power over some of the organizations people elements. Whilst some HR practitioners may wish to hold onto this with some vengeance or fear, there is an inevitable move towards automation and self-service that will negate this and create capacity in other areas. In those other areas there is rivalry.

HR advice and employment law are – of course – also the domain of qualified lawyers who are *not* HR practitioners necessarily. They are though increasingly commissioned to go beyond the advocacy and representation of cases taken to tribunal and to form part of the pre-emptive avoidance of litigious relief; to be more part of a more clarification process when new employment options are becoming more popular, demanded or desirable.

Good people management and development, when done well by well-equipped and warm-hearted managers barely, rarely needs any HR intervention or support.

Learning & Development is increasingly something that specialist divisions in corporate life take on themselves and service their own continuing professional development needs.

Organization development professionals may find themselves on the margins of change, comms, culture and values-related exercises with change teams, tactical units for innovation and design that are made up of business analysts, technologists and psychologists.

These are reasons why I believe the thicker trunk in the T-HR model of mine, is a proposition worth considering for these very reasons. Being equipped in areas that others are forging business value from (anthropology; sociology; entrepreneurial spirit and so on) we could see an unrecognizable HR function within the next 5–10 years. I may be seen as optimistic even in that timeframe yet I sense the planets are aligning and it is up to HR to take advantage of that combination of events and innovations.

And if not then there are already many progressive new organizations (I am fond of as case studies of the future of work) who have dispensed entirely with HR. No-one has that title in their role in companies like Buurtzorg, Nearsoft and AirBnB. Instead, HR is a distributed set of principles, protocols and practices that everyone has responsibility for. So there *are* warning signs that the current model of HR can and should be thought of as dispensable because it is. In even 1000+ organizations, distributed HRM can be delivered safely and effectively.

So Porter's five forces has something to offer transformational HR – or at least for a more attuned, business-oriented, outward-facing HR function. It does require what I can only describe as a kaleidoscopic view of the model – twist it, turn it and reimagine it for the 21st century in order to get the value from the model as an inquisition tool: disrupt the model a little I guess. Which leads me nicely onto disruptive innovation.

Disruptive innovation and its part in transformational HR

What is undoubtedly more transformational in its reputation (certainly a newer theory) than the five forces, is the theory of disruptive innovation (Christensen, 1997).

An innovation that creates a new market and value network and eventually disrupts an existing market and value network is something which seemed to overrule and overtake the five forces as an edge companies wanted to achieve. The term was coined in 1995 by Professor Clayton Christensen. Wikipedia is a disruptive innovation: destroying a previous market almost completely (expensive encyclopaedias and Encarta as a digital, CD-ROM version). A further example is that of the automobile. It was not the motor car itself, but the Model T Ford which made motorized transport more accessible to all and transformed the transport infrastructure therefore being a disruptive innovation.

So can HR become a disruptive innovation? Perhaps it can never be disruptive? Indeed is there a new market to create by HR? Let's look at some further examples of types of innovation.

What is disruptive innovation?

A *sustaining* innovation is an *evolutionary* (improvement-based) innovation that enhances an existing product or service in an existing market. Online-ordered movies on DVD through the mail was an evolutionary innovation.

Using an existing product and service (DVD movies and mail services) this took people away from store-based rental of movies to home-based and internet-based ordering.

The other sustaining innovation is *revolutionary*. Downloading movies from iTunes was a little niche to start with – it required superior bandwidth and whilst enjoyed on someone's Mac or PC, was a little out of the reach of the masses. It was though, a revolution to download the entire box set of *24* without the need to purchase DVD copies and have them delivered to you in a physical format. Sat around your PC might not have been that revolutionary a watching experience but it was a revolution in content delivery nonetheless.

And then a *disruptive* innovation – Netflix and the streamed content model. Increases in home digital bandwidth, online stores to rent or purchase digital download copies of movies and TV series negated the need for either a store to rent one from or a postal service to deliver the physical copy of the content coupled with SmartTVs and Chromecasts/Firesticks/Apple TV devices. This meant all the comfort of the lounge, couch and large widescreen TV with on-demand, streamed video content through a smart device and broadband connection. The ability to download to a mobile or portable device meant you could take your viewing with you wherever you went for added convenience. That was disruptive innovation – giving a product like a movie a totally different platform and interface, experience and utilization.

Unfortunately, disruptive innovation is now a little over-used and people tend to think of *any* innovation as disruptive when in reality it is probably evolutionary or revolutionary.

HR and its relationship with disruptive innovation

Using disruptive innovation as a principle or series of principles though, how *could* HR – and in this case transformational HR – be disruptive?

Let's start at the beginning of most HR journeys – hiring, recruitment and talent acquisition. Evolutionary innovation would be to go from submitting CVs by email to a web form and upload with automated response and tracking. This is a norm in most circumstances but still a little way to go before it becomes ubiquitous.

Revolutionary innovation would be where people apply and join an online community of fellow applicants and existing employees. They are then invited to participate in live chats with real (future) colleagues and complete an exercise and video interview, psychometric tool and work-related trial to assess not only competence, but cultural fit and innovation qualities. Decisions are made without ever formally meeting in person.

Disruptive innovation could be where you aren't even *hiring* people to vacancies. You are working with approved people (who are assessed for fit using an algorithm collecting data from their online presence on social networks) allocated to work on defined project assignments, by crowd-sourcing some of your inputs and work and bringing together totally flexible routines for all but a few core permanent people. As people begin to appreciate the work and you their contributions, they are then invited to work for a one week project to see if they like the experience before giving up their existing job and then a check-in conversation assesses the go/no go decision. Only then are more formalized offers made and an employment – not worker contract – drawn up. Even then, the design of their role is an entirely worker-led exercise where there is a value proposition between person and employer and not a vacancy the employer deems necessary. Using this (not totally unreal or made up) example shows us that so much of what we see in the HR space is evolutionary or revolutionary innovation. It could be argued that the most disruptive HR could be about itself is to disappear!

Some companies have created more of a disruptive approach to HR and disbanded the function and spread the work to those in leadership or coaching positions. Buurtzorg (mentioned earlier) – the now famous Dutch homecare nursing organization – has devolved all HR to teams and coaches within those teams. They have no HR function. Many other companies have outsourced administration and moved their HR teams to people and organization development/change/culture teams. In name and spirit in many cases. An evolutionary or mild revolutionary approach to innovation.

True disruptive innovation would take the form of radical models. Up until recently, Uber would have fallen into this category. With more established working conditions prevailing inside the technology company itself, their 'agents' driving cars and collecting passengers was done by freelance but 'vetted' and trained people. This is a disruptive model. The law though, has interjected and given Uber drivers workers rights (annual leave allowances and other quasi-employment privileges). So this was disruption that has hit the buffers of the law. GitHub, UpWork, Backscratchers, TaskRabbit and others are still attempting to disrupt the model of employ to create a new market – work as a platform. An eBay-like bidding of supply and demand; an alternative to hard-wired employment terms for people who genuinely want to gig so they can wrap their work around their lives and not the other way around.

Disruptive HR – a fallacy, fad or falsehood?

So what could be true HR disruption remains up for grabs. Disrupted out of existence? Or alongside a market-changing new-style company? Probably the latter. Although, there is a strong argument that given the right conditions, transformational HR could be a market-disrupting force to change the very nature of success and growth that a company experiences.

I could be bold and say that *true* disruptive innovation in HR (and HR's purpose for being) is unlikely and rare. Instead, HR functions could focus more on evolutionary and revolutionary innovation which in themselves would help it be more of a transformational HR force for good. I think it worth stating that it is my view that transformational HR does not mean you *have* to be disruptively innovative. Revolutionary and evolutionary innovation can, and will, help transform HR and be transformational for the businesses HR works with.

For example, HR teams *could* look to create the conditions for disruption in their companies by adopting something akin to the models mentioned in Chapter 5 – Atlassian's 24 hour 'work on what you want'; Google's 20% or Google X innovation time or ventures; the NHS have held 24 hour hackathons/transformathons which have delivered inventive, creative ideas to help improve healthcare. None of these are actually disrupting HR itself. They are evolutionary or revolutionary innovation – especially because they are building on other's innovation. It's hardly disruptive to copy. However, disrupting HR's own way of innovating would be a good thing in my view. I'll explain why with these following paragraphs, but in order to innovate more, I think HR needs to disrupt itself in this area – how it innovates.

HR innovation

Whilst there are undoubtedly innovative HR teams in operation, the function as a whole is not renowned for its innovative thinking. Quite the contrary, business leaders and practitioners I know (who aren't in HR) will often accuse HR of stifling innovation and being risk-averse. So I would decree that anything HR teams can do to prove they are being more innovative and embrace creative ways of working will curry favour with their colleagues. Don't be too quick to shut down innovation or be the ones to dampen the mood too soon. The more you get used to being innovative (and managing risks of course) the more you will be seen as helping other's attempts to innovate safely but purposefully.

So, it may be that HR teams set up a deliberate 'spin-out' of people who are involved in innovation, new thinking, creative application of HR principles and generally are like the special assignments squad within. Even in small HR teams, it can be part of people's roles for a certain portion of the week – they take an innovation lab approach. Or in bigger teams, a more full-time assignment for even a short period of time.

It may well create excitement amongst HR colleagues; that they won't always be the case worker or the administrator and they'll get a turn operating in a 'black-ops HR' manner. Let's face it, organizations are longing for some new thinking in how to harness the skills and talents of people and anything that breathes life into new ways is more likely to yield successful, competitive advantage than something which is tired, rule-ridden and predictable.

So whatever you think an HR team should do to become more disruptive, innovative and pioneering, I doubt it will be met with resistance from the business colleagues you work with. Quite the contrary – you might just find *more* support, *more* collegiate approaches and *more* belief that they are pleased and proud you're their HR cohort. With a strong reputation for being safe, it's not likely that HR would be deemed irresponsible and careless overnight. Especially so if it can be seen that there are ways to throw off the past shackles of predictable grey operating regarding people and organization design in favour of more technicolour inclusivity and innovation.

HR's road to innovation

How then should HR become more disruptive, innovative and creative when its footprint is one of rule-bound process being a potential hindrance? One very simple model is *skill* and *will*. Simply put, do we have the *will* to be more innovative, creative and possibly disruptive and then do we have the *skill* to back up the will? A place to start is to use established innovation and modelling tools and practices to increase the skill, which may enhance the will and vice versa.

Business modelling

I've talked a lot about propositions and business models in this book already. Some of my deliberate use of this language is to short cut the words used to get to the point of two things:

- what you intend to do (the proposition); and
- how you intend to do it (the model).

The *Value Proposition Canvas* and *Business Model Canvas* have influenced my thinking and vocabulary in this area and are two innovation processes – linked – that will give you a chance to edge your HR function towards something more inventive and disruptive.

If HR practitioners don't already know of these two tools, then the work of Alex Osterwalder and Yves Pigneur is well worth investigating. In keeping your head in this book and away from their resourceful creative commons website, https://strategyzer.com/, I'll share their work and some HR examples of where this has disrupted, challenged and reshaped the HR proposition to the businesses they work with.

We'll start with the wider picture and then zoom in – the Business Model Canvas. Osterwalder and Pigneur were curious, curious; about the way businesses were constructed and why some were roaring successes and others not so much so. They found an approach to business modelling that created a pattern – 300+ companies from the size of Amazon and Google to smaller enterprises were researched and the results smashed together in some deductive analysis. Out the other end of that hadron collider tube came the nine elements of the Business Model Canvas.

With a range of ways to construct this, the recommended type will be familiar to many of us: wall space, boxes and sticky notes. I first ran this with an aspiring Division in a not-for-profit world with big ambitions. How did they reconcile those ambitions with their own competence, resources and energy and then distil them into a schema that others would understand and participate actively and positively towards? We used the canvas. We mapped those aspirations, actualities, features. We created a visual on a lot of flipchart paper. We walked through it several times. We understood our business from a narrative, journey and pragmatic sense. We built something.

Those clever and passionate leaders took our *sketches for the future* (a great phrase introduced to me by Jon Husband), and built a strategy, a document and a briefing deck from it. They shared it with the team. They had already adopted the approaches of IBM and others to be strategically agile; to have resource fluidity and collective commitment. This seemed like the next stage in their developed approach.

It worked. A huge programme was endorsed, funding obtained and work delivered *because* they had such clarity and vision. For all elements of the work – not just the *why* but the *how* and the *what*. The Business Model Canvas exercise helped the team do this.

So back to HR. When was the last time you, as an HR professional, truly took the forensic approach to your function and modelled it? Looked into the DNA and spirit of who you are and what and how you can make better out of the mandate you have and the agenda you want to create?

Again, I took this approach with a large company. Digital transformation was on the horizon. The Board had said 'we need to digitally transform'. What that meant in its most wide but defined terms is be more modern, technologically enabled and forward thinking/working.

HR was charged with the *digital transformation* of the people who worked for the company. Many casual, nine months on three months off, from all parts of the globe, regulars and new entrants, with a very mixed degree of computer literacy. What was clear about this exercise was the lack of clarity about ownership, purpose and application. Lots of detail being shared about what digital transformation is and isn't. Tools and platforms forming the fixated thinking that provided more discord than connectivity.

So we walked the *entire* enterprise through the Business Model Canvas and paying specific attention to the people and digital transformation elements as we went through the nine elements.

And this led to a realization. That ownership of digital transformation was not just something people weren't sure about but was ill-defined if not even very badly defined. A realization that no strategy had been devised – no significant attention to a strategic outcome; the only why was 'the Board have spoken.' Not just a lack of strategy but a lack of perspective on supply; resourcing; partnerships; customer segments and more.

Did this win? Not really but it showed how losing the current approaches were. It showed how far apart the perspectives and thinking was and showed that it wasn't answers that were lacking but the right *questions* to even get to the answers. I left this to the teams to work through as my work was done. I disrupted their stalled thinking and activities and whilst I helped them tear that particular playhouse down, they were left to rebuild from a cleaner, clearer perspective.

That people – who had worked for years in the same profitable company – couldn't describe the value the organization created, their own HR function created and their own people were creating was telling.

So what is this magical tool?

The Business Model Canvas

Nine elements, constructed on a canvas with deliberately little prescription and allowing for complete customization and contextually specific dialogue. A team sport not a solo effort, an inclusive mechanism not an exclusive process.

Figure 6.2   The Business Model Canvas

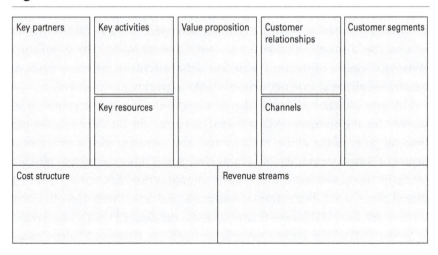

SOURCE Strategyzer and www.strategyzer.com

Starting, often at the centre, with the most important element to all businesses and business units – *the value proposition.* What is the value that you propose to the world? How do you create it and what does it mean for other people? Without this, there really is no point. There are questions to ask (both in the book and the accompanying website and numerous blog posts people have created since the tool was created). The value is there for you to define. Or redefine. The Business Model Canvas is that wonderful tool that can be both here and now, and there and then. Present and future, desired and actual.

Once you have the defined value proposition formed – or at the start of it – you can move on to other areas either where your interests lie: if you're in finance you might zoom straight into the costs and income elements; if you're in operations, then customer relationships and customer segments; if you're in technology or procurement you might go to partners. The canvas has several directional approaches to take dependent on the nature of your organization yet it really is up to you how you do it.

The remaining elements are 'channels', how people reach you and you them (and no this isn't just the web); 'key resources' (what do you have/ use); and 'key activities' (what do you do to create that value). Its simplicity is part of its beauty.

So my urge here, is for *all* HR functions with even a mild desire to be disruptive and transformational is *use this tool*. Sweat the HR value proposition, work through this entire model as if the HR function operating in your organization was a commercial entity that had to fight for the right to survive and thrive. Look at HR as an enterprise within an enterprise. If it were specifically commissioned and funded by a purchasing mindset, would anyone buy it and you?

Like all models, there's a method and there's an interpretation that means even unsuccessful ventures went through this process. A bad idea or lame application of an idea might not magically transform into a good thing *just because* people use the canvas. After all, someone might be so biased towards their current thinking that they don't use the tool to interrogate all elements of their thinking and let themselves be blinded by their own hubris.

When used with an open mind and a clear conscience, the tool works well. Really well in some cases like the one I talked about at the beginning of this section.

The Value Proposition Canvas: HR's potential killer app

I should also mention the spin out tool from the Business Model Canvas that is the *Value Proposition Canvas*.

So important is the value proposition to this entire process, that Osterwalder and Pigneur devoted some time to create the Value Proposition Canvas. A rather intriguing design with a face and a box to signify customers and a product.

Three sections in each aspect. Often starting with the customer and working right to left. What are the customers's jobs? What are the things the customer needs to do? The work they have, the services they provide and the activities that occupy their time? It's important to understand this because your product or service is likely to help them do this. After all, why would they buy? The job of the customer – for example if they are a consumer of video games – is to play games, learn, beat others, beat the machine, gain points, create a following and standing, push their boundaries of skill, enjoy

Figure 6.3   The Value Proposition Canvas

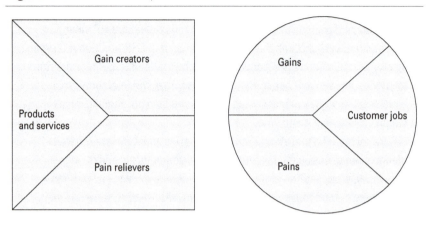

SOURCE Strategyzer and www.strategyzer.com

themselves and get to know others. If the value proposition of yours is to sell video games to these people, you need to know that's their job, their work, their thing. Some consumer data will tell you this but also knowing the people that are your audience and customers is vital here. Once you have ascertained what their job is, you can then look at the pains they experience in doing this work and the gains they are or might be after in order to maximize the impact of their work.

The next three-part box to complete is *your* part in this value proposition. What are the gain creators, what are the pain relievers and what are the products and services you offer? It is essentially, how you can map and demonstrate what you offer is of direct value to your customers either in the work they do/jobs they have, the pains they experience and the gains they are looking for. It can also be used to map new products/services – potential gain creators, pain relievers and products and services that *could* create value for customers.

It was using this model that 90 minutes with a famous health charity in the UK turned their approach to 'brand HR' into something much more powerful, aligned and clear. Mapping out the customer's view of the world; their issues and their opportunities may sound like an easy thing to conceive but we often see only the surface of the problems to solve. Taking their perspective adds a whole new dimension to what solutions, services and support you thought you offered for good reason and wondered why customers either didn't use or used but clearly not effectively as they were still having issues.

Working with this HR team some mini-revelations kept appearing as each facet in pains/gains/jobs was unpacked and added to the model. An entirely new way to pitch and support that client will make the biggest difference to them and the reputation of HR within that client base. All through thinking about things differently and visualizing a new and totally fresh way of presenting a model of the world.

So from two very high level conceptual models to two practical models/tools to the most dominant model in the HR sphere. The HR business partner – also known as the Ulrich – model and the transformational HR makeover of this stalwart of HR models.

Three key transformational HR takeaways and reflective questions to consider:

1 There are a range of models and theories which can be very useful to HR professionals and this overview of provides some insight into a more transformational approach to HR.

   Q: How can you use the five forces in a specific HR-related context to positively influence and advance your HR model of operating and strategic thinking?

2 Disruptive innovation has been one of the most transformative models the business world has seen and in the light of new markets created by AirBnB, Spotify and Kickstarter has become a somewhat overused phrase.

   Q: How can you use an appropriate level of disruptive, revolutionary and evolutionary innovation to transform both HR and the business HR supports?

3 Business modelling and the concept of the value proposition has helped shape everything from Google and Amazon to smaller entrepreneurial start-ups.

   Q: How can you use the Value Proposition Canvas (in particular) to reshape and enhance the HR proposition in your organization?

References

Bowyer, Jim (accessed 26 May 2017) 'The digital interview' [blog], 15/05, Penguin Random House, London [Online] www.penguinrandomhousecareers.co.uk/category/blog/video-interviewing/

Christensen, C (1997) *The innovator's dilemma: When new technologies cause great firms to fail*. Harvard Business Review Press, Cambridge

Huy, Quy (accessed 18 May 2017) 'Who killed Nokia? Nokia did', *Insead Knowledge*, 22/09 [Online] https://knowledge.insead.edu/strategy/who-killed-nokia-nokia-did-4268

Knopper, Steve (accessed 20 May 2017) 'iTunes 10th anniversary: how Steve Jobs turned the industry upside down', *Rolling Stone Magazine*, 26/04 [Online] www.rollingstone.com/music/news/itunes-10th-anniversary-how-steve-jobs-turned-the-industry-upside-down-20130426

Mauborgne, Rene and Kim, W Chan (2004) Blue Ocean Strategy, Harvard Business Review Press, Brighton MA

Porter, Michael E (accessed 26 May 2017) 'How competitive forces shape strategy', *Harvard Business Review* [Online] https://hbr.org/1979/03/how-competitive-forces-shape-strategy

Richardson, Adam (accessed 26 May 2017) 'Understanding customer experience', *Harvard Business Review* [Online] https://hbr.org/2010/10/understanding-customer-experie

The one model to rule them all? 07

Introduction

As I covered in the previous chapter, HR practitioners – possibly more than any other professional discipline in the world of work – love their models. Organizational design, development and effectiveness is particularly rife with a range of them. They are undoubtedly useful codifications of how systems and structures are and what can be explained through a model rather than a lengthy block of text.

We're yet to take a detailed look at the dominant model in HR: the *Ulrich* model and the *three-legged stool*. With this model's ubiquity, comes a familiarity that I hope many of the more experienced HR practitioners reading this can read this section at pace.

How will this chapter transform my thinking?

- This chapter provides a deep and detailed look at the dominant model in the HR world, the Ulrich model, and a look at where it has helped and miss-fired.

- It will explore in more detail a key component of this model – the role of HR business partners – and their transformation and overhaul the role so it is fit for the 21st-century needs of HR and the world of work.

- It describes an upgraded version of the Ulrich model and where it can be improved upon to provide a more transformational approach to HR.

Dawning of a new era

If we go back 20 years to 1996, HR was very different HR to the version we have now. So over 20 years have passed since *Human Resource Champions* was published by Professor Dave Ulrich which heralded this new era in HR (Ulrich, 1996).

Forever enshrined in HR – whatever the experiences you may have had as a people manager or HR professional, the Ulrich model is synonymous with HR practice. There are over 6 million people globally who work in HR. That means there's probably over 2 million HR professionals who have the title 'Business Partner' to define their role, which is a key differentiator of Professor Ulrich's model from previous incarnations of personnel and HR.

I can begin by stating that I'm not here to knock this model or to pull it apart any more than the average conversation in an HR team already might, and I'm not here to validate it any more than successful utilization of this model already has. Dave Ulrich is someone who I believe cares deeply about the HR practice field and the people in it – he's one of us. I think he has made some amazing strides into HR being more of a dynamic function and given us far more than we've ever recognized.

As Rensis Likert Professor at the Ross School of Business, University of Michigan he is renowned as the person who created the *three-legged stool for HR – shared services, centre of excellence and business partners*. Most of the HR practitioners I know have either been trained in this way, operated in it through their team adopting this structure or consulted in teams who are either working this way or trying to move beyond it.

Professor Ulrich has also had some criticism from HR practitioners (I think it right to say we can be a fickle bunch in HR) who have said the model failed to deliver what it promised. If I were Professor Ulrich, I would counter this by explaining that the model is a framework intended to work in your context – so it's not a prescription as a model and the actual execution is down to local teams.

How one person can be responsible for an entire function firing or misfiring is too big an ask. Adam Smith, F W Taylor and Henry Ford notwithstanding, there's a range of reasons why criticism of the Ulrich model hasn't really *moved the dial* for HR anyway. No-one has come up with anything to replace it although I will show how I feel transformational HR can be modelled later in this book. I would like to start with why I think Professor Ulrich's work is undervalued.

You may have had the same experience as I did – that prior to the Ulrich model, the HR team was a linear, hierarchical and functionally split unit as recruitment, pay and benefits, learning and development and employee relations. There were large and small teams doing this and many of them shared the same principles: they rarely collaborated with each other; were order-taking administrators; often had little or no knowledge of the work of the organization in its most customer-connected sense and enjoyed a very un-business like unmeasured life. Delays in recruitment campaigns were regular (time from vacancy for hire), there was an infamy in form filling and form processing that frustrated their operational colleagues, annual leave requests may have been centralized, long-term sick absences were unmonitored, there was confusion over maternity leave and learning requests took months to fulfil if at all.

Whilst many businesses tolerated this as 'just the way it is', many (rightly so) weren't happy. Modern threats like agencies; out-sourcing or offshoring presented themselves as more efficient options. Like most services, if the state of delivery isn't satisfactory, it's only a matter of time before alternatives are sought.

So against this mild crisis, many personnel functions (which was the prevailing moniker throughout the 1980s) were attempting to morph into a more responsive HR function. By this time, computer technology had infiltrated the workplace in all ways and one of the last functions to receive its suite of productivity enhancing technological support was HR. Some might say this was the low value perspective epitomized, which is potentially harsh but probably true.

Still things weren't necessarily improving much: training requests may be emailed but that didn't make them acted upon any more quickly – there was now simply a read receipt to prove it had been at least delivered.

The Ulrich model

So in 1996 influenced by the moves of other elements of the professional world, Dave Ulrich wrote and released his book, *Human Resource Champions*. In this book Ulrich described a (then) transformation that HR teams could deliver: realigning itself to be more efficient, more responsive and accountable and more business-like. IT and accountancy had done similar things prior to this with positive impacts. So producing this model and a template success felt like the natural evolution to many HR directors and it became the darling of the conference circuit – 'Have you adopted the Ulrich model?' became a regular question and it became the vogue model for HR.

HR delivery model (Ulrich, 1996)

- **Shared services:** centralized, technology-enabled HR service delivery excellence. Sometimes outsourced.
- **Centre of excellence:** HR experts with specialist knowledge who deliver leading edge strategy and solutions.
- **Business partners:** HR professionals working closely with business leaders to improve business outcomes through human capital solutions.

I think the genius in the model is its simplicity and using a method we all see in politics, rhetorical devices like speeches and in education – the *rule of three*.

In implementing this model, experiences I had, were akin to the following internal dialogue across the HR leadership team:

Shared services: customer contact – the start of the workflow, administrative support, recruitment requests, learning needs, changes to address, new bank account for pay, annual leave, maternity benefits queries – all started with shared services, a help desk, operators, technology to support it.

Great. Can set that up. One email address. One phone number. Efficiencies of scale: TICK.

Centre of excellence: learning professionals, employee relations, change, leadership development, equality and diversity (by now, a 'thing' at work), organization development/design, occupational health, graduate recruitment, assessment centres – all the stuff that formed the added value of HR and the things that the other parts of the business only had a basic knowledge of – experts, qualified practitioners.

Great. We have that – it's shared across teams but we can keep them in their functional areas of expertize. Commissioned by the HR administrators when there's a tribunal to attend; a course to deliver or a health issue to advise on. Collective expertise. TICK.

Business partners: strategic advice and support to business leaders, representatives on management teams to advise on people matters, client management for issues and functional problems, share new initiatives and key people management insight that helps their corporate clients – not advisers per se but can help with areas at a micro level and advise on the course of action to take. Respond to shared service calls and issues to resolve.

Not so great. Who has the skills for this all-new, customer-connected role? Largely people who are in my centre of excellence who do that already – hmm – what's the difference then between centre of excellence (CoE) and BPs? I have a lot of advisers who work on cases – I'll re-label them as BPs and they can take a more strategic role. Not sure what that strategic role is and how it goes beyond order-taking but I'm sure we'll work it out. Order taking goes to Shared Services anyway. At least it means that the HRD won't have to be at every management meeting now. Investigations – yes of course they can do this. Or should the CoE do it?

And so it went on.

This latter part – the *business partner* – was touted as the key differentiator in getting HR that fabled seat at the table. From having no seat at any table, we would have multiple representation through many tables. Yet I can remember this conversation myself and others have confirmed they've also had it. An operational manager to their HRBP: 'So what exactly do you do as an HRBP?' Met with a range of buzzwords, ambiguous objectives and slightly awkward statements of intent.

Again, perhaps harsh. I worked with some people who were outstanding business partners. What did they do that made them outstanding? Client focus, business understanding, advice on a more big-picture and long-term perspective and not a short-term problem solved but no causality analysis and fix to prevent repeat, and understanding human and organizational psychology and behavioural science. They were also influential through great insight, connections and analytical skills, and reputation enhancers with reliable, well-founded support and even provocation.

Nevertheless this 'patchy' implementation by some HR professionals left the model (remember three-legs) somewhat falling over in one direction. Combine that with inefficient shared services, some underwhelming 'excellence' from CoE and then little or no interplay between the three functions, and you have a heightened level of expectation, a degree of uncertainty and then a failure of the basics and we're not even back at basecamp – we've fallen back down the mountain.

Mine – and many others's – experience of moving to this model wasn't a simple transition though. Certainly relabeling HR advisors, caseworkers and team leaders certainly wasn't helpful – which I saw a *lot* of. Some HR professionals were a little confused about how to describe this new business partner role and that really didn't bode well for someone who was supposedly part of the organization that designed and rated *all* roles in the organization. I'm not being overly critical of the entire model, but there is a well documented trail of poorly implemented versions of Professor Ulrich's model leading many to point the finger of blame at the model creator.

As I said earlier and to avoid any doubts, Dave Ulrich has done HR a *huge* service and many of us will be forever in his debt for the careers we now have. This is not the time to criticize or attack Dave Ulrich who continues to shed some terrific light on HR from a point of view that many other professors will never do so. Yes, I'll hold my hand up and say that I've made some comments about some of the features of this model – not from a *he is wrong* point, but from my experiences of half-baked attempts at relabeling HR roles without due diligence being applied in transforming mindsets, processes and success criteria.

Time to transform the HR business partner role?

Why do I think we need a book about transformational HR when Professor Ulrich's model clearly *allows* for change and adaptation to be a part of the *modus operandi* of HR? I think to unhook our habits and orthodoxies in HR we need to consciously create something new, something *transformational* for HR and allow and direct HR to *be* more transformational in the businesses it works with.

For starters, we've already explored in this book how the world is changing in ways that simply weren't envisaged in 1997. Or even in 2007. We've also been through a great recession that has shifted some of our perspectives on safe, secure and even smart ways to work. Public sector cuts, austerity and a gap in the wealthiest to the poorest hasn't helped us mend societal rifts through enterprise, work and meaning. We've also simply learned more about ourselves. Our health and wellbeing for example. Our community spirit or otherwise, how the brain works and the discovery of new medicines, materials and methods of working.

So the 1996 Ulrich – or HR business partner – model was conceived in a different age. And yet bizarrely, we've rarely adapted the model ourselves as a profession. Not everyone of course, but there's a majority view that the *shared services, centre of excellence and business partner* triage is the solution in almost all corporate worlds.

The version of a changing entity in organizational life has largely been the *'R' word – restructuring*. I've experienced countless of these – many seemed to tackle systemic problems some even shifted to make a toxic leader redundant and not tackle their poor performance as a leader.

Yes, we've seen *endless* corporate restructures brought about by mergers, shifts in the market, the need to downsize (or even worse, a phrase I detest – *right-size*) and the almost fixated view that we unfreeze, change and then refreeze from Kurt Lewin's famous change model. One I feel has had it's day and is no longer as relevant in the fluid world we live in now. We appear to have seen very little *design for adaptability* or fluid states of being that are in need of no restructure and are a constantly reshaping and agile state of being.

The technology industry of course has a lot to offer to HR (as I've already mentioned) and yet not much crossing over of methodologies has naturally occurred. The technology industry has recovered from huge projects and failures during the 1990s into the dot com boom and bust of the early 2000s into the giants of success we now see. I don't even need to name the companies as their market capitalization and value is astounding.

The technology industry was, in my experience, the first to adopt a model similar to Professor Ulrich's own. I worked in this way in the early-mid 1990s before the Ulrich model was conceived and so when the model came into HR, I was more than familiar with it.

So I wonder why the HR profession has not learned more from their IT counterparts? I think there is a lot of realization now so I see this way of working more prominent in the learning and development/digital learning profession and in organization development practice fields.

Transforming the Ulrich model

Let's return to the definition I produced:

> Transformational HR is leading and delivering fundamental changes in how people and the organization conducts its business in order to control its aspirations, intentions and influence in an ever shifting world of work.

My definition takes a *fundamental change* approach to justify the tag transformational to HR and to the business it works with and is a part of. So do we need to *fundamentally change* the Ulrich model? I'd suggest we do. Not tear it all up and start again with a blank slate though.

I will use the quote by R. Buckminster Fuller again here: 'You never change things by fighting the existing reality. To change something, build a new model that makes the existing model obsolete'.

So I am advocating that we use some form of transformational HR mindset, approach and structure even to build something new that can reveal what is obsolete about our existing model. A parallel activity that will reveal the best ways to deliver effective and sustainable HR transformation to become a new norm (no unfreeze, change, refreeze going on here), an exploratory adjunct to inform the best way to pivot the existing practices, mindsets and skills – the spinout approach I mentioned in seeking the disruptive innovation to supercharge HR: transforming our three-legged stool into an adaptable product delivering human comfort and multi-purpose utilization.

Further chapters will share case studies and interviews with leading practitioners which share their view of the transformational HR world. For now, let's look quickly at the three elements of the Ulrich model and some elements that may transform elements within that:

Shared services now: HR administration, information management, supporting activities.

Shared services transformation: Exploring digital automation, friction-free administration; a culling of unnecessary but habitual bureaucracy, more intricate and bespoke support for people and organization development. Being HR's coders.

If you are an HR or people director looking to transform this function, you may want to take the mindset of the customer experience world and how we travel, buy, connect, join, share, challenge, administer and conduct our lives in the non-working world. It's that *employee experience* that may allow you to move to a more automated work of administration for HR.

A transformational project here is going to look at how the existing and future HR technology world is getting ready for this self-service, automated, chat-bot, blockchain world. And if you don't know enough about these areas, there's a great opportunity to start your project with insight gathering; research studies; and benchmarking in other industries who are exploiting automated and self-service technology that is secure and a superior customer experience.

Centre of excellence now: Talent acquisition, talent development, organization development, leadership, psychometric tools, learning and development, analytics, mediation, coaching. Lots of science, theory, practice and change mindsets already existing in this function.

Centre of excellence transformation: New frontiers of digital ethics; moral leadership; behavioural science; data mining; sociocratic ways of working; virtual reality and augmented reality; the singularity; augmented humans – may all seem some way off. Moving HR to being at the forefront of new thinking, emerging trends and innovations in the world of work.

The centre of excellence can expand its repertoire to include more research, scenario modelling and the futurology mentioned in Chapter 5.

This function can transform HR from within and not just be set upon the business it supports. Indeed, there exists a real opportunity that if the specialists in this world were to transform HR first, then the function could support and drive its business further and quicker than if it were a neglected part of the change process until perhaps, operations or customer service had been transformed first.

HR labs, transformational hubs, hacking squads. There is a lot of energy to be created *within* the HR 'reactor core' and yet I sense it is too outward active supporting its clients and customers to invest in its own transformation.

Which means it has to work ever harder in serving customers and clients and still coming up short because HR hasn't transformed. Catch 22.

I am advocating an approach where you service HR's needs first. With full support of the customer and client base and in pursuit of the new thinking and activism. Activism that I believe will help transform the people proposition in organizations for sustained success in that uncertain and challenging future we know is all around us and headed towards us.

HR business partners now: Functionally, geographically or strategically-aligned, client support to deliver a single point of contact and partnership advice, guidance and input to getting the best from people management and development. Commissioning shared service and centre of excellence colleagues as appropriate.

Understanding the context and operating ways of their clients to best interpret the HR processes, protocols and practices. Fixing problems and supporting HR activities like recruitment and selection, learning and comms.

HR business partners transformed: The ultimate intelligence source leading to being in the thick of transformational thinking. Relationships builder; agent provocateur; designer; coach; confidante; strategy consultant; learning partner; innovation catalyst; game-changing thinker and pragmatic solutions implementer.

Essential advocates and agents of a learning organization built for agility and adaptation. Leadership coaches, guides and straight talking enablers of ethical, humane and best in class people development and performance.

There are temptations for many HR business partners I see. Wicked lures into being a case worker, a trainer, a coach, a mediator. I see many clients insisting their business partner does this the centre of excellence or shared services could do, 'but you're here now...' is often the alluring comment.

I've seen some HR advisors, trainers not adopt the true spirit of the business partner model because they like their previous skills and feel worth and value in fixing something for their clients. Admirable but perhaps not in keeping with the true sense of the business partner. I'm still not sure *HR business partner* is the right title for this role.

From HR business partners to HR neo-generalists

Already out there in the business world – Kenneth Mikkelsen and Richard Martin have written a terrific book about the nature of our working times and come up with the phrase, concept and model of a neo-generalist (Martin and Mikkelsen, 2016). It encapsulates the brilliance of people who happen to have more than one area of expertise and a range of capability. In the past world of work, if you were a transient journey-taking worker, you'd be accused of being a 'jack of all trades, master of none'. Not in Kenneth and Richard's view of the world you're not. You're a master of *modern multiplicity*.

Peter Senge's seminal work on the *fifth discipline* called out *personal mastery* as a key discipline of a learning organization (Senge, 2006). Yet Senge didn't say *single subject expert*. Personal mastery might be that you are able to use the more traditional T-shaped model of a range of skills you know, can do to a perfectly acceptable level of competence, and then one or more areas where you have deeper experience and expertise.

So are HR business partners HR neo-generalists? Perhaps they are. They need to cover a range of issues and problems, interventions and applications for their clients or customers. And that's the important distinction for HR business partners – they are (in my view) first and foremost client relationship builders. They are aware of the work of their clients – their people. They feel and sense the world their clients operate in. They understand their challenges and difficulties. They appreciate their context and competence. They help their clients be great around their people matters because they know what it means to operate in that world.

Back to Peter Senge for a second – his account of the learning organization called out some 'learning disabilities' and one of them was being too symptomatic. Fixing a problem (an argument over a missed deadline between two people on a team) rather than zooming out to look at the systemic effects that caused the issue (a manager who is weak, delegates unfairly to one person over another favourite and allows one person privileges over others).

In one of the case study companies I've researched for this book (Menlo Innovations) there is an approach to technology design called 'Hi-Tech Anthropology'. Systems architects and designers who go and 'live' in their client's environment for a short time to appreciate their world. It helps get a better feel for design than the false environment of a design sprint workshop. It helps to see real people and talk to them about their flow of work, ideas and look at the systemic factors impacting on their jobs and work.

HR business partners are the business world's *people at work anthropologists* and should, in my view, spend as much time as they can with their people. They should become part of the world and understand it from a lived experience sense. Will they go 'native' and be less a part of the HR function not delivering strategic initiatives and becoming like a micro HR director? There is that danger so becoming part of a connected and collaborative forum with their shared services and centre of excellence colleagues together with different functional/geographical business partners is critical.

General Stanley McChrystal was former Joint Special Operations Commander of the US forces in Afghanistan. In his book *Team of Teams* he shows how intelligence, networking, combined with a reduction of bureaucratic friction were necessary for 21st-century anti-insurgent warfare and civilian relations. The Washington Times reviewed the book and shared the following: 'We had a large, well-trained, superbly equipped force, while insurgents had to recruit locals and smuggle in foreign fighters.[So] why were we unable to defeat an under-resourced insurgency? Why were we losing?' (Allard, 2017).

The drearily recurring culprit: US bureaucratic reductionism, sanctified in managerial thought and practice, honed throughout the military-industrial complex and wired together in a top-down hierarchy of electronic stovepipes and information silos. As sacraments of 20th-century warfare, reductionism and hierarchical obeisance were enshrined and reinforced from service academies through the higher military staff colleges. In contrast, 'Insurgent forces were native to the information-rich, densely interconnected world of the 21st century . In the course of this fight, we had to un-learn a great deal of what we thought we knew about how war — and the world — worked' (Allard, 2017).

Some of McChrystal's tactics were to forego armoured patrol cars from fortified yards and instead, have his people be *eyes on and hands off* – live with and get to know local people. This went against his military teaching yet was the right thing to do – build trust and gain intelligence.

An extreme example in a place of extreme conflict, but shows the power of new ways to work, using networked intelligence and presence and being.

HR business partners are those agents of intelligence. Where contact with the HR *command centre* is critical in both strategic alignment, sharing that intelligence and working out delivery tactics. So HR business partners are *outside in; and inside out.* This is ironically the title of a book co-authored by Professor Ulrich, *HR from the Outside In* (Ulrich et al., 2012), which set out six paradoxes facing HR in 2010–12:

- outside (macros trends, customer demands) and inside (working systems, employee demands);
- business (shareholder value, KPIs) and people (purpose and feeling valued);
- future (possibilities, options and threats) and past (reliable and proven practice);

- organization (what's best for the company) and individual (adapting to unique needs);
- strategic (seeing the bigger picture/planning) and administrative (keeping on top of essentials);
- process (Efficiencies and systems thinking) and event (fixing urgent needs and demands).

In order to be transformational, these paradoxes need to be worked through and any forces that keep them far apart negated. In essence, any interferences (mentioned in Chapter 3) are removed so that HR can perfectly manage the energy push and pull between these factors. If anything, a transformative approach would see them co-exist as creative tensions to spark innovation.

HR business partners then are able to be part of strategic and tactical solutions brokering. They are the networkers in the machine. They are the collaborative force for good. They are the pivot between short-term fixing and long-term systemic shifts to create more positive and productive ways of working and can effectively close the gap between these paradoxes.

HR business partners need transformational HR perhaps the most. There appears to be natural tendencies in many operating in the centre of excellence to be transformative. Change programmes; new leadership models; alternative structures; the creation of a new business venture – all call for the CoE to be engaged in transformational activities.

So how do we transform the HR business partner role without it becoming a field-ops version of the centre of excellence? For a start the capabilities of HR business partners need to be looked at critically and the design of the role given a good hard interrogation. If it's a hyper-specialized, case worker and mediator role, then it should live in the centre of excellence is my view. If it's an order-taking trainer for high volume customer care skills, then it should be in the centre of excellence.

If it's a *people at work anthropologist*, a strategy design consultant, a networking and connecting force and a sensing enabler of dialogue to explore new ways to deliver a great people proposition, that's a transformed HR business partner into an HR neo-generalist.

Battling for their client, yet compliant with a brilliant and well-crafted people strategy – the HR business partner needs to manage that ambiguity. They need to be a translator of people policies into operational covenants between people and the organization. They need to be stewards of change, adaptation and guidance on how to get the most of the quantum energy source that is the people their client/division has. They need to be teachers of great ways to operate with the rest of the HR function and they need to create enough tension that their colleagues who may be wanting answers from them, instead have better crafted questions to ask of themselves and others.

Transforming HR business partners

A from and to might illustrate some of the traps the HRBP role sometimes finds itself in and the more contemporary and progressive features a transformational HR neo-generalist might demonstrate.

Whilst some of these may be the result of clever wordsmithing, we do need – I feel – a new vocabulary for the HRBP role in particular. So whilst the role itself may need some reinvention of the key success criteria,

Table 7.1 HR business partners: mindsets and modus operandi: from and to

From	To
Focused down on delivering their clients wish list and acting in accordance with their every demand	Committed to their client enough to challenge their thinking and respect their potential and capabilities without undue reverence
Short-term problem fixers	Systems evaluators and solutions brokers – seeing the wood and the trees
Enforcers of HR policies	Guides for effective application of the covenant between people and organization
Rule benders in favour of their clients	Enablers of innovative approaches in concordance with fairness and inclusivity
Reactors to urgent fixes	Future-focused strategy co-designers taking the heat out of the heat of the moment. Rapid mobilizers and reflectors on avoiding future hijacks and reactive processing
HR generalists being able to turn their hand to a few different things in the HR world	HR neo-generalists adopting intelligence sourced approaches to better enable their HR colleagues and partners for the benefit of their clients
Order taking doers expected to deliver to demand	Quick response architects of great people and organization development solutions which may or may not include them in the delivery model

accountabilities and the like, the *fiction* we can create about the role – the strategic narrative, the sense of purpose for the role and the story the role is a part of, could help us realize that modernized take on Professor Ulrich's original premise. And yet, there is a stronger argument to not stop at transforming the existing roles, but take a look at the entire model. I will give this my best shot now.

A model fit for transformational HR

In thinking about an alternative model to the three-legged stool, I'm going for a four-wheel drive SUV. For a more professional sense though, I'll call it a *four-zone framework*.

HR People & Programme Support (HRPPS) Shared Services doesn't mean much to people except that there's something to share and it's a service. So HRPPS is exactly that – supporting the organization's people. This role will also form an essential hub of project and in-the-moment activity (programme support) coordinating the elements of the HR team just as a *scrum master* would do for an agile IT project – aligning task backlogs, project and product deliverables, data management and priority resource allocation in the HR team.

Figure 7.1 T-HR four-zone framework

HR People Performance & Development (HRPPD) A centre of excellence is all grand but to do what? A part of HR dedicated to the performance and development of its people is surely more understandable in what it does? All learning, talent, change, comms and design expertise will sit in this element. Importantly this function will also keep the HR colleagues fresh, challenged and on point with the latest skills needed to make the most impact.

HR People Strategy & Partnerships (HRPSP) Working collaboratively with all parts of the organization – and of course its own department – means this is where the true centre of connected working exists. Keeping the strategy in mind and constantly shaping the strategic and tactical level interventions aligned and relevant this role is effectively an intelligence, shaping and relationships force securing maximum impact for everything HR does.

HR People & Organization Transformation (HRPOT) The innovation hub, the challenger unit, the explorers of new and creative methods for working and developing people. The experimental *spin out*, the place where alternative thinking is encouraged and where the boundaries of known ways are stretched to get the best from people, process and potential. Feeding results of trials and research programmes into all other aspects of the HR team. This unit is a flexible *'special ops'* team given a wide and specific mandate and *tour of duty* and role to develop for others from HRPPS, HRPPD and HRPSP.

Important distinctions are that no-one is fixed in any of these elements. The principles are the best people practices and approaches that serve the people and aims of the organization. Just because you're a (former) HRBP you can fit anywhere where your skills and the need is. In current, slightly firmer designations, flexibility may have occurred but equally may have forced some unnatural duplication, crossover or uncertainty.

This model will use the HRPSP as a mechanism to direct, channel and bring together the other four parts so not just servicing the organization machinery, coordinating HR prioritization and resource fluidity. This four zones version will need agile, adaptive and flexible ways to keep its relevance and be consistently adaptable to serve the needs of the organization but primarily, its people. It's certainly a *hacked* way of looking at HR which gives us the chance to revisit the CIPD/MiX Hackathon.

Hacking the HR proposition

The thinking behind some of this model comes from Gary Hamel and Peter Cheese's MiX/CIPD Hackathon from way back in 2013. In this exercise, over 3,000 people enrolled from across the world to hack HR. The specific mandate was to create an adaptability advantage. As Gary Hamel says – 'to outrun change itself'.

Some great ideas and hacks came forward but no-one devised an entirely new model. Until now. In the report an adaptable organization was hampered by the features shown in Figure 7.2:

Figure 7.2   CIPD/Management Innovation Exchange: Enemies of Adaptability

SOURCE Based on 'The Enemies of Adaptability, Hacking HR to Build Adaptability Advantage, CIPD' with the permission of the publisher, the Chartered Institute of Personnel and Development, London (www.cipd.co.uk).

This list helped the 'hackers' focus on the issues that could really overcome these barriers. A range of alternative practices, mindsets and processes were devised in the form of hacks and largely they fitted into the following categories:

Figure 7.3   The design principles of adaptable organizations

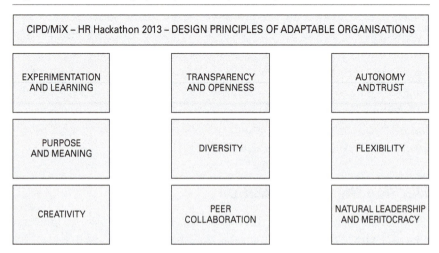

SOURCE Based on 'The Design Principles of Adaptable Organisations, Hacking HR to Build Adaptability Advantage, CIPD' with the permission of the publisher, the Chartered Institute of Personnel and Development, London (www.cipd.co.uk).

Nine areas that give a sense of where HR could really add some value to an organization beyond the conventional areas.

The areas of the four-zone model that I've just described find themselves hosts to some of these design principles where the *hacks* can be worked up as new practices and propositions.

Many of the areas identified as pathways to a more adaptable organization (such as autonomy and trust) cut across all four areas of this model but may start with transformational activity, before becoming more part of the strategy and then deployed through the people performance and development specialists. Peer collaboration feels like a natural fit between the people strategy and partnerships professionals and the people and organization transformation team. So the areas identified in the hackathon can map out to this more transformative HR model. The other aspects we can do with this model is 'roll' the work of HR through it. A little like a walk through and what we described in the Business Model Canvas of Chapter 6.

Figure 7.4　Characteristics of an adaptable organization

SOURCE From the CIPD/MiX Hackathon, mapped to the four-zone model for transformational HR

A scenario using the four elements of the transformational HR model

Let's look at an apprentice scheme with a difference that came from a hackathon. Instead of younger students, this is aimed at returning to work parents, carers, career changers. Talent but just not of the below 25 years old variety. Deb Seidman's Hack (Mix It) (2013) looked at experiences and alternatives to usual talent development processes. This is one from that stable.

To start with, our HRPPS team produces the project kick off. A backlog of tasks and a project mandate is constructed using the Lean UX and Agile methodologies now prevalent in HR. The backlog research, benchmarking and some design workshops. The HRPPD team are invited to facilitate the workshops.

A programme is designed as a minimum viable product (MVP) and this is then given to the HRPSP team to test with clients and colleagues. The team take it out to a small group of their most informed and analytical clients and get some further insight and shaping before committing to a trial in the research team. HRPPD are given a mandate to design an onboarding and culture awareness programme plus a link to the company learning partnership with a national business school with HRPPS team on logistics, payroll, devices and security checks.

The entire programme is run as an open and iterative exploration with the participants briefed on how they can shape the programme. A sponsor is found to act as liaison to the executive team and communications are handled from the people support team.

It is rolled out to the entire company after a six-month trial and after a year, the performance and development team commission the transformation team to enter into an award and win at a national ceremony.

Hopefully this illustration (albeit with a very movie-style ending) shows a more agile, responsive and transformative approach can be taken across these four disciplines.

Is this easier than in the three-legged stool model? Perhaps it is, because of the presence of a transformation unit. And a clearer line of responsibility between the other three units. Of course many three-pronged teams make this work but I believe this is more innovation led than the majority of existing formats.

Conclusions

We need a transformational HR model to decouple ourselves from a model that we've been operating in for over 20 years. It has changed how we are and how we view the world but it's time to build on that and create something more dynamic and progressive for the 21st-century world of work.

This is recognizable enough that it plays to current strengths and professional disciplines, and in combination with the thick stemmed T-HR model, demonstrates a new depth and breadth – especially in people and organizational sciences – that we must attain as serious, forward-looking progressive HR practitioners.

Using things like a hackathon is just one innovation tool that a HR people and organization transformation team would readily use – which would then give a mandate to the HR strategy and partnerships team to go and share the ideas and test the viability of an innovation whilst the HRPPD team are already working on the software and the skills support to get ideas from concept to delivery.

It may not seem transformative to have three recognizable elements of HR discipline in this new model, and yet, it *is* transformative to have a flexible and changing team acting in the transformational space as an allocated resource within HR. It's this subtlety that could reveal the biggest gain for HR in the 21st century.

Three key transformational HR takeaways and reflective questions to consider:

1 In reviewing the existing utilization of the HR model, this book has taken a generic overview of the successes and issues in operationalizing Professor Ulrich's framework.

   Q: What would be revealed if you conducted a full and comprehensive review of your own implementation and utilization of the model in terms of successes and areas to improve upon? A self – or collaborative – audit would reveal insight to use in shaping up a revised way of working.

2 The HR business partner role is so key to the success of the Ulrich model that this would require a review of its own and a chance for those working as business partners to help reshape the role for a more progressive and transformational impact.

   Q: How can you create a more transformational approach to the HRBP role?

3 The revised model here is a suggestion based on the author's 14 years of working with this model. It is a conceptualized upgrade deliberately aiming to create a more transformational element to the way HR works.

   Q: How could you take this model and adapt it and deploy it in your organization or with your clients?

References

Allard, Ken (accessed 20 May 2017) 'Book review: 'Team of teams: new rules of engagement for a complex world', *The Washington Times*,13/07 [Online] www.washingtontimes.com/news/2015/jul/13/book-review-team-of-teams-new-rules-of-engagement-/

CIPD (accessed 20 May 2017) The Ulrich model: business partnering factsheet [Online] www.cipd.co.uk/knowledge/fundamentals/people/hr/business-partnering-factsheet

Grams, Chris (accessed 20 May 2017) 'The enemies of adaptability', *Management Innovation Exchange, CIPD/MiX Hackathon* [Online] http://www.mixhackathon.org/hackathon/contribution/12-enemies-organizational-adaptability

Martin, R, and Mikkelsen, K (2016) *The neo-generalist,* LID Publishing, London.

Ulrich, D (1996) *Human resource champions: the next agenda for adding value and delivering results*. Harvard Business School Press, Boston, MA

Senge, PM (2006) *The fifth discipline: the art and practice of the learning organization*, Random House, London

Seidman, Deb (accessed 20 May 2017) 'Mix it up', *Management Innovation Exchange, CIPD/MiX Hacakthon* [Online] http://www.mixhackathon.org/hackathon/contribution/mix-it

Ulrich, Dave, Brockbank, Wayne, Yeung, Arthur K and Lake, Dale G (accessed 20 May 2017) 'Human resource competencies: an empirical assessment', *Human Resource Management* [Online] http://onlinelibrary.wiley.com/doi/10.1002/hrm.3930340402/full

Ulrich, D, Younger, J, Brockbank, W and Ulrich, M (2012) *HR from the outside in: six competencies for the future of human resources*, Mc-Graw Hill Education, London

PART THREE
Narratives

Transformational 08 tales from HR game changers

Introduction

It isn't just me – honestly – that feels like HR is in *need* of transformation and that it *can* be a transforming force for the businesses it works with. I have quoted some inspiring sources in this book and can add to that with further insight from some inspirational practitioners – people like you and I.

People involved in the reality of the world of work and brought together in this chapter to give their views and experiences as people who want to transform, are already transformational and have more transformation to come.

How will this chapter transform my thinking?

- The chapter includes tales from entrepreneurs, practitioners and innovators who are linked to the 'business' of HR for further provocation, validation and challenge to our existing ways of doing HR and transformation.

- It has examples of business approaches which have been transformational and led to new ways of looking at the world of work which may influence your thinking and practice.

- There are links to previous messages and theories espoused in this book and it builds on new thinking from a range of perspectives, geographies and experiences outside of mine as author.

Methodology

Networks are a terrific thing and these people come from my network. As clients, partners, colleagues, collaborators, co-creators and just good-hearted, innovative, sharp-thinking people in the world that HR operates within. These are my chosen commentators and now also yours as a reader. Giving us their views on the transformational need within the world of work and the chance HR has to become known for its transformative capacity, capability and creativity.

I was after more narratives than scores. So being a big believer in conversational practice, and rather than a numerical approach (for example on a scale of 1–5 how transformational is HR...?) I crafted five questions for interviews, exchanges and considerations. These questions were intended to reveal just how much people feel about the *wider* context of transformation and then a specific zoom into HR. This was to not bias results too much towards the HR profession in itself and the widely documented belief that HR *does* need to transform. Not all the professionals interviewed would necessarily describe themselves as being in HR but many would identify themselves as recruitment, learning, change, communication, performance, leadership and organization development professionals.

Before you read what those practitioners say about transformation and transformational HR, you may want to record your answers to these questions on a notepad, keyboard or recording device. They are questions we might want to ask ourselves at intervals and see how our responses may be changed by circumstance.

---

1 How would an organization sense and then decide it needs to transform?

2 Who typically designs, drives and delivers transformational activities in organizations?

3 What do you see as the main barriers, challenges and obstacles to transforming an organization?

4 Specifically looking at HR, what do you think it has to do to be more transformative about itself and for the businesses it works with?

5 What are your three killer apps/key skills needed to be transformational?

People and their views on transformational HR

The people included in this chapter have had some form of transformation in their working lives to use as of experience and information to share. Some are now independent practitioners and some are working for large or small organizations. Some have set up their own enterprises and some have moved from one sector to another or from one level to another. Engaging in transformative work at the systems level and a personal level.

So let's see what other people have to say about these five elements of inquiry into transformation and transformational HR.

Our roll call of game-changing HR transformers

- **Miranda Ash.** Miranda is Chief of Community for WorldBlu.com – accrediting and supporting the world's most freedom-centred and democratic organizations.

- **Su Askew.** Su is a recently-independent voice in the HR consulting practitioner world and has an acute interest in performance and what we know as performance management. Su is based in the South East of England.

- **Karen Beaven.** UK HR Director of the Year in 2015, Karen leads a multi-award winning HR team in a highly competitive retail environment with a flair for progressive thinking.

- **Shakil Butt.** Leading HR and OD at Islamic Relief gives Shakil not only a practitioner and professional view of the world but also a humanitarian and charitable one. Shakil is based in Birmingham, UK.

- **Catalina Contoloru.** Catalina is COO at creative agency 90 Digital and a former HR graduate scheme practitioner from Romania. Catalina is also an ambassador for the Alternative University in Bucharest and a champion of next-stage working environments.

- **Nebel Crowhurst.** Nebel leads on talent and organization development at River Island and formerly Virgin Holidays. Nebel is based in London and lives in Sussex, UK.

- **Eugenia Dabu.** Eugenia is a practitioner in employer branding at ING Bank, Bucharest, Romania. A co-founder of the HR Hub, an inspiring community of HR practitioners and a proponent of a more user-experience (UX) led way to consider HR and people practice.

- **Gail Evans.** Gail is a HR practitioner doing her masters at Liverpool John Moores University and working in the facilities management sector.
- **Barry Flack.** Barry is a very experienced and expressive practitioner with global HR experience and a challenging view on a range of areas in the HR professional field. Barry is currently an independent partner in HR consulting, based in Hertfordshire, UK (via the Emerald Isle).
- **Lisa Gill.** Lisa is founder of Reimaginaire. A writing and consulting force in alternative ways to work, learn and lead. Lisa is truly global. Lisa is currently based in Barcelona and is from Leicestershire, UK via Singapore.
- **Roger Gorman.** London-based founder of ProFinda.com – an innovative AI and machine learning platform which powers expertise finding and shaping enterprises to become Workforce Of the Future (WOF) ecosystems. The outcome is far better utilization of talent for bids, projects, etc. from internal teams, contingent networks and alumni.
- **Meghan Keeley.** Based in Minnesota, USA but from Wisconsin, Meghan is a new practitioner having just completed a Masters in Organizational Psychology from Nottingham University, UK. Meghan has researched self-organized and self-managed enterprises as part of her study programme.
- **Jaana Nyfjord.** Based in Stockholm, Jaana recently moved from organization design at Spotify to return to academia and now leads on research at Swedish Institute of Computer Science.
- **Erik Korsvik Østergaard.** A forward-thinker in leadership and organization design from Copenhagen, Denmark, Erik is known for his love of inclusive and human ways of leading, learning and working fused with technology. Having an engineering background and a passion for people is an interesting mix.
- **Nathan Ott.** Nathan is a founder of the GC Index® and a serial innovator in the design and development of great teams, challenges and high performing ways of working. Nathan's enterprise EG1 is based in London, UK.
- **Lara Plaxton.** Head of HR at a technology enterprise, and a quietly dynamic force for more agile and responsive ways to do HR from Brighton, UK, Lara has some very progressive views on HR's future.
- **Karin Tenelius.** Karin is co-founder of Tuff Leadership Training from Stockholm, Sweden. Tuff is Karin's own methodology for a new strain of leadership and management which gets to the heart of how dialogue and trust can turn around companies, teams and individual relationships at work.

- **Garry Turner.** Garry is a passionate business leader interested in the next stage of organizational life and ways of working. Garry is based in the South East of England.

To the power of 18. Eighteen people – all in their own ways transformational and all helping us get a better grip on what we mean by the term 'transformational HR'.

Here are their views on the five key questions to decoding what is transformational HR.

1 How would an organization sense and then decide it needs to transform?

Of course, it we look back to my use of Yuval Noah Harari's work, then organizations are inanimate fictions. However, this term is used in its *collection of human beings* sense. How does either a team of customer service representatives, a member of the executive board, or the shareholders convention sense and decide it needs to be more transformative (in order to be more successful)?

It is often systemic

Lisa Gill gave us a pretty vivid way to imagine this systemic element about the organization's sensing instinct and used a great metaphor from Margaret Wheatley's 2006 book *Leadership and the New Science* – that of a natural system like a spider and its web. In the book, Lisa describes the 'web' is the quantum nature of organizations and that there may be a disturbance in that web caused by a break or a failure somewhere. In science and mathematics this is described as a part of the *bifurcation theory*. Essentially, where in the system there is a break or a failure then the system reacts to fix itself using its own resources. Lisa felt this was particularly acute in self-organized or non-hierarchical structures as there was more of a pronounced interconnectedness to any *bifurcation* points and a tendency to fix things without the need for external intervention. In hierarchies, such breaks may be found in the boardroom and attempted containment eventually fails as it does if in a discreet part of the business (customer loss or competitor attacks perhaps). The web an organization creates means that any break or failure is felt by the rest of the network despite others attempts at covering things up or using spin to convince people otherwise. HR's role in this networked, tremor-sensitive environment should be to help people create fixes as part of that system response.

Any *bifurcation point* cannot be resolved by a minor repair – either because of a big breakage or a number of smaller, aggregated failings. This tipping point means the system will never be the same again – hence it needing to be transformed – which necessitates a systems-wide reaction to stabilize and strengthen the newly-shaped system. **Lara Plaxton** has clearly been considering this for sometime and envisaged a loop to transformation. Lara's progressive and advanced thinking (my words not hers) are of the systemic variety; and in creating a loop that gives us all the chance to spot the tremors and any breakages in the web and adapt to them with more pace and power. The system of Lara's links *employee experience* and *customer experience* to create a *shareholder experience,* and has HR as the energy source behind this loop, to create a new sensibility and systemic chain which creates an insight channel to inform any transformational needs.

Insight-led transformation is also the thought of **Eugenia Dabu.** Business intelligence gives us the 'what happened' to either system-wide failures or successes. In order to transfer, this data needs to help us at an organizational level answer the question 'What next?' Transformation – and not just change – is a continuous process in Eugenia's mind – knowing how to transform and at what speed are crucial.

Catalina Contoloru elegantly describes sensing and deciding:

> Healthy organizations develop a system of listening to their environment and people in order to grow this practice of sensing when a transformation needs to happen. Most of the time, there's an external factor that drives change in organizations: Another company challenging how the organization works; or an idea someone had from their network; or insight from a customer. It's usually people who build their role in a way that makes them open to the signs the environment sends and they put together all the pieces of the puzzle. The decision part depends on each organization, on where this decision making power is concentrated. If the power is distributed among all the people involved in the organization or just some of them can choose the direction. If these two processes, sensing and deciding, are well connected, that's when the true transformation happens. That's when good decisions are taken based on real insights people developed and shared.

Gail Evans adds that organizations need to become more savvy in a version self-awareness, asking of themselves *are we the right size and have the right skills?* Question why are there good people leaving? What power are the people bringing to the organization? Where are we losing cohesion or heading into energy-wasting internal power battles? Gail builds on this self-awareness dialogue and of the need to look at change and transformation as a necessary good; needed to survive commercially. **Miranda Ash** agrees 'In my experience organizations tend to realize a need for transformation through a combination of pain and enlightenment. There are some critical success factors to consider which include leadership at the top. Typically it begins with a "call to action" both at an individual and collective level – a realization that you can't go back and have to continue to move forward. This is the Hero's Journey!'

Roger Gorman admits to looking at this from a multi–national corporate perspective and has this to say:

> Major transformation programs are typically around 'burning platform issues', and there is (understandably) rarely scope for important 'nice to haves'. Goal 1 is almost always around saving money initiatives. A distant 2nd, and follow up areas, include new ERP programs (and all the work around these), new hiring plans and securing better revenue channels.

So, there are three lead reasons for major change programs:

- Money out: namely cost savings are the number one catalyst for investment. Often it's because they are in 'catchup' mode and are spending too much money in the wrong areas. There will be ongoing tension from the board to find new cost savings, and a burning need for utilization improvements.

- Money in: namely new revenues. Small investments are made to help firms make or retain their income streams.

- Competitive tension. Sometimes direct competitors have just launched a new initiative and they need to respond and this needs a response.

Secondary reasons for large change programs are:

- hiring new, better talent, faster;
- M&A;
- L&D; and
- growth/efficiencies.

Far less reasons sadly stem from smart, progressive investments which would actually make for key, longer term benefits such as; culture, insights, harmonizing tech, etc. Most companies are suffering from staggeringly archaic, unused technology, poor ROI, near zero people data and living with contracts they can't break. The pressure from the board – unhelpfully – is to ensure the past £X million isn't wasted, and this leads to why companies can't swallow sunken costs.

So for Roger, it's less transform to thrive and a lot of transform to survive which comes with added emotional weight and uncertainty of course.

Nebel Crowhurst describes this aspect 'It's about having an outward focus. Seeing beyond the "four walls" of your organization and horizon scanning. Looking at what is happening not only in your industry, but within business in general as well as having an awareness of what's happening globally and what may have an impact on your organization'.

Shakil Butt adds that organizations can become blinkered and sometimes it takes a new leader or financial alerts around costs or income. Forward-thinking organizations though, keep abreast of this by challenging themselves; using diversity of thought; and encouraging others to voice the challenges.

Meghan Keeley shares her thoughts which really resonated with me:

> While it may be an idealist opinion, I think an organization must first sense a need to transform based on input from employees primarily and customers secondarily. An organization's employees are the heart of the organization and there wouldn't be customers if it wasn't for the work that employees do. And for employees to be able to express a desire for some sort of change, the organization should have a culture that allows for such expression.

Jaana Nyfjord feels the network is all important here in picking up the need to transform: 'Human sensor networks. Use signals to decide the need to transform. Most importantly, don't neglect weak signals. They might be the most critical ones'.

It is also about skills and information

Barry Flack shared how he sees stagnating business performance and reactionary hires are often used to overcome this failure to act in time or in having insufficient data/information. He believes strongly that predictive modelling, use of data and trends is a key to understanding tremors in the web and that HR is key to helping create strategies which can correct poor leadership, ineffective hires, low morale or a talent exodus.

Garry Turner says it's all about listening: 'Effective communication and feedback structures that allow speedy, candid insight, in any and every direction, such that the 'truth' (or clarity) is always known. This will allow the organization to know if and when transformation is required'.

Karin Tenelius has experiences of where only at times of great pain will an organization's most influential people decide transformation is necessary and that inspiration alone *rarely* causes transformation.

Su Askew agrees that there are indicators that should and do cause painful realization that transformation – not iteration or minor improvements – are necessary. Su asks clients to share their assumptions about people and that some biases or behaviours can create a series of blind spots in the organization where assumptions are made about people which dismiss such tremors for a range of reasons other than the need to take a good hard look at the organization's culture, reward or leadership (for example). Su has seen examples of typical growth stages in entrepreneurial success which loads more bureaucratic operating systems and erases the ways success has been achieved. Su has seen and been a part of programmes where HR has led transformation to almost re-load the previous systems reflecting the newer, larger organization it has become.

Erik Korsvik Østergaard agrees that sensing is based on data, listening and connecting to information sources but feels that organizations at the most influential level need 'headroom'. Particularly at the apex or most in command positions, rarely is headroom found to listen to and analyse what are tremors, warnings and breakages and instead it only comes to their attention when meltdowns are already underway. He feels that change agents and *grassroots* movements are there to be listened to but there is often a disconnect between high-ranking officials or HR influencers who aren't tuned in or part of these sources of early warnings.

It is personal

Nathan Ott feels that there is a challenge in modern-day business that he is trying to address: who are the *people* that will help you change the game (or system)? Not just relying on systemic tremors but having people who are predisposed and even tuned in to changing the game is key. His *GC Index*® is aimed at using psychometric profiling to help organizations appreciate who – and therefore where – their natural transformers are. Nathan's experiences of HR has often been one of admiration and frustration – committed professionals that are very busy. So busy, Nathan contends, that they are often left out of transformation activities until the plans are cast and therefore any innovation quotient is omitted. Nathan's *GC Index*® tool could help organizations reconsider how they identify and utilize their game changers from HR as well as marketing, R&D and customer insight teams.

So personal is an important and challenging aspect of change in the light of an organization sensing and deciding it needs to change. Transformation has to be effected at an individual level in order to truly succeed.

Summary

Organizations are complex, adaptive systems – a web of interconnected threads holding it all together.

We, the people, are all like the spiders tending to, and benefitting from, that web.

Where there is a bifurcation – a tremor or breakage – in the web that can be either an opportunity or a threat. We are mobilized to act. That may include paying attention to whether we need to simply repair or indeed something larger; a transformation.

Decisions are often taken at the most 'mature' part of that web, and yet at the edge of the web is both it's strongest, furthest outreach and yet its weakest spot. Insight is critical. Data is telling.

In order to transform, we need a loop that allows us to listen to the words of warning and chance, tune in to the mood of change and feel the tremors of danger, that help us decide to take a transformational approach to our organization's future.

2 Who typically designs, drives and delivers transformational activities in organizations?

Eugenia Dabu offers that transformation could become an *automated* routine in response to data; although for now, it tends to be the senior leaders who design, drive and orchestrate transformation. The REAL designers and drivers are the customers/users/consumers – listening to those people is our key to delivering success.

Su Askew reports that HR does drive (and design) so ultimately delivers transformational activities in organizations, be they change programmes, new terms and conditions following mergers/acquisitions and so on. Much of what feels transformational (or as the result of a transformation) has a different sense of belonging, role, location, brand and more.

Meghan Keely says that typically, transformational activities seem to be driven from the top down as a result of a hierarchical structure. While organizational structures continue to flatten, then the average organization's change is driven by employees in upper-level positions.

Roger Gorman offers this: 'Regardless of the near-endless number of areas firms need to address, the main checks are moving around utilization issues, and these are around ops/resources and tech, you'll find the lead decision makers are COOs CFOs, and C-Suite. Influencers are of course CEO, HRD, CTO etc.'.

Miranda Ash has direct experience of a leading force but distributed transformational power:

> In the organizations we work with, it's typically the CEO who drives transformational activities and then collaborates with relevant colleagues on design and delivery. For example, when DaVita undertook their incredible transformation back in 1999, the new CEO, Kent Thiry, held the space together with his leadership team but decentralized many of the decisions around the creation of core values, the new company name, etc. to individual clinics using a very clear trickle down process of communication. This gave the power to the people and has been the key to the success of their transformation having gone from near bankruptcy to a $17 billion public organization.

Garry Turner adds his view that it can even be that transformation normally occurs from the 'middle out'. As such the identification of the need to transform can come from anywhere but it is a curious, listening, proactive, forward looking HR/OD leadership team that is required to design and deliver transformation, with the support and input of various stakeholders. Garry sees forward and outward looking internal innovators in R&D and OD that create and lead to a transformation agenda.

Erik Korsvik Østergaard recognizes just how much management of an organization is in the lead on these 3D elements (designs, drives and delivers). He believes managers's abilities are enhanced by strong change agents and *guilds* of other players. Something **Su** also believes in – active participation by as many people as possible.

Catalina Contoloru adds that truly powerful leaders will always find a way to bring their contribution to transformation and more importantly to empower others.

Nebel Crowhurst builds on this by sharing how typically the driver of transformation comes from the top, however truly collaborative organizations foster an environment which enables transformation to take place at all levels: 'to me transformation doesn't always have to be big, it can be the small changes that can make big differences'. Nebel adds to Lisa's *bifurcation point* example from earlier.

Lara Plaxton has an interesting thing to add in the tendency for other leaders (HR included) to want to take over and lead all transformational activity. Truly transformational leaders don't get caught up in this ego-fest and so HR – for example – should be enablers of transformation not always leaders of.

Karin Tenelius talks about visionary 'intrapreneurs' – bold courageous people no matter their title. Insightful CEOs are sometimes in this category but Karin says they, visionary CEOs, are too rare.

Which is backed up by **Shakil Butt** – it doesn't have to be the CEO (but often is) and if it isn't the CEO driving a transformation, then it has to be bought into by other leaders. Shakil believes that bottom-up changes are always best whereas top-down shifts from one leader to the next. Not all transformation of this kind is good.

Gail Evans offers this: 'I've found it to be a combination of senior leaders linking in with employee voice councils and even using engagement data. Consultants are used to support the outside view but not enough planning goes into engaging or utilizing those on the front line. Organizations could highlight four or five key points and let people share their thoughts and ideas and see what is functional to put into plan'.

Whoever drives it, communication is an obvious but vital element. Gail found it helpful through past transformational programmes when regular updates were shared in a timely manner, i.e. through specific change sessions to be clear on messaging, having open sessions through Yammer or a general inbox with rapid responses so people can ask questions to stop fear setting in.

Barry Flack has seen the external dimension (contractors/consultants) in the 3Ds seat – and also shares how his experiences have seen HR in the pre-ordained plan of hire, retrain and retire based on the strategic imperatives of others. He believes that where transformation programmes have not lived up to their billing, is where there has been a *dislocation* of the leadership team and the change process; a lack of time and energy devoted to understand the complexity of the organizational body and a failure to build true connections and relationships – usually a distraction such as near-term tactical issues. Indeed, Barry states that getting organizations to truly envision the future appears to get harder and harder and HR – working with its partner functions – can help break the myopic nature of many business strategies.

Nathan Ott has called out the curse of busy HR professionals and their (perceived) lack of commercial awareness, bottom-line impact and/or use of data as always giving them 'second fiddle' roles in transformation programmes. This then leaves a disconnect between some psychological and emotional factors unknown, unrepresented and therefore potentially damaging to the success of the programme.

Eugenia Dabu believes the HR professionals should help the CEO see beyond short-term profiteering and into the listening and culturally sensitive areas HR occupies and has access to. The mood of the people if you will – which can, where fear takes hold in transformational programmes, hamper the speed or depth of shift the transformation programme delivers.

Jaana Nyfjord says that in practice, unfortunately, it is very often people hired into doing the job of transformation, who are not part of the core production.

Lisa Gill talked about the sensors in the web as being anyone and that transformational activities are ever-more a part of the self-organized features seen in many progressive and democratic organizations. Multi-directional (so not top-down or transversely bottom-up) but coming in and being activated from a range of points.

Summary

There is a recognition that senior decision making leaders and HR are often in the driving seat for transformational programmes of change.

Of course there are others – expert consulting partners; and people from the organization themselves. What appears evident though is, that the more people that are *engaged* in some form of activism around transformation, it is likely to ensure there is more success in transforming beyond surface-level structures or titles. Yet many transformation programmes are very tightly controlled and defined including who is at the heart of the programme.

Deep emotional and psychological connection to the transformation is a key to truly transforming versus simply making changes that are big but perhaps lack the fundamental shifts transformation sets out to do.

In designing, driving and delivering a transformational approach to your organization's future, there is a need for a *coalition* and *guild* of transformers which could include our customers/users.

People from a range of perspectives will help to create a programme being designed and delivered by the very people transformation will impact upon. Paying attention to logistics, structures and naming convention are all – as Edgar Schein would call them – cultural artefacts, and yet what really deepens the transformative effects is the psyche of people at an individual and collective level.

HR has a real opportunity and challenge to become more prominent in transformation activities: in essence be the psychological centre of transformation. Creating as much widespread interest and activity in the spiritual and cognitive discourse with transformation to complement the structural and logistical focus.

3 What are the main barriers, challenges and obstacles to transforming an organization?

Lara Plaxton has it nailed: 1) not having the evidence and insight to support the reasons for the change; 2) not having an agreed shared purpose/goal; 3) not having the right skills or knowledge on the transformation team and not empowering them to deliver.

Lisa Gill has a clear barrier to transforming in her experiences of the world of work: design. Badly designed organizations are often those most in need of transformation, but this design in itself often inhibits the very thing that would transform its success and human factor.

Catalina Contoloru is also clear on barriers:

> I think one of the biggest challenge that people are facing is to let go of what they learnt in organizations that are rigid and hierarchical. These old practices are so well embedded in people sometimes that they don't even realize there's a better way to do things and they fear the transformation will affect their work and what they gained so far. When egos get in the way, the transformation process becomes even more complicated. I think this is one of the essential things that leaders should check as often as possible, that egos, theirs and others, don't get in the way of meaningful work.

Meghan Keeley agrees that layers of management, difficulty scaling transformation in large organizations, change-resistors, lack of transparency throughout organization, lack of input or access to providing input from *everyone* in the organization can be seen as real and perceived barriers.

Garry Turner builds on this with senior leadership that have very fixed mindsets out of kilter with the need to evolve the organizational culture and structure. Garry adds that the ability of the organization and its ecosystem to continuously learn and improve – if hampered – is a major obstacle to transformational success.

Eugenia Dabu also offers that the existing culture *and* the scale of the transformation could combine to become serious obstacles.

Miranda Ash continues this narrative:

> Ultimately the main barrier to transforming an organization is rooted in fear. The self-worth of leaders is also a barrier. Those organizations led by leaders with a high sense of self worth (not ego) are better able to traverse the complexities of change and help people to identify and overcome their fears. Fear is a killer. It's vital to address fear at the get go. If not, you run the risk of designing a fear-based rather than freedom-centred organization.

All the research we've undertaken demonstrates that organizations with a freedom-centred design based on the WorldBlu 10 Principles of Organizational Democracy achieve greater growth and are more resilient.

Roger Gorman sees many solutions (technology in particular) that are ready to transform organizations yet there is user caution, i.e. fear again: 'While there are some incredibly advanced minds out there, many are also lacking the experience and technical knowledge to advance the right opportunities'.

Gail Evans's experiences are slightly different barriers where the most amazing *sounding* transformation project can be designed/developed, but it isn't a good fit for the people or culture (plus not shared through powerful and open communication) it will fail to transform. To get the design right and inspiring people to engage and participate throughout should overcome original design flaws. Another barrier is the need for 'skills upgrading' which if not sequenced with need fails to build confidence, could lose productivity and morale may suffer. It's a point well made as there is a competence and confidence issue at stake with transformations.

Jaana Nyfjord puts it simply in two things – a lack of domain knowledge and time.

Barry Flack has some very firm views having seen many good and indifferent attempts at transformation: that the design – 'the lofty ambition' as he calls it – of the transformation itself can see unachievable timescales set and see the change impacts lessen. He too decries the lack of involvement of others and the alienation that comes from this disconnect. Barry goes on to also point to the real lack of capital investment and short-term viewpoint as denying transformation the fuel and vision needed to really get off the ground. Barry also identifies what Peter Senge might call a 'learning disability' a lack of transformational skills across the organization aggregating into an organizational deficit. We rarely see people 'learn' their way into a transformation. Restructures, sure. True learning programmes, not so much.

Shakil Butt adds that groupthink is one mindset issue that can create an inhibitor to success; especially where there is a lack of clarity on what's causing the need to transform. **Shakil** adds that failing to understand long and short term trends can place an organization out of touch with its key stakeholders: customers, people; partners. Too often the focus is only to satisfy shareholders rather than all stakeholders. Shakill goes on to share this about risk: 'Increasingly risk management has become the crutch that organizations have fallen back on but sometimes that becomes a double edged sword with organizations opting to take fewer risks on being innovative opting to play it safe not realizing safe translates as stale'.

Karin Tenelius is much more certain about barriers to transformation: top management. Their lack of insight and focus on what *really* makes organizations great hampers of transformation (and particularly their lack of interest in what matters to their own people).

Nebel Crowhurst picks up this thread:

> Although there may be a desire from the top to transform, most commonly what I see blocking organizations actually taking leaps to move forward is effective leadership. Having the skill to inspire and bring people on an emotionally connected journey is often the barrier. Many leaders are very good at presenting a vision two dimensionally, but making that vision truly compelling for people within the organization to want to be a part of is a real skill. I genuinely believe that leaders who are highly self-aware and have a desire to develop their Emotional Intelligence have a greater chance of success.

Erik Østegaard calls out a list of deficiencies and barriers:

- 'sensing' the urgency;
- decoupling from reality – a discord between management and frontline perspectives on reality;
- taking bold enough moves (and then *actually* transforming and not just minor improvements);
- courage and willingness ('we're used to...' and habits that may hold people back);
- making 'fake' transformation projects just to 'tick it off the list'.

Summary

Surprisingly, not everyone believes bad leaders are those to blame for a lack of transformational success. Yet there are still many who see and have experienced that disconnect between inspiring, visionary and connected leaders and their people.

Design – of both the organization as-is and the transformation programme itself – can be a disabler of success in transforming the organization. Careful attention to this and the way in which transformation is conceived, articulated and then delivered is much needed. Knowing how the design of the organization influences people; their ways of working and therefore being will help overcome barriers.

Bravery also appeared to be an issue with many of those interviewed. Not of the foolhardy variety but more boldness, confidence and belief.

Where this is evident need for bravery this appears to be best given prominence in the rationale and dialogue about any transformational activities.

Skill and will are needed in transformational approaches to change, so there is a need to seek out not only those who want to be part of the transformation but also check on the capabilities you have in the people of your organization, as well as those areas to boost and skill up in.

Dialogue is therefore critical in overcoming barriers and potential disablers of transformation.

HRs role in engaging people about the transformation and assessing the mindset and skillset of people is a useful component alongside the budget, timeline and governance arrangements.

4 Specifically looking at HR, what do you think it has to do to be more transformative about itself and for the businesses it works with?

Nathan Ott is clear – HR *can* change the game of work but it has to change itself and its game. Perhaps HR should transform itself first, perhaps it should do so alongside wider organizational transformation. Asking something as simple as 'if HR inside this company were a commercial concern, would the organization buy us?' gives a sense of the value that is either already created or the potential value that can be created. Through impactful and commercially astute people development approaches. Nathan recalled a CEO who told him he'd invested heavily in a talent programme that produced one leader – something he felt let down by. He expected more and it caused him concerns about the capability and impact his HR team created for the organization. That damaged belief would need a transformative approach to restore and then build something on.

Lara Plaxton is *really* clear on things so is quoted here in total:

HR should work on not calling itself a 'partner' to the business but being seen as an integral part of the business.

We concentrate on our employees and tend not to look beyond. As people experts, we should understand how our employees impact our customers and how our customers impact our employees. This should shape the employee and customer experiences and result in the desired behaviours required by the business to be successful. With this human insight, HR can then work with the various functions to understand the insight collaboratively and turn it into transformational actions. Whilst we have transactional activities to deliver, transformation requires a completely different approach. It's not about what changes HR want to see take place, but about what changes are required to meet the needs of the business and its people to remain competitive.

By ensuring we are the curators of human insight and critical in creating the right culture and environment, we can empower those at the front line of the business to deliver the results. HR then becomes a necessary function of organizational performance rather than sitting at the side-lines.

Karin Tenelius also sees getting tougher as a need for HR. Karin's management methodology – Tuff Leadership – would call a restorative approach needed in the greater closeness with HR and their business leaders as 'a relationship conversation'. HR would have to take its shortcomings on the chin. Not avoid it and not try and mitigate too much over it. Take a blow; apologize and look to get back to a position of faith and trust. Indeed, Karin feels that HR should instead work more firmly and closely with leaders about the impact those leaders and managers have on their people, therefore their business and on any strategic HR applications/processes. Well crafted talent development programmes can be impaired by leaders who (for example) want to hoard their own talent. So they don't encourage their best people to go on the programme and instead, promote them within or over-occupy them within their own realm. If HR is closer to this mindset and approach, it can call this out and be part of a dialogue to overcome any fears and self-serving measures. Fairness, strategic alignment and a bigger picture approach to this could result in more people being promotable *through* the talent programme instead of *in spite* of it.

HR giving leaders 'people dialogue' (and not just via once-a-year surveys) is a vital intelligence source in keeping leaders tuned into what matters to people and what inhibits strong performance and continued growth.

Barry Flack agrees that this narrative has to be more powerful and convincing. Data will help this cause and be used to show the cause/effect of any short-term stings on long-term impacts. Constant fear over role security, for example, may cause inappropriate actions on over-promising benefits to customers who then (expectations unfulfilled) do not renew. Short term sales figures massaged but long term relationship totally ruined. There is rarely this form of interrogation and the fixation with convulsive priority shifting and doubts over success can harm people's commitment to the doing the right thing for sustainable success. HR getting into the heart of more complex issues such as these gives the organization's leaders more to consider when making decisions and setting a prioritized approach. How people feel is a huge factor on how well they perform. Nokia's burning platform being a large point in case (*The Wall Street Journal*, 2017).

Eugenia Dabu believes a focus on HR's own capabilities and skills will help this. HR Technologist and HR Analyst roles are needed to get to the heart of the data that will be convincing to others in making the right decisions by customer, company and colleague and not just the former two with disregard for colleague impact. Eugenia believes there is insufficient exposure by HR professionals to the work of the organizations people. Not enough 'anthropological awareness'. Eugenia also believes (and we will cover this more in Chapter 10) that a more agile and iterative approach (in much the same way the IT function has) to their work would be transformational in both efficiencies and effectiveness.

Lisa Gill echoes this. Referencing the impact that aluminum factory *Alcoa's* CEO Paul O'Neill had on his organization. O'Neill gave a memorable address where he declared safety of employees as their priority. This was effectively the pivotal moment in this story of this business turnaround (Baer, 2014).

This *'what matters to me'* approach (for people in an organization) can become HR's most useful ally – getting hold of information that will highlight what will make the most difference to people so they perform at their best and deliver outstanding results.

HR can help the leaders of the organization close any distance between them and their colleagues and increase their understanding of what will make the most positive and negative differences to their own people. HR will need to be sensing the environment and doing something like a *coup d'oeil* – a knowing glance that takes in a comprehensive view (Cooper Ramo, 2014).

Patterns, a sense of what would happen *if*, and a belief that people will be shaped by the dialogue and the events around them at that time. Not to mention the energy being displayed to transform or indeed, to resist or reluctantly accept the transformation.

Lisa also describes how HR can state 'three i's' that can help an organization transformation plan gain an appropriate level of support from their own people:

- **Identity** – what does this transformation do to who we are and what I am a part of?

- **Information** – what do I need to know and what can I help the transformation with?

- **Involved** – who is in the inner circle? How is it proposed to involve me and how do I wish to be involved in this transformation?

These three i's are where HR can add a real human factor into the thinking of the transformation programme and help leaders make more *Aloca-like* decisions. HR can do this through dialogue and exchanges; through the connections their 'field' staff could naturally come across and so they would all have to activate their *vigilant instinct* to make the most of the network capability they have.

Meghan Keeley adds to this by suggesting better organization-wide communication, transparency and actively seeking the opinions and ideas from all employees. HR should constantly be evolving to best serve employees which means a team that never stops learning and innovating.

Catalina Contoloru also adds 'it needs to get different perspectives, by putting themselves in someone else's shoes for a while, looking at problems from different angles. By experimenting in other roles, HR professionals can get insight on what people in the organization really need, for them to facilitate better conversations and think in a more strategically aligned way'. Experience is key for Catalina clearly.

Jaana Nyfjord concurs HR has to shift: 'HR should be a role model. HR has THE window of opportunity to re-position itself. The future workplace is happening. You are the experts. If not, then bring in the missing piece(s). Or travel light, leave old misconceptions behind and focus on the difference you make and want to make'.

Garry Turner believes that the current model for HR, should be decommissioned. For too long HR has been seen as a football to be kicked around and used as a scapegoat when senior leaders, cultures and organizational structures do not work. Welfare and employee support are critical but he feels the need for a renewal of what and where HR stands for and is positioned. Indeed Garry feels that more people outside HR should spend time working within a revised model for it. To lead on and experience deeply what HR's challenges are and bring new thinking and solutions into the refreshed function.

Gail Evans recognizes that transformation in the business presents HR with an opportunity to transform how employees feel and align to the company's refreshed vision and values – the binding principles during and as a result of the transformation. HR could also transform the state of its relationship with the ever crucial line managers and employees alike – offering more accountability for their impact in a human and commercial sense. HR professionals should maintain an alertness to transformative approaches in the wider world of work and by using their network to develop personally along with supporting change in the organization.

Erik Korsvik Østergaard also agrees that relationships with business leaders, managers and people more widely in the organization needs transforming. Erik feels HR has somewhat ensnared itself in its own administration and instead, needs to become more of the sensing and intelligence source we describe earlier through better relationships.

Nebel Crowhurst thinks HR and L&D need to be innovators and challengers. Accepting something is just how it is and never striving for better isn't good enough. HR and L&D need to be seen as real business contributors and enablers. We should be bringing new ideas to businesses and challenging the thinking of our people. If something isn't working we should be working with the organization to find progressive solutions.

Roger Gorman adds:

HR needs a major new raft of talent into their own departments, and more authority to author longer term investments. They have been woefully underinvested in for the longest time, had restrictive decision-making powers, and been criticised when everything goes wrong. They have had it hard! But beyond better budgets, the single biggest way HR can help itself is to hire into its own teams a new generation of highly strategic, dynamic holistic HR folk. They need to enter the workplace.

Shakil Butt believes that HR's transformation is overdue. The Ulrich-type model still has a part to play but it needs to be adapted to mirror what the organization needs HR to be. Business partnering alone has not delivered because simply serving your 'customers' and understanding the business is not enough. HR professionals need to match and outdo their business colleagues. Tough sales organizations need tough HR professionals – that's the arena they're in – so show what tough *and* fair looks like.

Shakil continues: 'The world of work has changed and will continue to change with talent choosing when to work, where to work and how to work forcing HR to adapt in order to secure the best of the best for their respective organizations'.

Miranda Ash adds that business leaders should already understand that HR is not limited to a transactional function. Rather HR is a strategic function and frankly needs to be front and centre in any organization. This means that HR teams need a balance of transactional and strategic skills and a solid understanding of the purpose and vision of the business.

Summary

From these exchanges, It is clear that HR's role should be more about *relationships* and *representation*. Not just the will of the people, but as an intelligence source for the impact of transformation on the organization's people and inclusion for ideas and activities that would accelerate, not hamper, the transformation. The voice that will help close the distance between leadership vision and receptiveness and commitment to transform.

It requires a braver and more networked HR function to do this. To be more analytical about its data, evidence and therefore its impact.

HR's role as a voice of reason, organizational justice and democratic influence is evident from these comments and this – not just the unilateral decision of boards – is a challenging convention to the way many businesses choose to transform.

HR should not be considered the handbrake for transformation, more the gear change mechanism, to ensure the smooth acceleration along a challenging journey. At a time when ethics and morality are (potentially) more under threat through technological disruptions, continued profit making and of course short-term growth targets, HR's role as a conscience and agent provocateur could become a welcome shift in emphasis. If anything, transformational HR could be as simple as It being a more *radical listener*. If the trust is damaged or broken in an organization, that is in need of transformation.

If you as readers were hoping for the *uberization of HR* then transformational HR is NOT just to be technologically disruptive; only about innovation or indeed unrecognizable from previous incarnations. It is *whatever* is contextually in need of transformation. That appears to be about relations and relatedness if these comments from smart people who care about work are anything to go by.

So HR can transform itself into being:

1 Chief relationships officers and the voice of impactful representation;

2 more adept at using evidence and data to influence outcomes for the better; and

3 smarter in the ways it networks and deploys itself to listen, understand and build trust in people.

These appear to be the elements in need of transformation: HR that is founded on connectivity to people, of intelligence *about* people; that positively impacts on organizational transformation whilst enhancing trust in turbulent (for that read exciting and challenging) times.

5 What are your three killer apps/key skills needed to be transformational?

In asking this question, I wasn't prepared for such a literal response to the first part of this – by killer apps I meant human applied elements but have gladly allowed this to mean technological applications.

Digital apps

We live in a world where our devices and their apps becomes our toolkit for the knowledge and connected era. **Erik Korsvik Østergaard** believes in internal social tools, visual planning and video meetings as three killer apps to a more connected, plan-based and collaborative way of working.

Meghan Keeley adds killer apps Slack and Twitter. 'I've loved using Slack since I was introduced to it about a year ago. I don't necessarily believe zero emails is possible... yet... however emails are often ineffective and inefficient and Slack is a great alternative to quick communication, sharing of documents, group channels and even calls'.

Garry Turner also goes for the openness and energy of Slack and adds Impraise's feedback application as step in the right direction to fuse dialogue with technology.

Gail Evans agrees that a communication app or platform to accommodate audio visual media means important messages can be recorded and dispersed to wider coverage and increase awareness. Where possible some interactive elements are powerful such as threads, chats and posts on a two-way Intranet or Yammer. Broadcast messages can use Webex (screen share) even Facetime.

Nebel Crowhurst add this 'In the hunt for seeking out insights into new trends *tw:in* [http://twin.trendwatching.com/] is a global trend watching network which is something relatively new to me. 'A glocal community of 3000+ savvy spotters, tapped into the new, the next and the novel innovations from across the globe'.

Human apps

Lara Plaxton challenges us on her three skills/apps:

- **Question limitations** – humans, machines and organizations all have limitations. Whether we are looking at changing human experiences or implementing new technology within the organization, we need to understand what the limitations are of these resources within the new systems and processes so we can account for them. We need to question HR's limitations and more importantly our own individual limitations so that we look to work with others who fill those knowledge/skills gaps.

- **Understand context** – we talk about commercial acumen but how often is that put into practice. Commercial acumen is not about being able to talk about what you do as a business but rather knowing the challenges that the various business functions experience, talking the same language and applying people insight to the commercial context. We often create people analytics which we align with the overall business goals, without any thought for people insight beyond the realm of HR, with the sole purpose of proving our own value. If we aligned our analytics around employees and customers then we contextualize that insight into something meaningful to all functions. The insight only becomes credible when all functions contribute to the diagnosis of the insight, create actions and then finally link those actions to overall business goals.

- **Be human-centred** – having a human-centred approach means our employees and customers are at the centre of what we do. Therefore, the design process for the employee experience is not driven by the latest trend in HR, but is driven by collaboratively working with all functions to understand how to transform our human experiences. Ultimately, transformation is best when it's simple. The environment that employees and customers operate in is continually changing but their needs on a more simplistic level have not changed that much over time. Avoid over-complicating and using HR terminology that is not relatable by most business functions or the leadership team.

Erik gives us three key words for the skills transformational HR practitioners will need: courage, communication, collaboration – building out from Lara's, questioning, context and human-centred trio.

Garry Turner also builds on this with curiosity, collaboration and humility as three top skills for the transformational practitioner of the future.

Eugenia Dabu believes the trio is: questioning reality; exploring scenarios; and connecting data to emotion. More links to Lara's three key skills.

Bolstered by **Meghan's** view that openness and willingness to constantly question and learn aren't exactly skills but more of a mindset or attitude but I think these characteristics are key to embracing transformation.

Echoed by **Lisa Gill** who has three key frames of reference for transformational HR practitioners: a coaching leadership style; the use of Liberating Structures for more dialogic problem solving methods and multi directional conversations (often found on social networking tools).

Roger Gorman adds two attitudes and a focus: a *can-do attitude* added with a '*we not an I*' attitude right through the organization from CEO to the new intern. The focus – in Roger's view – is that business and human outcomes should come first. Sadly, too often it becomes about systems, processes, plans and they take too much of a lead role in people's thinking and doing. People should develop the skill to be attentive to, and follow/ support the 'business and human outcomes' over all else.

For **Catalina Contoloru** it's these three, starting with a digital app: Medium is a wonderful blogging platform and a great way of keeping that flow of inspiration that's needed to be in a state of continuous transformation. The skill of listening is essential, as a practice that can't be ignored. Every time you get the chance to listen to a new story, to understand other people and their way of living and thinking, it makes you see things differently. And finally experimenting takes a lot of courage but it's mandatory for anyone who wants to go through a transformation. The experiment can be a failure or a success but the key is to continue. Don't stop because you failed, but also, don't stop when you succeeded, experimentation is an ongoing process.

Miranda Ash has a clearly defined three top skills for transformation (having seen so much of it with helping companies move to freedom-centred):

1 Active listening skills – absolutely vital in transformation – we need to be able to *listen* first in order to be equipped to make the best decisions.

2 Open book management skills – this is all about transparency with the numbers – the more *everyone* understands the numbers, the better equipped they are to make educated decisions about the future of the organization.

3 The use of a communication channel such as Slack which give people a platform with which to communicate and collaborate with each other.

Karin Tenelius agrees on more freedom and has gone for a non-hierarchical state of being; empowering and coaching ways and the ability to work with imperfect processes (especially through transformation where new ground is being broken). It's a rough ride to transforming people and their organizations so we should expect some letting go of control, power and perfection in pursuit of better, more dynamic and transformative ways to be and do).

For **Gail Evans** language and code is all important. Not too much jargon, bring in the new words gently. Transformation may need a new language being used (such as a merger and acquisition). Playfully, Gail would also like a magic wand that can release a spell to measure morale in real-time and deliver useful data. Transformation can be turbulent and people's mood will change potentially hourly before, during and after transformation and rarely are these interferences and fluctuating energy levels accounted for during change.

For **Shakil Butt** it's about this: having *more*; being *open* and strongly *connected*.

Having *more* than HR to bring to the game if you really want to win support from fellow leaders. Knowing you do not have all the answers but having an *open mind* is the best starting point to be transformational. *Networking* with peers who have made the journey or are on the journey – they can always help you with your journey but remember to use not abuse as relationships only build if it feels real and is a two-way street.

Nathan Ott sees the need for innovation *and* invention as critical. In his work assembling the GC Index® – a psychometric tool which identifies *game changing* and associated complementary skills – he has seen how innovation be a *thing*, yet nothing new was truly invented off the back of those innovative thoughts or actions. It is why his GC Index® doesn't just categorize those who have innovative thoughts, but those who can strategize, implement, coordinate and finally polish a product, service or initiative. He has seen, and believes, that there is balance to ideas with pragmatic and practical implementation (even if to test the innovation and shape it for wider replication). He also states how important it is that HR professionals can manage both old and new states: of mind; process; behaviours whilst in transition. During any transformation there is a state of transition and this needs careful, attentive and analytical consideration.

Jaana Nyfjord adds the need for competency an extreme sort. 'My one and only killer app is eXtreme Programming' – something we will touch on later in the case studies in Chapter 9. 'Use its values wisely and you have what it takes to be transformational: communication, feedback, simplicity, courage and respect'.

All five questions in summary

Karen Beaven has given us a terrific summary of all responses thus far received and therefore worthy of its own section.

1 How would an organization sense and then decide it needs to transform?

I believe that the signals that transformation is required come from a variety of sources, all of which leaders within the business need to validate and then decide if they want to act on them. You could start at the global economic level and establish if changes there are likely to impact the way you operate. Then come down to the specific industry in which you operate, this includes analysing competitor and consumer activity, this tends to be the most immediate trigger for change and transformation given the immediacy of commercial impact. Then you come to the individuals within the organization, and the need to listen to and observe the trends of the people within it as real transformation (for better or worse) generally starts from within an organization as opposed to outside of it. When the leadership of an organization have their eye on the economic landscape in addition to being aware of industry, consumer and competitor activity they will start to have a sense of the degree of transformation or re-invention required. When leadership can combine that with their own personal expertise and emotional intelligence, and also be humble enough to listen to the people within the business and see the human trends impacting the future of work, they then have a more rounded picture and it's this 360 view and an ability to bring people on the journey that then drives transformation.

2 Who typically designs, drives and delivers transformational activities in organizations?

I think this is likely to be different depending on the size of the business and the mindset of the CEO. In some organizations it would be the norm to have a dedicated 'transformation' team. However, for most the direction is likely to come from the Leadership team, hopefully informed via the insights mentioned above. It's then a case of determining what work needs to be done through from scope to delivery and then bringing together the relevant people to do it. It's my observation that some organizations operate a more collaborative approach on this than others, and I don't think there's a specific right or wrong here or a model that could be deployed cookie cutter style. It's going to be determined by the scale of transformation required, the resources available to deliver it and the culture within the organization.

3 What do you see as the main barriers, challenges and obstacles to transforming an organization?

The main barriers to transformation as I see it can be firstly achieving real buy in from leadership and management levels within the organization. There needs to be a compelling case for doing it and that case needs to be communicated in such a way that it engages and inspires action. The leadership and management populations need to believe the story and be clear about it in order to engage their teams and lead them through it.

People within the organization need to believe that it's the right thing to do and only then will they back it. Then you get into practical transformation delivery activity and here it's about making sure that the required resources are in place, the budget has been allocated and that people have clarity over their role in the transformation process, the all important 'so what does it mean for me?' question has to be answered. Then finally on a practical level there's a need to look at existing legacy tech and operating systems and consider their impact, it may be that they are in fact the thing that needs to be transformed. They will undoubtedly be a factor that will impact the pace of the transformation and on the flip side noting that new advancements in tech, should be positioned as an enabler to transformation just as technology is now an enabler to the way we live our lives today.

4 Specifically looking at HR, what do you think it has to do to be more transformative about itself and for the businesses it works with?

HR professionals need to ensure they are current and commercial, that they are open minded and able to make informed decisions and to then be brave enough to act. I see a lot of great things starting to happen in HR so I think we need to celebrate those stories and start sharing ideas. I think HR has a unique position of insight within an organization which enables HR professionals to be well positioned to spot trends and inspire change. We understand the heart of the business, the people and the culture and that's a very valuable thing. Where HR starts to have real leverage is when this can be combined with commercial awareness and financial acumen in order to present a sound and robust business case for the transformation journey. Ultimately we need to focus on the results we want to achieve, plan for how to get there and then act, knowing that we may need to make a few brave decisions along the way.

5 What are your three killer apps/key skills needed to be transformational?

I think three traits of transformational people could be as follows; *curiosity, networking and bravery.* There needs to be an ability to spot trends, link themes and then actually do something about it. People who are transformational also know how to engage the hearts and minds of people too, they bring them on the journey. They have effective networks inside and outside of their organization that they draw support from and also that they add value to, they know they don't need to have all of the answers all of the time, they just need to know where to find them.

> **Three key transformational HR takeaways and reflective questions to consider:**
>
> 1 Strong voices and opinions are common in the HR profession from stage-walking thought leaders to us as practitioners in the world of work. Often there are urges and calls for action to transform. Often these fail to effect the changes we need.
>
>   **Q: How can you add your voice and experiences to this with the organizations and people you work with, to create a compelling narrative to transform key areas of your work and those of your colleagues?**
>
> 2 The calls to build better relationships and make representations from this strengthened approach are evident from all those I interviewed. People see this – and not technological disruption – as transforming HR.
>
>   **Q: How can you, as an HR or people professional, create a more transformational approach to these elements with the people and the organizations you work with?**
>
> 3 There are skills identified in the fifth question that may need strengthening and developing as part of your HR transformation approach.
>
>   **Q: How would you identify and develop those skills in you and your HR colleagues which would enhance any transformational programmes of change?**

References

Baer, Drake (accessed 20 May 2017) How changing one habit helped quintuple Alcoa's income, *The Business Insider*, 09/04 [Online] www.businessinsider.com/how-changing-one-habit-quintupled-alcoas-income-2014-4?

Cooper Ramo, Joshua (2014) *The Seventh Sense*, Little, Brown, London

The Wall Street Journal (accessed 26 May 2017) Nokia CEO Stephen Elop's 'burning platform' memo, *The Wall Street Journal*, 09/02 [Online] https://blogs.wsj.com/tech-europe/2011/02/09/full-text-nokia-ceo-stephen-elops-burning-platform-memo/

Wheatley, Margaret (2006) *Leadership and the New Science*, Berrett-Koehler Publishers, Oakland CA

Transformational 09 organizations

Stories of the future

Introduction

In Chapter 5 we introduced the concept of futurology and the element of *asymmetry*. That something can be the *same* yet so *unequal* by comparison. Like the state of the most advanced hospitals in the world versus the shacks of a rural outpost administering inoculations. Both are dispensing health-care but one must seem like a science fiction movie compared to the other.

In this chapter we will look to close the gap between transformational *thinking* and *doing* by showcasing organizations who have transformed or have some elements that could inspire your organizational transformation. It will be looking at the orthodox and unorthodox. The traditional and contemporary.

It isn't that easy to find transformative organizations with stories that haven't already been told. With the connectivity we now have, many pioneering people and organizations are more known to us. Indeed, some of those we mentioned in Chapter 5 have their fans and their sceptics in equal measure. This may depend on your view of their transformative nature or that they are part of some new 'school of cool'.

Not everyone appreciates those doing things differently and many watch such experiments willing them to fail to confirm their model of the world as 'right'. Others cannot wait to hear about the next challenger to convention and go a bit starry-eyed at those companies with dog-friendly offices; nap rooms and on-site masseuses. One person's remote working heaven, is another's idea of a hellish disconnect.

In reality, there appears to be an ever wider range of alternative working models; operating asymmetrically alongside traditional approaches. As a consequence, the way HR is operating is similarly widening out. In Chapter 4, you may recall we covered the now significantly expanded modern HR portfolio. This even wider range of organization design, ways of working and employment models therefore stretches HR's *modus operandi* horizon even further. HR it seems, isn't up for simplification any time soon. And in this book, we haven't even deeply explored the *gig economy* and the nature of *work as a platform*.

The companies included in these case studies are *not* particularly traditional in their way of operating. Indeed, some don't even have a role labelled HR. They do though have a range of people practices, development options, hiring philosophies, care and well-being and of course, legal compliance. They also have an integrated approach for workflow and decision making; investment and spend; business development and client relationships and product/service quality. They have transformed how they used to work to what they have now and they provide examples of how you might transform. Not a straight copy of course – this book isn't about best practice more *next practice*. It is intended that these case studies are used as inspiration; for your transformational ideas and ideologies.

What is evident is that when you spend time with these organizations or talking to the people who work there, there is a sense of something different that they now take for granted and have absorbed as their norm. They may only feel transformative themselves when compared to more traditional or outmoded companies. You may well have out-transformed these companies and be further along a journal of radically altered states of operating. And if so I'd love to hear from you. Yet it's all about context and relevance.

Transformation is very much contextual and so we return to our definition for a second: these organizations have, at some stage, transformed *from* and *to* something different. Fundamental changes in how they have conducted their business in order to control their aspirations, intentions and influence on an ever shifting world of work. They will never be the same again (unless they – bizarrely – transform in a *retrograde* sense).

Transformation is that state: a shift to something that will be forever different. These companies feel they will be forever different not only to others but to how they may have been when they were first conceived.

How will this chapter transform my thinking?

- It will look into the ways some organizations are providing their HR support and enablement, in some cases in very non-traditional ways, provoking new thoughts about how you might adapt your practices.

- By identifying where transformational practices exist and that these may feel at a tangent to existing methods of HR, people and organization development. Such approaches are works in progress and are continuing experiments in transforming the way work is done and people are developed.

- This chapter appreciates that context is king and whilst these models are working in their environment, straight replication may not be the desired model for your organization. Instead these posts present insight, challenge and new mental models to look at and inspire you to think and approach things with a fresh perspective based on others endeavours.

Case study one: Widen, Madison, Wisconsin, USA

In a leafy part of the gloriously pretty state of Wisconsin is Widen Inc. One of Madison's most reputable businesses and a regular feature in Wisconsin's best companies in terms of performance but more importantly, its way with people. Spending time interviewing people about what it was like to work in the 'Widen way' was an experience I'll never forget. A sense of something more family-like (without the falling out) than any other business I'd visited and worked with. A sense of belief in the way things are done there as a privileged, appreciated, adult environment and of course the clear success in a world I'd never heard of before – digital asset management.

Widen is approaching its 70 year anniversary and has a heritage in marketing solutions and an early adopter of new technological advances. Proud of its heritage, you can also tell Widen people are proud of their direction of travel. I spent two days, in sunny August talking with a range of great people about Widen and I had one particular question I wanted to find out more about: 'Why do they love their work?' When I walked into reception, I was immediately confronted with an artefact of how things are done in Widen: a wall of fame – a series of postcards where members of the Widen team was celebrating the help given to them by another member of the team. Clipped on a card to a kind of tree of life. If you're in any doubts about whether a company is people-centred, this would remove that doubt. Like a Facebook feed of likes but in real life and with more heart and substance.

Leadership letting go

It is important to know that the CEO of Widen is responsible for a lot of the feelings at Widen. About how it is to work there. Matthew Gonnering is a former marketing director, now CEO who has taken a strongly principled approach to how Widen operates. He has introduced a more self-managed approach to teams; kept an approachable and flat feeling to his hierarchy and included an entrepreneurial spirit where activism and innovation is encouraged. Everyone I spoke to over two days reported how much they believe in, admire and feel privileged by Matthew's vision for how to run a human, freedom-centred company. Matthew has very much let go. Let go of power, of decisions and of control. He has built an organization which thrives because it is alive with a sense of purpose, pride and belonging.

Decision making is more open source than prescribed. Inclusion means influential roles can be taken by those with the belief, stamina and ability to do so, and his entire approach at Widen is covered by the term *well-being*. Not just free fruit and foosball tables either. Widen has no slides, no cheap gimmicks and no sense of immaturity. Internal communication there is all on the channel *Slack*. A free flowing, thread based communication tool, this serves Widen folks well in being open, participative and conversational approach about everything from the expansion of an additional building to the car parking and new business leads. Whilst this may not be a revelation to some, it is indicative of how open things are at Widen. Open.

A spirit of adventure

Shortly after I was there, I interviewed – by Skype – Libby Maurer. Libby came back from a European vacation and so we grabbed a drink but we didn't get the chance to share stories. Libby had introduced *User Experience (UX)* thinking to Widen. Libby tells me that this realization came about because of a potential loss of clients/work and that this approach wasn't part of the way Widen worked at the time. So Libby took it upon herself to learn about the intricacies of UX. Libby then made a pitch to Widen's leading people about why this approach could result in better products; more client wins and would serve the company well. The response was a positive one and also one of hands-off support. Libby effectively became the UX Lead and changed her role to become that. She wrote her own job into existence and (perhaps coincidentally perhaps not) Widen began to win some rather large clients who are now using their DAM (Digital Asset Management) software. Libby now delivers talks to others on UX. An intrapreneurial approach if ever I've seen one.

This thread of 'enterprise spirit' was evident in others I interviewed too – there is clearly an openness to activism and participation.

Conducting and jamming

Widen's management was described by the people there as being so pro-democratic, and therefore likened to having a conductor of the orchestra who also jammed with the musicians. Their friends all reported envy at the openness at Widen so there was no doubt that this was a place of regard to work in. The closeness of the leaders to the customer was also felt to be an advantage to both manager and team member alike. Whilst 120 people isn't vast, there could still be a disconnect to the day-to-day needs of customers that Widen's managers felt right in the thick of. Open exchanges of issues, resolution and good feedback were norms. No-one appeared to have to check-up on anyone but check-ins were regular. Short and useful conversations about performance and developed happened in any of Widen's themed meeting rooms, and stand-ups and creative sessions were part of Widen's non-bureaucratic and friction-free ways of working.

Inclusive by design

Widen operates on three distinct premises – which were not something they had ever classified or made a conscious effort towards. They were simply a part of the Widen way. As an outsider, I recognized them perhaps more clearly.

The premises are:

1 **Consensus design** – the majority element of democracy directs decisions and system constructs.

2 **Consumer idealized design** – the role of the end-user or customer directs a group of people to design things based on their understanding of what would be best for customers

3 **Circular organizational design** – no single individual has ultimate authority; power is circulated or distributed equally across, say three or five people. Each person participates in decision making.

Widen is using all three and particularly the *consumer idealized design* principle. It was more than evident that customer is everything to Widen people. The rest of the 'Widen way' forms around what is known in sociocratic organization concepts as *interactive idealized design,* i.e. things emerge and are adapting constantly to the need at that time. It's well understood at

Widen – from all my interviews – that everyone is an active participant in this dynamic way of working. So much so that there is an understanding of the order of things in the way Widen has a psychological contract with its people.

Transformation through development and growth

The frame often used in referring to democratic companies is that *development* and *growth* are distinct but related factors. *Development* is referred to with four subsets: development for truth; plenty; good and joy. *Growth* is an increase in potential and attainment.

Development is often analogous with *quality of life* whilst *growth* is referred to as *standard of living. The quality of life* at Widen felt good from the moment I arrived there. The *standard of living* is a code of conduct and being that keeps things from slipping back to more controlled ways of working.

Companies built on this type of social system of self-management, develop in order to grow. Therefore, the three key aspects of the social system to support this are that:

- communication constantly improves;
- consultation is more active; and
- co-determination builds for decision making and inclusive direction setting.

Such active verbs as *development* and *growth* give people a sense of something highly participative. So how do people feel about their personal contributions to Widen and the personal satisfaction – and love – they get from their work?

The genuine affection for their work and the company helps people understand the role they play, and that it is made up of their individual and personal application as part of their *membership* of the system they are in. Some researchers and academics refer to this as *corporate citizenship*. The flow experienced by people at Widen is therefore like this:

person > role > member of system > social expectation/pressure > behaviour

People are a *microsystem* (their personal settings); belonging to a *mesosystem* (personal network); part of an *exosystem* (the organizational network); part itself of a *macrosystem* (their operating world).

Cultural influences are found in each system and relatedness to the culture at different levels has an impact on how attached people feel to their settings/values at each level. This can determine their commitment, performance, adaptability, positivity and more. Within Widen, it's clear that their is a pronounced attachment to the three nearer systems (micro, meso and exo) and in some cases a link to the macro (technologists – clearly see themselves as part of that world). Being a WorldBlu listed freedom-centred organization is part of that macrosystem. That people can create teams and new ventures within Widen is highly regarded and puts people in a position of respect and responsibility. This was appreciated by everyone I spoke to.

Dedication and loyalty

The ability to experiment, to be considered a trusted entrepreneur was felt to be a key differentiator to other workplaces and showed the company as a whole, and people within it (exo and meso systems) supported the personal systems. This allowed people to go and experience the macrosystem and bring back insight, new tools and ideas that impact on the other three systems positively. Encouraged latitude and creating enterprise within, are important energy and advantage creating sources. Workaholism and presenteeism are seen as danger signs and none of these feel part of Widen's bear traps. There is a clear indication that balance, wellness and compassion are strong and believed in.

Wellbeing as a corporate belief

At Widen, being a responsible company, a suite of benefits were provided which took the form of a company spend. This started as a point-based wellness system with tracking and incentives, intended to do good.

Widen folks had an idea though. They worked out, financially, how much this cost the company. They then worked out how this could be invested in a basement refurbishment to include a fitness centre and other wellness resources. There was a trade. Give up those benefits and equip the workplace with its own. Matthew was delighted to agree to this, and on my visit, work was underway for this installation and in full progress. Of the people, for the people. A delightful turn of events.

So where's HR in all of this?

HR is an invisible force in Widen. Well not totally invisible as I met and spoke with Heather who has the title of HR Manager in her role. Heather has a low friction job and by that I mean she is definitely NOT in any policing role or *inflicting* directives and policies on people. In fact, *everyone* does HR at Widen – which arguably makes Heather's job an easier one. Yet Heather still has to manage a pool of applicants who have heard of Widen's fantastic culture and want to join their ranks so believe me, Heather is as busy as any HR professional I've come across, just in a different way.

So HR is an invisible but active force for good. It's just not called out that much in Widen's parlance. Check-ins aren't called performance reviews; permission to recruit is a business case made with clear understanding of the investment needed and the returns that will give and there's *never* a restructure as there is always a state of that interactive, idealized design in place. For some veterans at Widen this is a little unnerving but they are fully participative in the process if sometimes a little unsure of just how much autonomy they have.

Organizational design 'sign off' sits in Matthew's domain but is a consultative process and an open chain of dialogue. I shared with Matthew what I thought his design was. It was a learning organization and the most pure interpretation of it I'd ever seen, a shared vision; known mental models (in this case particularly openness and wellness being two strong models in people's minds when they think of Widen); personal mastery (Libby's UX adventure being a prime example); team learning – a constant witnessed on the two days I was there; and systems thinking – there is constant attention to the systems at play across Widen.

Chief eudaimonia officer

Widen has a participative CSR-like approach with several local employees on the payroll with learning disabilities. One utterly fabulous role is the popcorn manager. Andrew provides a much needed service of just-in time confectionary relief to the creative minds at Widen. From a partnership with the Community Support Network (CSN), it is part of Matthew's approach to work called *eudaimonia* – happiness, health, prosperity and he is the *chief eudaimonia officer*.

To inspire his people, to remind them of the multiple, complex and societal needs an employer can fulfil, Andrew's cheerful and pick-me-up attention is as much an incentive to work well and be well, as it is to help the community with meaningful roles for people with daily challenges in life.

When Matthew announced Andrew's arrival it received more positive responses than any message he'd ever delivered. Andrew also then revealed his love of growing things, so he also takes care of all of Widen's plant life. Andrew also loves gaming and is part of Widen's Xbox tribe and is a constant participant in looking after the smiles of all across Widen's two floors. Matthew feels the sense of social responsibility and goodness that comes from employing Andrew (and his five other CSN colleagues). In keeping with the Widen way, Andrew is just as much designing his own role, as Libby Maurer did. Enhanced empathy and a deeper gratitude for one another was also evident in people in a much more noticeable way then before Andrew's arrival into the fold.

If anyone reading this has a sense of warmth but a colder realization that sounds like this question 'How does this create value for customers?' are reminded by CEO Matthew that Peter Drucker once said, 'The purpose of an organization is to enable common men to do uncommon things'.

There is something uncommon about Widen and the people there. Something that may indeed be the common of the future of work and the role HR plays.

Summary: how does this case study help us with a transformational HR approach?

1   It points to the future of technology and humanity co-existing.

The business of Widen has been transformed by the explosive percolation of digital technology in their chosen field. Instead of becoming more like an efficient machine, Widen have kept a strong family and inclusive feel by being more self-directed and non-hierarchical in their way of working. People at Widen believe this creates a maturity of application and a sense of coming together that enhances their technical and digital skill. In essence, as we get more digitized in our work, we become more human in the way we work.

2   It demonstrates how 21st-century leadership is defined by human values and letting go.

Matthew's approach as CEO is to focus on wellness and well-being. Of people first and then the organization becomes a well-being operation. Of course Matthew has to get the numbers right; the pipeline healthy and report to the board but he trusts his people and therefore they believe in him. It's not easy letting go like this but Matthew has checks and balances in place where people will share with him if they feel it's too loose or too tight.

3 Understated HR still means good – and even better – people practices.

Far from HR professionals feeling this proves they're not needed, the work of organization design, leadership, personal and technical development, recruitment, pensions, benefits, and more still need to get done and do get done at Widen. It is a more distributed effort which means it feels less done to people and more part of the way of working. The invisible force I mentioned is given the name of a wellness approach to work and a wellbeing approach to each other.

4 Transformation might feel episodic but it can be a constant series of major and minor shifts.

No doubts that Widen has been through transformation and appeared to be settled when I came across them. Clear on who they were and what they did, there was though, a constant attention to evolution. At some point a major transformation at Widen then settled into the new normality yet – and the UX venture is proof – minor transformative elements kept a sense of freshness and energy. The attention to decentralization and self-management is a longer and more regularized transformation rather than a spike of activity that then settles down.

Case study two: Nearsoft, Mexico and USA

Celebrating their 10th anniversary this year, Nearsoft is a technology innovation company of over 250 people across four sites (three in Mexico – Hermosillo, Chihuahua and Mexico City as well as two in the United States: San Jose, CA and Las Vegas, NV). Founded by Matt Perez and Roberto Martinez, from the outset, they set out to transform. The vision of Matt and Roberto was of a human-centred, bureaucracy-light company built on innovation, commitment to clients and distributed power.

Spending four days over two consecutive years with Matt and his team in Miami (as part of a conference) led to some fascinating conversations and discoveries about their way of working. Like Widen, they are a WorldBlu-certified, freedom-centred workplace and have been since 2009 – symbolic of their commitment to democratic workplaces of inclusion and more dynamic ways of working.

Scaffolding not structures

Matt and Roberto are 100 per cent committed to self-management. In fact Matt detests much of what we take as norms in the corporate world. He has an allergic reaction to the term 'human resources'. Matt is all about people. Resources to him are capital, equipment, technology but *not* people. So it's a surprise to feature someone so averse to a term that is part of this book – transformational HR. Yet this company is transformative and has transformed itself from a small beginning to being one of the most progressive companies that only a select few of us know about.

In order to make sure self-management is totally understood, the joining process at Nearsoft is a discovery-based six-week adventure across a range of roles and with a variety of people. Conversations and time spent with others forms not only a fluid, personal and highly immersive programme, they also bond people to each other, the company purpose, and the ways of working. To most new people, controlling ways are the only things they've ever experienced until they come to the free and liberated sense of how Nearsoft works.

Staying tight but free

Matt believes in the power of social capital. So much so, that he has some affirming blog posts shared across *Nearsoftian* internal channels with 'bad word of the day'. He uses it to highlight how the language of business can create negative emotional connotations. He deplores Human Capital (as do I) and so offers alternatives. Alternatives that not only let you into Matt's mental models of the world, but also to the things that are important to Nearsoft's way of being.

Social capital, exchanges, and belief in each other are key factors in the design of Nearsoft as an organization. It is because of this that *Nearsoftians* can maximize innovation, stay close in relationships to customers. People at Nearsoft are fiercely loyal to their customers and build up years of relationship *capital* with them, (which fosters trusts and creates stronger commitments to each other), and be adaptable at the same time – to respond to new demands and help out colleagues in need.

What *is* clear at Nearsoft are the processes and ways of doing the work. Everything is recorded, so there is a library of content to help people understand how to work with a client and the standards of operating are clarified. This becomes clear during the six-week orientation stage as does the flow and allocation of work.

With no management and no specific role titles given to people, it is important people understand the flow and the route to success alongside the standards and guidelines for how to do the work for clients and each other. Decisions on who works on what normally starts with the skills a person has (that may be the expertise in a coding language) and then in the team, a backlog of tasks indicates what work is to be done. Either by self-selection or in discussion with colleagues, the work is then allocated in an open and discussive way. Normally, the teams at Nearsoft are dedicated to a client, so the skills that brought the new developer to the team are part of the client's need firstly; then integration with the purpose of the work; the client's preferred way of working and then the work to be done is allocated or opted into by the team members.

Values that truly matter

It's the oldest cliché in the book that many company values are window dressing and yet at Nearsoft they are the epicentre of all decisions: hiring, new clients, investment decisions and innovation.

Career changes at Nearsoft have a whole new dimension because the organization has no static hierarchy. The 'climb the pole' success is replaced by naturally occurring, situational and responsive leadership principles. Roberto says he is continually amazed at how people step into that role when not expected to do so. It doesn't mean people lack ambition but competition is replaced by cooperation. People freely mentor, guide and teach others, give space and credence to those with drive and skill to make things happen and generally are more a 'band of brothers and sisters' than they are a corporation of roles.

Instead of the usual formality of corporate meetings or the perceived state of anarchy in start-ups, Nearsoft decisions are made with the democratic process of dialogue and discussion. Their leadership team process is the primary mechanism for *Nearsoftians* to frame problems, make decisions, and take action (e.g. how are year-end earned dividends assigned).

No managers, no HR

Fiercely independent of the normal view – having no managers is a way of life at Nearsoft. Matt and Roberto have introduced a systematic way of operating that simply does not need management to deliver on it. Democratic decision making is hard baked in the Nearsoft way.

Matt talks about an example when, one year, there were some concerns over training. Instead of the normal solution – either a management/HR problem to solve – at Nearsoft they form a leadership team of three to nine people who are bothered about the issue and want to resolve it. In this case, those people would have to go back to their teams and share they were stepping up to do this additional, but useful work. The rest of the team would either back their request or work out how much they needed to do to keep the client work in focus whilst allowing for their involvement in the leadership team.

This is the way things get done, and how things stick that reaffirm their values and make a difference. When you feel you have the chance to actively work on things that will make your workplace better without conflict, tension or a clash of priority, why would this need any more bureaucracy and further layers of control or bureaucracy. Leadership teams then disband and others will form around other needs so it's a perfectly fluid arrangement very much akin to a murmuration of starlings.

Roberto and Matt admit that not all decisions taken by leadership teams are things they would be in favour of. But they are not all-knowing, nor do they claim to be the most reliable decision makers anyway. They have faith, and it has been proven, in the people and the system they've created, as being the best mechanism for success. Ten years of growth and impact are testament to this faith. The only veto they reserve is the right to make sure that the company doesn't slide into an old-style hierarchy. They see themselves in the role of creating the conditions for the culture that makes Nearsoft a brilliant place to work.

Roberto, Matt and all at Nearsoft believe in freedom not fear, in collaboration not competition and in unity not untidy. Nearsoft is proof that you can create something where adults come to learn about a new way to work together.

Summary: how does this case study help us with a transformational HR approach?

1 Culture really is everything.

At a time when products, systems, processes and other business factors are all known to the world, culture is yours – it's unique and it's the key differentiator. With all companies chasing the 'thing' that makes the difference, an intentional and deliberate cultural design is a winning formula. HR is often seen as the shaper and guardian of workplace culture and yet so often has to fight against a toxic, competitive, fearful culture created by the leadership and heritage of an organization. Nearsoft's way is deliberate, magnetic and guiding all who work there.

2   People step up to lead on merit not by role.

When we face the challenges of adaptability, responsibility and creativity we need more people to step up to take on challenges, bring ideas to life and lead. Titles may appear to ordain that responsibility but at Nearsoft it's situational. When everyone has the chance to lead, it's always *their* business not someone else's. Engagement is therefore not pursued or a number on a survey it's a way of being that matters. This form of self-selection needs no nine-box grids, needs no artificial layers of management structure and therefore no HR processes to manage the heart and soul of human endeavour.

3   Transformation becomes everyone's role.

Collective belief, responsibility and activism is rife at Nearsoft and yet there are checks and balances with the system and everyone else to make sure all intent is going to be good for the people, the customers and ultimately Nearsoft. HR's role as systems creator to get the best changes out of the people is often a thankless and fruitless task and it finds itself convulsing from restructure to restructure. Yet at Nearsoft the state of fluidity negates the need for this and simply points everyone towards better versions of what happened the day before. A truly complex adaptive system.

Case study three: Competo d.o.o., Ljubljana, Slovenia

Slovenia is the one country in the world with love in its name. And through the wonders of the internet I was contacted by one of the co-founders of an executive search and recruitment company called Competo d.o.o., Laura Smrekar and I had a Skype call and we agreed that I would be the keynote speaker at a live event in December 2016 about the 'future of work'. Not that uncommon a thing for me but Slovenia wasn't somewhere I had ever been to before. Intrigued, I looked into this company more and liked what I found. It looked like an entrepreneurial company and so in further conversations with Laura and Tina Novak Kac, I arranged to go out and find out more about this new client. A short stopover in October and the chance to meet and talk to the entire team and then the story.

Matic Vosnjak and Laura Smrekar are the two co-founders of this enterprise. And both from previous roles in conventional recruiting and talent acquisition roles. After several years of working in that system, there was a determination to do something different. So Competo was born and the translation is quite literally fit. The perfect fit. An approach for recruitment that isn't about 'who have I got on my books' but more 'what's the perfect fit for the person and the company?'. A small team of occupational and workplace psychologists; flexible consultants who have industry knowledge rather than recruitment and HR knowledge; an inventive and creative culture based on research, data, people and organizational design.

What's so different about the Competo way?

The company strategy is more than it's stated 'When passion becomes work' – it appears to be more that they help transform the lives of people and organizations by finding the perfect fit.

In order to do this, the philosophy at Competo is on relationships, partnerships and a networked approach to business. Instead of cold calls or relying purely on inbound, Competo's people have experience of the markets they serve: automotive, technology, manufacturing, leadership, knowledge work – so not just being good at spotting a decent CV these are people who can feel the symbiosis between a prospective candidate and an organization's role.

The psychology element is looking at a richer data source about people so there is more than instinct at play. Scenarios, tests and personality assessments routines are included in the conversational exchanges and a deep understanding of the culture and world of the organization.

The work of Competo might *look* a lot like other companies in recruitment yet when you talk to Competo people, they are part of an entrepreneurial approach to work and other people. Should the teams need a new researcher or a new project manager? The individual who sees the need works up the case, validates their decision with colleagues and the company decides democratically what major changes they make in the way they hire, work and expand their portfolio.

Leading with intentional direction

Matic made the conscious choice that people would feel part of an enterprise and that had transformational qualities. He has had a transformational journey into his current role. One he recognizes is the starting point of any business-level transformation. In his past, he has both been able to achieve that – (in his time with volunteer-based education not-for-profit AIESEC) and not (within larger more corporate environments). Matic recognizes there are three levels at play here: *personal transformation, corporate transformation* and then *market transformation*. Some come in a linear form: you personally transform, to then generate a corporation transformation into a market transformation. Matic recognizes this is pretty rare but it has happened in his career.

Where one is immediately blocked by another in this chain it can create frustration, cause tension of the negative sort and totally derail any transformational proposition of any nature.

If transforming a market that impacts on corporate and personal, this could cause people and companies to be left behind. If a corporate transformation fails to create a market and not bring its people with it, it will fail. If people want to transform but the corporate level and market are not conducive, that transformation often ends up in them going to work somewhere else. It is through understanding this dynamic that helps Competo be the most interesting recruitment firm I've experienced.

For Competo is also somewhere with a family feel, which you might expect for a small startup. And yet there is little parenting going on here. It was the fabulous **Fons Trompenaars** who first alerted me to a smart model around enterprise growth and the stages of development. In his model he talks about four stages:

- **Incubator:** is as it sounds: a fresh, almost lab-like environment where everything is an experiment.
- **Family:** where the enterprise is growing and hierarchies develop where some take responsibility and more senior roles.
- **Guided missile:** where clarity, alignment and management by objectives defines targeted work.
- **Eiffel Tower:** where the business is a monument to success. And also at risk from calcifying and being stuck.

Competo is a fascinating mix of the first three. Something I've rarely seen in one company and that's why I find it so fascinating and why I believe it is transformational. To simultaneously see these three is rare as many people move through the stages, leaving the previous stage behind. I suspect Competo's people don't even realize they are in a constant state of movement between these three elements.

Competo have worked with, and now actively promote, the partnership approach to transformation. This is either in the way you use internal and external collaborations, or the way you fuse new people, more experienced colleagues and people of a range of ranks and roles in a company. Indeed Matic believes in self-starting transformation much like Lisa Gill described in Chapter 8.

Small energy-creating activism which becomes more systemic as there is realization it could replicate out/up and impact on the entire company. At Competo, Matic and Laura encourage active innovation and therefore transformation from all in the company and with their clients and partners. They believe you can make more convincing arguments this way for transformation with clients by showing smaller-scale micro-transformational ventures Competo itself uses as part of its way of operating. So they experiment and learn fast with their clients in a trusted way. Be that the use of their psychology assessments to their interview and scenario-based assessment techniques. They build and believe in bespoke solutions co-created with clients.

Matic and Laura back this up and have deliberately made it clear that Competo is designed to maximize everyone's contributions not just to create economic value. They encourage creative tension and to challenge conventional thinking that may impede the success of the company.

Bravery and resilience go hand in hand

Matic has experience of the skills needed from his own transformation – resilience being a key one. Holding one's nerve and the courage to take on something huge and far reaching. He also restates the ambitions to foster good relationships with others as a key skill in the future especially with digital transformation changing many of the ways we had that were touch points to build human connections.

And with resilience and a strong and deep network, Matic sees the need to have bravery as part of the essential skills of the transformational HR practitioner of the near future. Bravery that can come from more convincing cases for transformation through strong evidence and support from others. This comes across in the way Competo looks to match people and their future potential to organizations with a need to identify a perfect fit for now and in the future.

People at Competo are encouraged to grow quickly and be independent but connected in their ways of working. Not being overly prescribed to but allowing for emergent and adaptive ways of working together.

Willingness to listen

I ran a small but powerful hackathon with the team – all were invited to discover what would make Competo a better place to work and a better service provided to all their clients. An all-hands event with an openness and a dialogue many other companies would be afraid to expose people to. Shaping the future of their own enterprise gave a sense of ownership, democracy and participative leadership.

The same happened when we looked at the psychometric profiles of the team using the GC Index® – we discovered that Competo had a high level of energy towards innovation and creativity; a high degree of energy towards implementing and refining quality products and services but a deficiency of energy towards making strategies. This is not the sort of thing that many management teams would openly share in public. In Competo, everyone is an opinion-sharing, business-shaping activist.

More widely, in looking at the role HR professionals play in the world of work – Matic and Laura feel that a heavily networked professional is an intelligence source across the organization to aggregate views, inputs and reactions that would otherwise be locked into individual manager/colleague discussions and all but lost to the overall transformational programme's source of influence and impact analysis. Sure, surveys and working groups can represent (along with unions or other representative fora) yet everyday conversations and in-the-moment reactions can be as, if not more, valuable to making the right decisions and avoiding anxiety or detrimental impacts to people.

Summary: how does this case study help us with a transformational HR approach?

1 Entrepreneurial spirit and including everyone in this as a system.

It is fair to say HR isn't *renowned* as entrepreneurial and yet this energy, commitment and creativity is a sustainable force for good at Competo. It feels like an established enterprise with an urge to constantly reinvent and experiment. Orderly and artistic is a closer relationship in a company like Competo – science and instinct; data and sensing; now and the future. Competo have closed the gaps between many things that perplex professionals in the people 'game'.

2 Bravery and astute business sense.

In a highly reputational environment, being brave is a risk. Yet, being adventurous and still delivering high quality services to clients is a mix Compeo has perfected. Understanding the client's world helps craft new solutions to age-old problems in hiring the perfect fit. Competo has organically grown and attracted people with a range of skills and disciplines that in itself make a perfect fit. Using intuition and openness to creative thinking have become trademarks whilst delivering to complex and challenging situations in hiring the best people.

3 Strategies can be emergent as long as belief in the philosophy is deeply felt.

A CEO of a 9,000-person company once said 'we've never had a strategy because no-one's ever asked for one'. There is an unfussy and yet highly professional way that Competo has become a thoughtful *doing* organization. Allowing for an adaptive and emergent way of building a thriving business with a warm and inclusive workplace isn't as easy as Competo has made it look. Listening, ideas sharing and open exchanges create a place people feel part of and own the future of. Shared successes are evident at Competo and it always feels like a team game. Something many HR teams can do well to be mindful of.

Case study four: River Island, London, UK

River Island is a family-owned and run business – Ben Lewis (CEO) is the nephew of founder Bernard – and a brand introduced to the world in 1991. There are over 300 stores worldwide and an organization HQ in West London. Karen Beaven is the HR Director and in 2015 the HR team there scooped four awards as part of market journal *HR Magazine's* annual ceremony. Karen herself won HR Director of the Year – a truly prestigious honour. I had the pleasure of working with Karen and the HR Team in 2014 and 2015.

There's something the HR team at River Island are doing that is best in class for certain, and transformational, arguably. Indeed the HR Magazine's own materials in profiling the Gold Award (overall) winning testimony opens with this quote: 'Anyone wondering how to take HR from a transactional function within their business to a truly strategic one could do a lot worse than take a leaf from River Island's book'.

Recognizable transformation, is still transformation

Much of what River Island HR did in transforming themselves and their role in the business may not appear that radical to some. And yet, it was transformational in context. Things were never the same once they had been transformed.

For example, the team created a learning and development academy – accredited by the Institute of Leadership & Management – giving managers at River Island a professional qualification for their work leading people. A first for them and so management development will never be the same as it was before. Yes, this may have been done in hundreds of organizations, and yet daily, I come across thousands who are neglecting their people through poor development of managers.

Their recruitment practices – notoriously challenging in a highly seasonal and high-turnover environment that is the retail world – saved a huge amount of money whilst establishing a stronger employer brand, and delivered more responsive and effective recruitment methods. Many HR teams fight a daily battle of volume and process efficiency. River Island HR transformed their recruitment proposition.

An apprenticeship scheme was introduced way ahead of legislative changes from the UK Government. Alongside this, a new work experience scheme developed and launched enhancing the contact with academic institutions and people looking for experience of a dynamic working environment. A mid-senior level skills and recruitment strategy – a key role in operational management – and targeted sales periods being effectively resourced and sustained whilst also using less agency hires and better use of social media for not just employer brand activities, but also vacancy management. Improvements in this area were transformational. Hence the scooping of the award for best recruitment strategy.

The company's own expansion into new global territories and with a new venture (The Style Studio) championed from HR, commercial awareness was rated high on the judge's assessment of the River Island HR's team list of achievements. Something many HR teams have been aspiring to for some time.

Show intention

River Island HR created a three-year transformation plan which would not only transform the services needed for a fast-paced, competitive business, but also the way the HR team conducted its business to support and create a better place to work as part of that growth and diversification.

The HR Magazine article concludes that the examples set by River Island's three years' transformation strategy is one of future-focused, business-aware and adaptable HR practices in a highly demanding working environment with a strongly forged awareness of their customer's needs.

It is the most HR-like example I have in this book and proves that you don't have to *over-radicalize* what you do to be transformational.

The transformational HR playbook

There are several key activities from their strategic approach that I will share with you:

1 There was a *transformational HR strategy*. Deliberately set to prove and communicate to others that HR meant business. It wasn't about to just improve a little here and there, HR wanted to *transform*. That intent is important.

2 The team managed simultaneous streams of transformation whilst delivering core HR support. Each divisional lead was responsible for transformation in their areas. Distributed transformational activities, co-ordinated and aggregated through the strategic level plans.

3 The perception of HR was integral to this. People felt HR was shifting hugely, actions backed that up and so no false promises were made yet intent was signalled. This was all improved through the dialogue and relations side of how HR people worked with their business counterparts.

4 There were commercial figures attached to the results. Whilst there may have been new hires into the team to grow in numbers, and therefore reach and capability, the returns were savings on recruitment costs lost on agency hires; recruitment per person costs reduced and retention of new hires increased through better joining and development routines.

5 Commercially focused learning programmes improved customer service, management of people and a skills programme *for* HR staff. Investment not just in others but in themselves powered transformational mindsets and strategies.

This continues with River Island's HR team responding and supporting the improvements to their much needed e-commerce and technology teams and continuing to build greater links to charitable pursuits with their relationship with the Retail Trust being just one example.

This is not a technology company from Palo Alto, or a platform enterprise in Rotterdam; or some fancy distributed website maker with people working in the mornings and surfing in the afternoon. This is the challenging world of retail design, distribution, sales and market share. This market – 18–35 year old fashion – is probably one of the most competitive buying markets there is.

People are critical, product is of course also critical. Yet River Island's HR Director Karen Beaven brought them both together in a new business and retail concept Karen led called the Style Studio. This is a classic example where the style of HR matches perfectly that of the business, its people and its services and yet still holds onto rigours like employment law and protective rights of workers.

Transformational HR doesn't have to be *The Jetsons* meets *The Matrix*. Transformational HR is contextual and means that you take a version of what you are and transform it into something that is radically different, drastically better and sets a new tempo and direction for what else you can deliver. River Island HR and Karen Beaven did this and proved so with four awards in 2015. It certainly proves that even a traditional look and feel for HR can be a transformational force for good.

Summary: how does this case study help us with a transformational HR approach?

1 Declaration of transformation can shift perceptions of HR.

In making sure others are aware of your intentions, and secure their help and support, you really do need to name your aspirations and create something people can see, read, hear about and feel. Giving yourself a sensible timeframe but showing ambition, courage and flair all help enamour people to your cause. River Island HR's three-year transformation plan clearly did this.

2 Commercially astute transformation will win favour with your business colleagues.

Knowing your costs and where savings can be made is one thing that will get people's attention. Also improving speed, quality and accuracy at the same time will really help them believe that a transformation has occurred. In order to do this, investment is needed and so River Island HR took time to ensure their HR team had the people and the skills to do this through partnering and developing whilst being involved in the transformation programme.

3 Transformation and business-as-usual can operate side-by-side.

In River Island's case innovation – and transformation – *became* the business priority and through clear planning and resourcing, was delivered in a harmonious and absorbable way by both the HR team and their colleagues across the company. Much of the HR transformation was about the work that was needed to help people more – better hiring, better managing, better retention, better leadership, better reward policies. Transformation of this nature fits the shorthand version of the definition used earlier in this book – *things will never be the same again* – and arguably, is also perfect fit for the longhand version too.

Case study five: Menlo Innovations, Michigan, USA

We close as we started, a technology company in the USA. This time, in downtown Ann Arbor, Michigan. The organization whose reason for being is *to end human suffering as it relates to technology.*

At Menlo Innovations the 70+ people who work there all believe in and experience *joy*, which was also the title of CEO Rich Sheridan's book *Joy Inc.* Because at Menlo Innovations they have transformed a workplace to become known as the 'joy factory'. I spent two days experiencing joy and talking to Rich and his people in August 2016. Two memorable days where the hype I'd experienced in videos and through the book were exceeded by the experience. And I was not alone in coming to Menlo Innovations in Ann Arbor, Michigan. Over 3,000 people had come for tours of the way things work here. Courses and experiences are put on to experience what it's like to work here in the Menlo way. Menlo's way is a much a product as it is the software they build for clients. I was privileged enough to sit, stand, walk and talk through their joyful way. It was a learning experience which, yes, I really enjoyed. And man, did I learn a lot.

The Menlo way

What's wonderful about Menlo is that their way of working is neither chaos or bureaucracy – it's a way of maintaining a sensible flow of culture, tasks and performance. Rich describes their experiences of experimenting with the ways of working are:

- culture without process = chaos
- process without culture = bureaucracy
- culture + process = joy

The way Menlo have set this up is the equation:

Structure + Human Relationships + Human Energy

This is personified no more strongly than in the daily stand up. Now *lots* of companies have stand-up meetings, or perhaps their teams have stand-ups. Yet this is different. Passing around the ceremonial plastic Viking helmet, and introducing who you are and what you're working on plus anything else of interest; charity work, significant life event, fun thing, achievement, whatever. It's something people feel is necessary, willingly participated in and keeps the information conversational, human and clear. It never takes more than 15 minutes and that's for over 60 people. There's guest included and mostly it is a personification of the pairing aspect of working here – people share their joint endeavours.

Togetherness through pairs

Pairing is one of the most important things to note about Menlo. They have a stack of great things but perhaps pairing is one of the most important. For example, when Nick (one of Menlo's Development team) came back to the welcome event I was part of in August after missing the *entire* thing to work on a project with Kealy, he asked me what did he miss. I jokingly but also mildly seriously said 'it's all about pairs'. Not teams, not trios, not just you – pairs. So instead of working on a project as a developer and being given your modules and projects you work on the same working assignment but in pairs. As a duo. So you effectively are a tag team, two heads better than one in ideas and problem solving and checking each other's work to avoid bugs and mistakes.

Is it really cost effective though is the obvious question most people will ask? Doubling the resource means it looks like it is double the cost but this has to be set against not the ROI (return on investment) but against the RUI (residual unintended impacts). The RUI of mistakes, glitches and all the 'knowledge in one person' risk are counteracted by working in Menlo way. Knowledge, creativity, accountability, perfection, support, feedback, help, excitement – all shared amongst you and your working partner. Pairs are rotated regularly; pairs are allocated to projects and pairs cover each other and when there's holiday or other issues, cover is picked up from others. It's very self-organized without any confusion and like managed process without the overbearing bureaucracy.

When I thought about cost but the result that Menlo achieves through this method I said it like this: *there is a cost to products **in pairs** and there's* definitely *a cost to products **impaired**.*

That's the simple economics. As CEO and architect of this method Rich said – 'you're closing *significantly* the gap between error and discovery of error'. In 12 years of operating Menlo Innovations has had no software emergencies and has no support team to handle calls. Their software solutions work. Clients pay for that certainty and they believe in the pairs working methods and that this is a part of Menlo's joy at work philosophy. Experience the joy of success in building great software with your pair; other pairs and the whole Menlo family.

Designed for cooperation

Even interviewing for a role at Menlo is done in pairs format. Pairing people brings accountability to each other; brings consistency in two sets of eyes working on code and design solutions; it brings dialogue and feedback and most importantly it brings a solid reliance on 40 hour working weeks.

Menlo have also created something unique in one of their roles; a high-tech anthropologist. This is a philosophy of Menlo's that means analysts and designers go and spend time with their technology users. To truly understand their customers's world and design for them not just for a technology blueprint or archetype. Not just walk through functionality and design with a few project co-opted managers, but talk to the people who will use the software in everything they do. They watch and observe their world. Looking at the routines, the demands, the variations the challenges their end users face. This approach helps the design methods be sharper and more attuned so that when personas are created for their users, there is a clear link back to the world their users operate in. High-tech anthropologists also work in pairs – as do designers, testers and coders.

A joyful environment

If I were to shout 'Hey Menlo' right in the middle of the office, everyone stops; responds and I can ask them how they feel. They'd tell me, I'd thank them and they'd get on with their work.

There's a noise here: of people talking and working together to solve complex technical issues and meet ambitious technical requirements.

There's no cubicles or offices; the furniture moves and is reassembled meaning people create their own environments; and there's a sociability that is palpable.

Despite this appealing sense of a youthful environment, Menlo is an adult to adult place to be. Firstly, the openness by which work is logged, recorded and planned. Via an open and visible board at the far end of the office, tasks are plotted on handwritten cards with notes and coloured stickers denoting progress/status. This means you don't need some bureaucracy of reporting (that often no-one reads) or a manager to interfere and direct your working efforts. There's no shame in being behind or being ahead as you can ask for help or get help because everyone's aware of your progress. If you're shirking, your partner will let you know. If you're both struggling, others will help.

Secondly, there's learning *as* work in this model. If you're new to a piece of software or a client or a design concept, then you're paired with someone who knows. They won't just do the work whilst you *spectate*, they will show and tell and observe and guide. It's how come someone can start on the most long-standing client's work – in sensitive medical software for example – and still be in your *first three days of working at Menlo*. There's no hollow induction period or lengthy wait until you're unleashed, just instant application and productivity and learning. It's how come in your third week at Menlo, you have a brand new person join *you*, because you're learned so much from your partner the previous three weeks. It's like mentoring and coaching; instructional guidance and protocol compliance happens naturally as you're working. No time offline practising with fictional case studies to learn: straight in but with a wise partner.

Thirdly, there's autonomy that if you need to head out to a course on iOS features for tablets you and your partner agree; arrange and whoever goes brings back the learning for whoever needs it. No need to have allocated budgets just an agreement in the pair that there is a need that can't be solved by others in the network.

Fourthly, people are recruited because they are good coders/designers/testers but primarily because they show in the interview/assessments that they can work in pairs. It's so important to Menlo's methodology (pairs) that they set up situations and scenarios that people have to demonstrate they can work in pairs.

Learning is in pairs; decisions are taken in pairs; working is in pairs, as a result Menlo needs no management. Let me say that again, Menlo needs no management. Menlo also needs no email between each other – they talk; meet; talk some more and working in pairs means the act of programming is one machine/keyboard between two who take it in turns to 'drive'. And because of the pair working and very low friction on bureaucracy, there is no visible HR department, once again, HR is a distributed and invisible force. Hiring, contracts, performance conversations and development still happens, so HR work does happen.

Rich has genuine regard for HR professionals, saying to me that Menlo 'would like to rescue HR from HR'. I guess in the same way that their mission statement about ending human suffering as it relates to technology. Maybe the twist here is to *end HR suffering as it relates to bureaucracy?* Transformational HR could, should and potentially will do that.

It's refreshing to see such an approach to people as I've seen and experienced at Menlo Innovations. The reason this is so refreshing is down to:

- **Working in pairs:** that rotate and have focused schedules of work they accomplish together.

- **No management interference:** planning is done by the team who work on the project in dialogue and agreed with the client.

- **It's about the client need:** demonstrations and show and tells are done with the client driving the demo for increased openness and ownership.

- **Low tech and high tech coexist:** the manual, highly visual planning process means progress and accomplishments are present for all to see; recorded; validated by others and feedback is constant and as ongoing as the 'how you doing' conversations we have around the water cooler.

- **Dialogue builds trust, trust builds caring:** openness, transparency, caring about each other's work is commonplace and creates a healthier working duration and cooperation which in turn, creates the most superior products for clients.

All of these – along with interesting work; good clients; professional pride – come together in a place where joy is the by product of the belief in a better way to work; in each other and in joy itself.

Summary: how does this case study help us with a transformational HR approach?

1 Working in pairs could be the adopted way for HR professionals to operate.

OK it may be tricky if you're it – the only person doing HR – but invariably your work is often helping others and so pair working could be instigated with colleagues. I think the essence of this is bringing people closer together to operate not as lone workers in a team framework and have more people understand each other's part in the process of people and organization development. I would at least love HR teams to experiment more with this method. It can't be any worse than sat behind a desk emailing policies and jumping in on meeting after meeting surely?

2 Adopt the design principle of HR anthropology.

Spending time with people on roles, understanding their world and making decisions on HR initiatives, policies and guidance from an informed and observational, lived experience *must* help HR professionals make better choices and more informed decisions. If nothing else, better relationships will be forged, more visibility will prove HR cares about the people whose work HR impacts upon and we might just innovate more with a sense of what the working world is like for all our colleagues.

3 Balance well being with working hard.

Menlo has a unique way of allowing people's lives to seep into work. So pets, babies and working hours appear in the office that some companies feel they couldn't replicate. Yet the principle is more about design. Design the work so that accurate assessments can be made on how long it will take to complete; make sure people are as friction-free to do that as well as possible and help them work things out and get the help they need to make it work. Craft, quality and creativity appear to do more for our well being than hard-deadlines, bonuses and shortcuts. So Menlo design the former to never have to take the latter.

Conclusion

So what have we learned from all five of these case studies from the USA, Mexico, Slovenia and the UK?

How people feel about their work is important

We are in a position where it isn't just the financial stability that work and a wage brings, it's how people are treated and the fulfilment they get from their work. If you're thinking 'that's easy in knowledge working environments' then perhaps it is. My next phase of research isn't to just find outliers who have challenged the knowledge worker hierarchies and high-stress white-collar factory mentalities, it's to look into the world of other work. And yet, labour statistics show us that only 13 per cent of us are engaged in manual work. Knowledge work accounts for a vast majority of working lives across the spectrum.

Regardless of sector and type of work, how people feel about their work IS important. Whether it is physical and strenuous labour or whether it is cognitive and highly mental what isn't fair is exhausted, poorly treated, under-appreciated people in whatever area of the working spectrum.

The people from the companies in this chapter care about how colleagues feel about their work, and see the results of this create thriving, successful businesses. Their belief in sustaining a humane workplace is something I hope more people are inspired to replicate.

Working against tradition is, in itself, hard work

Everyone wants you to justify difference. Yet rarely do we question the same. We blindly believe that because we replicate what others have done we will achieve the same outcomes. Which is why difference is so hard to work at. Years of conditioned, experienced and entrenched beliefs need to be surfaced, scrutinized and subjected to the same rationale that people expend on different propositions. Yet we rarely do this.

These five organizations have the gift of stoic, creative and warm people. People who believe their way is good because it's good for the wholeness of better ways to work, share and learn. Those companies in this chapter that are decentralized, self-managed and flatter than the traditional corporate layers provide a general model of inclusion that appears to be more promi- nently positioned as a next stage evolution of organizations. More natural, adaptive, human and less fixed, mechanical and machine-like. This kind of shift IS transformational. And hard work.

Wellness has value

How well we, the people, are appears to ultimately impact on how well the organization is. In relation to adaptability, relating to customer need and in retaining a sense of safety, protection and regard for its own people. The just nature of an organization – its fairness, dignity, generosity, compassion, warmth – are appearing to mean something to job seekers and consumers alike.

Shiny glass and concrete temples of graft no longer appear to the lure of a converted warehouse with non-matching furniture. Its sterilized versus organic. It's becoming a factor in what matters. So designing workplaces is less technical drawing and more artistic creation of community space. We see the opposite of the dark world of Karoshi – literally overwork to death – in the companies in this section. We see how being well matters because that's how you also then do well.

Of course it's not the inanimate organization that does this, it's people and they way they act, lead, work, influence others. So it's why HR is so important to this realization that macho overwork is as much an addictive and damaging property as illegal narcotics and other compulsion-creating pathogens.

The way people operate in these companies proves transformation can be done and I hope gives HR professionals who believe in this type of transformation some hope, options and examples to build on to create their own transformation stories.

You can change your culture when you change your structure

It is an oft-quoted reason that things have become stuck, not as fulfilling or toxic behaviours are let off – the culture. And yet in these examples, there's been a shaping revolution to effect a cultural transformation. The way things are structured – physically but more so logically – has meant people think, act and do things differently.

It's all connected to will, and belief and other factors of course but there is a clear indication that symbolizing the need to be different and more responsive means the hollow words of change need to be backed up with the structural shifts to make it feel different as well as sound different.

Symbolic of this is the demise of the organization chart. Much less defining people by their role in the squad (like a sports team) and more like the team photo – letting you know who people are and they let you know what they believe in and what they do as work.

Three key transformational HR takeaways and reflective questions to consider:

1 Declaring transformation – and knowing what from and to – is important to bring others into your world and join in with your efforts and aspirations.

   Q: How would you describe and then declare your transformational intentions at this precise moment?

2 Greater autonomy (self-management and working in pairs) came out from our case studies. This appeared to be one key reason why these organizations achieved success.

   Q: What can you do to create more autonomous ways of working for you and those around you, in order to drive your transformational agenda with more power?

3 Wellness and well-being formed a part of our case study organizations approaches to their work and transformation.

   Q: What does well-being and wellness mean to you and what strategies can you design to transform the approach to wellness for others around you?

PART FOUR
Future

Transformational 10
HR

Putting it all together

Introduction

So, we continue our journey into a transformational HR mindset and we come to a sense of *how*. How, if inspired, stoked and curious about what you have read, could *you* start to transform yourself, your HR team and your organization: How could you create a transformational HR approach?

How will this chapter transform my thinking?

- We will bring together all the thinking and examples from previous chapters into a narrative-based approach on how to 'do' transformational HR. We will walk through elements of the HR proposition and how the transformational HR model will work whether you are a smaller, medium or larger organization, or a consultant, activist or leader working with HR professionals.

- We will explore in more detail the personal, team and professional/ strategic levels of transformation and how all three dimensions influence, shape and enable each other. Whether there is an impending transformational need at any of these levels, we will look at how to start, where to start and how to continue and sustain a transformative approach in all three dimensions.

- We will be as practical as possible about the ways to activate transformational HR and introduce the concept of more use of agile project methodology in creating a more flexible, responsive and rapidly deployed way to manage improvements, change and even minor pivots in the way HR works.

In my avid reading of books, I've always appreciated those where the author gives away as much as possible about *how* to activate thinking, models, theories and methods. So not just why, what and where, but how. It has sometimes been referred to as *a field guide*.

The final three chapters combined becomes that *field guide*. A handbook for turning transformational ideas, aspirations and plans into a sharper focus and to the realm of *doing*: Be that doing experimenting, full-blown implementation and that metamorphosis I have mentioned earlier in this book.

In Chapter 5, we saw how some of this comes together in the T-HR model and then the four-zone framework/reinvention of the HR operating model into a transformational HR model. Their inclusion earlier in this book was to help the flow of the journey from:

1 where we have been;

2 where we are; and

3 where we *could* be with HR.

This chapter is about scenario modelling (in line with one of the four aspects of futurology referred to in Chapter 5). So – as with much new thinking – if you're looking for evidence of how it works, you will have to adopt a more concept-mindset with this chapter than an evidence-based mindset.

The thinking behind the recommendations in this chapter though are far from *devoid* of experiential evidence. Fourteen years of operating in HR counts for something, five years of operating as a roaming consultant and being exposed to a range of organizations and their culture, leadership, HR people and awareness of emerging methods for working, counts for something. No empirical research though I'm afraid.

Professor Gary Hamel said in a keynote address to the CIPD conference in 2013 'someone's got to be first to go to Mars'. And of course, what he means here, is that sometimes being first, new, different, inventive, means there is no research trail to test that theory in its *entirety*. So I'm calling that out before others might. This is speculation. This is aspiration. This is also based on experience and experiences. And that counts for a lot in being pioneering and transformational.

So this chapter set outs to be the *possibilists guide to HR of the future*. Starting with you.

Transforming me

If there's one thing that writing this book has led me to believe, it's how important – and how seriously overlooked – *personal transformation* is, and is necessary to make transformation in other areas successful.

Giants of the consulting and professional services world *Boston Consulting Group* have recently described a concept of *bold transformation*:

1 We must reimagine ourselves in a digital world.

2 We must be adaptive in an uncertain world.

3 We should seek simplicity in an increasingly complex world.

4 Leaders must be purpose-driven in a world searching for meaning.

Earlier in this book I contradicted point 3 when I said complexity is here we'd best just get used to it. I stand by that, but that doesn't mean we don't make it *our* understanding in that complexity so we therefore are simplifying it – because we put ourselves in the eye of that storm. We have to make sense of it for *us*. We cannot be expected to individually master the economical, social, political, commercial and ecological complexity of modern life.

Yes, we've had change before but we haven't been headed to 10 billion people on the planet; assets being stripped from the planet like they have this past 100 years; disease mutation that resists medical treatment and social anxieties like we have now. Yes we change, adapt and survive but we hadn't had Ebola before; we didn't have a war in Syria so complex we didn't really know who to support; and we didn't have the digital technology capable of doing what it can do and with so much more to come. We haven't been here before like this.

So please, don't say 'there's nothing new in this change' and use it like a weaponized contradiction to the way we should look at how to make good for life. When this is a world with elements that we just haven't seen before.

It is precisely for this reason that we have to start to look at transforming *ourselves*. At an individual level. Perhaps not since the birth of existentialism has the question 'who am I?' so needed to be asked.

Not being a qualified or trained psychologist gives me no right to play with people's minds and pretend or assert I have deep enough knowledge to proclaim a new sensibility in what it means to be human. What I will do though, is look at transformation through a lens of personal metamorphosis I've seen, experienced and been part of in years of working, leading and coaching others.

Knowing me

In Chapter 5 we introduced you to the transformational states of knowing about *you*.

We have been able to codify self-awareness and understanding of self for some years now. Daniel Goleman's discovery of the series of mental models that became known as 'emotional intelligence' captured our attention and whether it is scientifically proven or otherwise, there are a range of data points and stories of personal transformation that started with a sense of knowing self. It is here that I start to introduce you to the transformational HR model for people professionals of all denominations.

In this model we look at several emotional states, several capabilities/ skills and mindsets. There is no prescribed method to develop skills in any of these areas as this is more a model for consideration of what the components of self-derived transformation are. From this, of course, coaching and other learning will help you improve your understanding, confidence and ability in any of these areas.

It is a recommendation of mine that in order to react better to transformational elements around you and your work, and to therefore be part of transformational activities; in order to better navigate transformation that happens to you and so that you feel less entrapped by transformational programmes, starting with *your own transformation* has some significant value and even comfort. We often think about what would help us and look outside to 'things' that can help us. When inside us lies something we may not readily realize, discover and then utilize.

Starting with some self-awareness, self-analysis and deepen the understanding of who you are and why you feel how you do about transformation is, I would argue, vastly under-utilized. I've identified six areas based on my 20+ years of transformation programmes and described them around 'knowing'.

Exercise: your knowing quotient

Either through reflective practice – i.e. thinking and working through this model alone – or with a coach, mentor or trusted confidante, there are a series of activities offered here to help you increase your KQ – your knowing quotient.

You can either use these questions with someone as a prompted coaching conversation *or* you can simply sketch them out yourself and see what you reveal about yourself.

Once you've got some answers, you could look at themes, areas and topics with which you can make a development or knowledge gathering plan to put into play and help you with your KQ.

Table 10.1 The six states of knowing

Knowing self	1	Describe what brings you to life with the work you do or have done in the past.
	2	When are you at your best – under what circumstances have you achieved your *peak* performance?
	3	Please recall those situations where you felt at your peak level of performance – what was it about that combination of factors that enabled you to be on top of your game?
	4	When others describe your more vital aspects of who you are, what would they list and why?
Knowing others	1	When others create a strong connection to you, what are they saying, doing and being that causes this strengthened feeling?
	2	How do you begin to open up to people? What are the conditions where you feel comfortable to be yourself truly and share vulnerabilities and strengths?
	3	When you begin to work with someone, how do you 'contract' to ensure you're both clear on what's needed to make things work well between you?
	4	How do you approach giving useful comments to people on how they conduct themselves and how do you like to receive such useful feedback?
Knowing skills	1	When you identify what you are really good at, how do you compile that list and what factors lead you to the prioritization?
	2	What have others identified in you that surprised you? And why do you think that is?
	3	When you assess others's skills, how do you decide on what are their strongest skills and areas where they meed work?
	4	In assembling those around you to complement your skills, how have you identified and approached this creation of a learning network?
Knowing systems	1	How do you create an understanding of the nature of the system you're operating in (i.e. trust, commitment, energy, empowerment)?
	2	How do you design systems that work for you?
	3	In thinking of your answers to (2) above in knowing self, what was it about the systems at play there, that you could describe as a perfect model for getting the best from you?
	4	What do you understand about the range of models and theories about working systems such as autocratic, agile, democratic, self-organized and their governance requirements?

(continued)

Table 10.1   *(Continued)*

Knowing need	1	How do you come to identify a need for you – be it stimulating work, development or type of environment that suits you best?
	2	When you are given a need from others – a problem to solve, a piece of research to conduct or a task to complete, how do you like to get across what you need to complete that work?
	3	In looking at how you identify what others need from you, how do you go about identifying to get to the root of their need?
	4	When you have differing views on what the precise need is from others, how do you go about challenging or pivoting that need?
Knowing Energy	1	Under what circumstances are you at your most energized with almost endless verve for the work you're doing?
	2	How do you identify energies in others?
	3	When energy is lacking in others, what do you do to investigate this and what tactics do you use to lift the energy?
	4	When you need to restore your energy, what are your strategies for doing so?

You can now use this data to help you with your own personal transformation. More than your usual learning needs analysis, this helps you understand more deeply where are the key areas for you to up your level of KQ about yourself and what transformation really means to you.

In bringing solutions to mind, you can consult others, creating coaching and learning partnerships, conduct research and knowledge gathering exercises, activate your networks and communities that you are part of and consider other learning programmes that will help you in areas you have identified through this reflective exercise.

Knowing others

Knowing others is so critical to success in life and work it would be churlish to leave it as one component in the model of self. We are so impacted upon by our family, friends, colleagues and even strangers that knowing others is a vital element in understanding and positively impacting on transformational activities that are needed to sustain improvement.

A second model to consider in thinking as a design and development tool is that of transformational HR at a *partnerships* level. Rather than being a team/function design concept, this includes all those who are part of our transformation aspirations and application, so they are essentially partners in transformation. They may be the customers or beneficiaries of transformation (of course they may be the precise *point* of the transformation) yet there appears to be a lot to gain in specifically calling people partners in this process. It may save us from transformation done *to* people as a norm, and include them more in the realization, concept, design, decide, deploy, do, deliver, measure, refine and sustain stages.

In creating a strong sense of what this model exists to serve, it was envisaged by me as:

> HR professionals working *with* each other and their internal and external partners (often in a deliberately paired approach) to realize an enhanced impact for their work through collaborative learning, innovation and application creating increased confidence, belief and trust through shared philosophies and understanding.

Transformational HR: partnerships

In order to contextualize this for HR professionals this model looks at five dimensions and uses the squared metaphor (^{2}). The premise is that through a coming together with others in *partnership* (around, say, learning together) doesn't make it a simple 1+1. It means a deeper and more *multiplying* source for energy and effectiveness. The Menlo Innovations application of pair-working covered in Chapter 9 has revealed not just two people's efforts but a significant uplift in quality and rigour without management bureaucracy. This approached is encouraged using this model.

Figure 10.1 Transformational HR at partnerships level

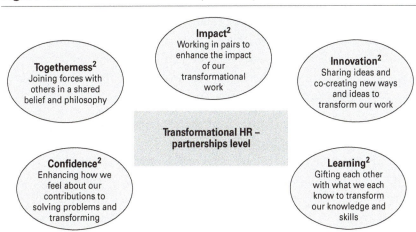

Impact^2
Working in pairs to enhance the impact of our transformational work

Togetherness^2
Joining forces with others in a shared belief and philosophy

Innovation^2
Sharing ideas and co-creating new ways and ideas to transform our work

Transformational HR – partnerships level

Confidence^2
Enhancing how we feel about our contributions to solving problems and transforming

Learning^2
Gifting each other with what we each know to transform our knowledge and skills

Togetherness² Sounds a little clichéd, but is genuinely intended to work out what you share as common with others. We often transact our way through work without ever truly understanding what others value, what really matters to them and what their code of life and work is all about. Whilst we may not always find a match – and indeed may even have a totally opposite approach to others – we will at least have a deeper understanding of what makes us tick, what ticks us off and what we can then watch for in terms of harmony or respected differences. This can simply be achieved by asking the question of each other 'In what ways are we *together*?'.

Impact² We talk about goals, outcomes, results, sales, figures and all sorts of other ways to define success and yet at times we're ignoring the most regular and perhaps most fundamental aspect of all of those definitions – impact. What we say, do, deliver, don't deliver – all creates an impact. Emotional, physical and logical impacts happen all the time. When we're working with others – especially if we've discovered that in looking at our togetherness we're very different – the impact we want to create with our collective endeavours can also be the moment of togetherness. Impact is a broader term than goals so doesn't just say what we'll deliver it gives us a chance to describe how we and others will feel about what we do. And impacts can happen all along the way, so it eliminates the big goal as the distant and difficult thing to achieve. We can have many impact milestones – hourly and even daily – so we can feel our progress as much as track it and record it on project plans. Working in closer ways with people will help us realize the impact as we'll have someone else give us a narrative on our performance other than us or a (sometimes) distant line manager.

Innovation² Creativity can be deeply individual but also an energetic team sport. In conversations with others we often get our most amazing 'a-ha' moments. We can also get instant validation or consideration on our idea which means we can cull pointless flights of fancy or give life to amazing breakthrough thinking. In co-creating around innovation there is also a spirit of participation that negates the need for overly cautious or even obstructive bureaucracy that dampens creativity.

Learning² Being able to share insight and experiences brings people closer together and as philosopher Alain de Botton said at 2017's Changeboard *Future Talent* conference 'helping someone develop is an act of love'. With such a rapid pace of change, where things can quickly date and be replaced by new methodologies and theories, joining forces with others to learn is more than a nice-to-have – it is essential. In the recent past, it was *the* competitive advantage to know more than others. Now, it is more powerful to be known as someone who *shares and gives*. Adam Grant's work on researching the successes in those at work who are *Givers* illustrates this point. What can you give people in the way of great knowledge, insight or experience without any need for reciprocity or trade will inevitably result in reciprocity?

Confidence[2] We should talk more about confidence in the world of work. How confidence is a non-permanent, often fragile and influential state of mind. In athletes, confidence is a must – tennis and motor sport, football and swimming – performances can be enhanced or diminished by a state of confidence. In our working environment it is the same, we can be convincing and get the decision our team needs or get flat-out refusals and a display of confidence can be the difference. Working in pairs is a great confidence boost – we don't feel alone for a start. We also feel a sense of someone having our backs; someone with no agenda other than to succeed and not at my cost. Having managers and leaders who care and inspire can bring confidence but some managers are intrusive, distrusting sorts who overly direct effort and can erode confidence more than build it; through admonishment of mistakes and favouring others. In the adult world of work, I think we vastly under-estimate how much of a productivity inhibitor low confidence can be. In a transformational situation, confidence may wain, and we need others around us to show belief, support and encourage us in often uncertain times.

Extreme programming and the advent of HR professionals working in pairs

In Chapter 9, we discovered how Menlo Innovations was able to not only create the highest quality digital apps and platforms, but also create a rapid learning environment through pair-working. Born from the concept of extreme programming (XP).

There are a number of elements of XP which we see in operation in most technology companies. In essence it is a way of developing software with a more focused approach to improve quality and responsiveness to changing customer requirements. It is part of the agile software development methodology, and it is built on regular 'releases' of software in shorter development cycles for review by customers or users. Some call this aspect a part of the minimum viable product approach to software build. Releasing in shorter cycles is intended to improve the overall productivity of development and introduce earlier and more regular checkpoints for users so their customer requirements can be adapted following feedback and reaction to the releases.

One feature that interests me the most is programming in pairs or doing extensive code review. This is where two people share accountability, effort, creativity, testing, designing, writing and deploying the code. It means two pairs of eyes are reviewing work in the moment and two pairs of hands are making the product. This method is proven to need less management by a team leader. Each pair holds each other to account within the pairing process and only where irreconcilable differences occur, does anyone else need to be involved.

This way of coding takes its name from the idea that the beneficial elements of traditional software engineering practices are taken to 'extreme' levels (Wells, 2017). It is this concept that I believe can herald a new level of proficiency, efficiency and therefore impact for the work of HR professionals. My assertion is that for too long, HR practitioners have become isolated from each other in attempts to service clients and professional needs. Bringing more pair-working to HR will naturally create collaborative approaches but it will need some redesigning and rethinking of how work gets done.

Before you go running to your resource management spreadsheets to work out how this impacts on HR's own paybill, I'll explain more of why I believe HR adopting this practice could create the renaissance or metamorphosis I refer to in this book.

Scenario: pair working in action

Hannah is part of the recruitment team. She acts as a campaign coordinator for a national retailer's store manager and regional manager roles. She also acts as an employer brand manager posting to social media sites and sharing information on campaigns, culture, awards, industry articles and so on. Hannah uses the internal tracking system to track recruitment requests, works with hiring managers, helps form panels for interviews, liaises with candidates and keeps an eye on social media traffic. Hannah gets emails from internal clients and links to marketing for on-brand imagery to use and for social media data analytics. Her days are made up of emails; posting and reviewing content on social media platforms; meetings (lots of meetings); phone calls; data collation and reporting; directing Amy, the HR assistant's workload in managing candidate applications; candidate liaison; contract drafting and completion and agreeing start dates with candidates.

In a pair-working scenario Hannah's work will shift somewhat.

1 **No meetings about work; only working together.** Hannah will not just go to a meeting with an internal client about a vacancy that needs filling at store manager level, Hannah and the hiring manager will sit and do the work together on either Hannah's or the Hiring Manager's PC. No order taking: real time work. This will include some conversations but largely any time they spend together will be *doing* the work together and not just talking *about* the work, and then Hannah departing a meeting to then *do* the work.

2 **Hannah and Amy will spend most of their time working together** – either at Hannah's workstation or Amy's. Together they will manage the flow of work for a range of campaigns and therefore will be reacting to candidate submissions; making arrangements for the interview timetables; posting on social networks; collating data; producing reports; processing contracts and start dates and putting together onboarding plans.

3 **Amy and Hannah will never have to have any meetings about work,** they will be active, agile and adaptive during the day spent mostly at the same workstation. They will quality check each other's work and will understand each other's workloads and demands through this close collaboration. At times, Amy will be processing high volumes of applications whilst Hannah uses her mobile device to post to social networks and check on feeds and traffic.

4 **Hannah and her manager, Janine complete campaign data reports** for end of month submission so, for three hours each month, they will share the same workstation and instead of meeting to talk about this work, they will co-create the report and discuss (as they're going along) the implications and together they will draft the report. Amy is in a learning partnership with Sabrina about reward so they spend three hours working through pay modelling concepts.

5 **Hannah spends two hours a month on social media data analytics and reporting.** She spends this time working WITH Jonah from the marketing team. Initially he wasn't sure about doing the work together and tried to do a half-hour meeting just to run through the reports. But after sticking with it for two months, Jonah realized he could help Hannah and she had discovered some platforms and accounts he wasn't aware of. They turned this two hours per month of desk sharing and working on something together into a shared learning experience. Amy is also interested in knowing more about learning metrics and spends time with Aimee from

L&D – they spend two hours compiling reports and looking at consistencies between recruitment data and learning data.

After spending seven months operating in this way – with some initial struggles to throw off old, bad habits of being stuck inside an email inbox, here's what Hannah found:

- Hannah has reduced her meeting time by 90 per cent. Whilst this is offset by sitting with Amy and working together on campaign management then working on campaign specifications with hiring managers. Trust, understanding and relationships have improved significantly including the time management of campaigns and turning around urgent requests for vacancy postings.

- Error rates and administrative slip-ups have been eliminated. HR no longer has to fix anything as they have a 100 per cent success rate on administrative and management support for recruitment campaigns.

- Candidate satisfaction and candidate experience has shot up from a Net Promoter Score of 5.5 to 9.1. Glassdoor.co.uk reviews have seen a 220 per cent increase on people posting how they found the recruitment experience outstanding even if they weren't selected for the post.

- Data shows that social media postings on the slickness of the experience is resulting in more positive social buzz. There has been a spike on Twitter and Facebook feeds with compliments on the level of service provided.

- Marketing were now much closer to HR and more involved and interested in Employer Brand. They were turning more customers in potential job applicants and vice versa (witnessed by purchasing/vacancy statistical analysis).

- Hiring managers were starting to invite their teams to work in pairs; having seen HR do so and eliminate non-productive meetings and exchanges by emails, they were adopting this process too. HR started to give advice and help people to move to this form of working.

- Meeting room hiring showed a 75 per cent decrease in use. A cost calculation on this showed an average of £40,000 a week being saved by working together not meeting to talk about the work that needed doing.

- Amy's confidence is sky high. With Hannah absent on occasions through leave or training, Amy is capable of covering the entire function for short periods of time. Amy and Hannah also have daily check-ins on performance and development and no tired appraisal chats needed at monthly or yearly intervals.

- Internal relations with clients are at an all-time high. HR is held up as an innovator and creator of productive and efficient ways of managing previously tricky issues on staffing and vacancy management.

This isn't a real example but it *could be*. The concept, I am sure, is worth pursuing based on the potential gains and higher quality working relationships that come from this shift.

It seems very bold that HR should make such a shift yet there are clear signs that our working habits – particularly in office environments – have stubbornly held us back from more efficient workflow, stronger relationships with colleagues and better service to customers and clients. To not even experiment with this process could miss out on huge gains to transform HR and its impact and value to its clients.

It will take transformational approaches to unlearn; and relearn this approach as it really is work's best kept secret. *HR XP* should become a thing to work with the philosophies and models contained in this book. This is an important shift from HR *business partnering* to HR *working in partnership*. Which leads me onto the oft-talked about strategic influence that HR aspires to, but in most cases, lacks.

Reference

Wells, Don (accessed 20 May 2017) 'Extreme programming: a gentle introduction', *Extreme Programming*, 08/10 [Online] http://www.extremeprogramming.org/

Transformational HR 11

Strategic-level shifts

Introduction

Being a strategic influencer and player in this space has long been the aspiration for many an HR professional. I suspect in many cases, this hasn't really been thought through, deeply and philosophically thought through.

What do we even *mean* by strategic? *Influencing at the highest level of operating to shape the future destiny and success of the organization* would be one way of describing it. For now, let's return to the definition of transformational HR here to help us calibrate this thinking:

> Transformational HR is leading and delivering fundamental changes in how people and the organization work and conducts its business; in order to control its aspirations, intentions and influence in an ever shifting world of work.

Get this strategy started right

In order to achieve this, HR professionals *may* want to start with the *transform self* stages and then *transform partnerships* working as described through HR extreme programming (XP). The strategic level transformation would then be as a result of the aggregation of *self* and *partners*.

Of course another option is start with a strategic level of transformation that influences and shapes the transformation of *self* and working in *partnership* within. Indeed a strategic level transformation will normally set the tone and direction for *self and partners* to feed from. Whichever comes first – strategic-first or self-first – this level of relevance and influence is vital for the continued success of people professionals as creators of transformative practices that sustain the performance of people, and cause a company to thrive.

In reviewing tales from game changing professionals in Chapter 8, the case studies in Chapter 9 and generally looking ahead to a very uncertain and challenging future of work, strategic influence from HR may be more relevant than ever.

With the decline of union power and individual voice, the difficulty of legislators and policy-makers to keep up and shifting societal views about what is allowable and ethical in the way we treat each other as fellow human beings, HR's role as upholders of a 'just and true' organization may need to become a more critical aspect of its strategic role.

A strategic-level transformational HR model

It is with this in mind – and several other macro-level challenges facing organizations, leaders and all people at work, this third model I have conceived may help with a strategic-level playbook.

Some very deliberately vivid language is being used here to distinguish a shift from cliché-like statements like 'be business savvy', 'be more commercial' and 'be digitally competent'.

We will start with the one of the most pressing of needs: information externally and internally. Firstly this is captured through *external vigilance*.

External vigilance   External vigilance is a perhaps extravagant way of describing what is increasingly an essential element of business success – being tuned into, and thinking through, the complexity and pace of change in the world: largely – but not entirely – driven by advances in digital technology. The more interconnected the world now is, the more the world is

Figure 11.1   Transformational HR at strategic level

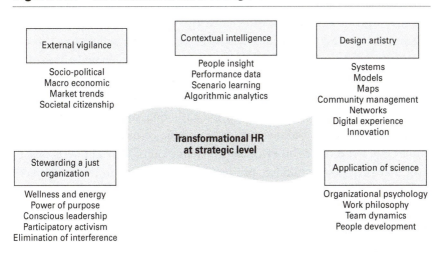

only a *chaos theory event* away from some major incident that changes the course of an organization. Being aware of, understanding about and reacting or pre-empting potentially damaging, limiting or disabling actions is where HR can add value.

For example, the so-called *gig economy*. Being extra vigilant in this area would mean the difference between overreacting, being frozen or understanding the impacts of the increase of non-employee partners in delivering services to customers. Let's face it Wikipedia's volunteer curators and GitHub's enthusiasts have been pointing the way to this for some time – work as a platform. Yet, I have experienced HR professionals feverishly taking notes over the recent court rulings in the UK on Uber employees as if it were some long-awaited proclamation of clarity. HR was caught up in zero-hours hype and using procurement to secure additional resource and expertise in the form of contracted expertise. It's been brewing for a while and even been operating in the world of media (journalism and film) for a long time. So why do many HR professionals seem caught out by the 'Uberization' of work? They've been focused inwardly and on the job proposition when lots of enterprising types have gone for what NIlofer Merchant proclaimed around 2011 – '*work not jobs*' (Merchant, 2012).

Being externally vigilant would have meant more access to emerging trends, to networked and virtual organizations popping up and the awareness that from 2012 onwards, the UK's self-employed market was only showing signs of upward shifts. So enterprising HR professionals would look at this and their work needs and review how they could make the most of this increasing trend and to adjust their policies, contracts and ways of working accordingly.

Contextual intelligence Using more data-led approaches and understanding the fullest possible picture of people's energy, commitment, ingenuity, application, and process architecture helps HR present compelling cases to the most influential decision makers. For the focus needed in certain hard-pressed areas, under-valued individuals or teams and where excellent practices can be replicated for smarter commercial and employee experience improvements.

The context is all important and the gathering, analysis and reporting of data that isn't just rudimentary demographic or basic information, that makes HR stand out as an evidence-led champion of the right decisions, to help that keep people fulfilled, productive and adapting to the demands of this transforming world of work.

As well as data that can be captured, HR can be responsible for predictive analytics through the analysis of small-scale experiments and scenarios that model potential adaptations that can help create more flow than friction.

'But not everything can be measured' may be the challenge – but everything leaves a data point; there are stories, anecdotes and examples of superhuman feats and innovative ideas that deserve recognition, support and scrutiny. HR can become a champion for people and their committed application, energy and ideas prompting the most influential decision makers to better understand what they are really gaining from the investment they have in their paybill and contractor budgets.

And as more data analytics will become the signature of a transformational HR practitioner, so will their understanding of the application of machine learning and evidence by algorithm. Understanding the opening of a new branch or shifting the scale of a division can be modelled through an algorithmic simulator to show timelines, friction points, leadership needed and how to engage people with communication and involvement throughout this programme. No more hopeful restructures and more planned adaptations, already modelled through digital simulation, could help businesses smooth out their often bumpy road to change and transformation.

Design artistry This follows the accumulation and utilization of more useful data and insight. Having a deeper understanding of a range of progressive and robust models for the way the entire organization or aspects of it can be structured, mapped and deployed is more an art form *with* science, than purely a set of boxes with people's names on linked through hierarchical structures.

And looking at not just physical or competency-based allocation but of the need for communities (of practice or interest) and the deployment of networking power are as much a consideration and to some degree, will *overtake* the more physical location/line management decisions.

Designing for adaptability and innovation means the lessons of smarter and more successful technology organizations will permeate other professional functions. Agile, Scrum and project-orientation will overtake static, allocated roles, with more time spent on iteratively *doing* than traditional cascade drip-down over-planning and documenting. These techniques have shifted the digital technology profession's performance from tolerated to business enabling and vital, to be as much a 'must have' as finance/capital.

Which is where HR's role as organizational architect goes beyond technical drawing and into the understanding of the art of human relations. Communal and human systems. The need for social connection, for belonging, for companionship and in even for creative solitude, providing a more complex design need than simply square-foot per desk, rotas or high-viz jacket sizes.

For what good is cutting-edge consumer-facing technology when your own people professionals have to make do with outdated databases and disconnected data streams, when they have to help the very people who need it the most – your own people? Design artistry will help all factors come together in order to create the conditions and the environment (physical, virtual, psychological) that gives people that belonging they want and the flow they need, to get things done.

Application of science Application of science will support the *design artistry* and all other facets of this five-dimensional model for strategic-level, transformational HR. We've seen the need for more 'ologies' in the world of work and not just for academia, with an interest in researching and teaching about the world of work. Business, and occupational and organizational psychology are getting to a deeper understanding of the *now* of work, and not just previously long-held orthodoxies. Practice and research combine to help keep the teaching of new professionals, and those wanting to acquire more academic certification to deepen or diversify their careers, as sharp as it can be. And yet, I hear many practitioners studying programmes like HR, finance and PR who claim the taught materials are already out of date. So it's up to us, as professionals in the game, to be applied well and with good sciences to make sure those topics are exposed to the transforming world of work we're adapting to. Studying programmes and mixing them with work can be hard on us individually, and yet the two can be so symbiotic with work-based projects used in assignments and assignments used to trigger useful work-based projects.

Even if degree programmes aren't for you, there's an increasing bank of popularized insight in books, blogs and online programmes to help you understand behavioural economics, philosophy, sociology and those we discussed as vital in the thick trunk of the T-HR model in Chapter 7.

Therefore this is an area for all HR professionals to seriously consider as development areas: more science-based study areas in keeping with personal and strategic direction/need. Full qualifications e.g. Masters Degrees and the likes are great but not, in my view, an absolute necessity. There are a range of alternatives from the world of MOOCs to coaching or mentoring by an experienced academic and/or practitioner. There is enhanced credibility and influence to be had by effective utilization of the sciences of work, which isn't only via a certificated programme of learning.

Stewarding a *just* organization This is perhaps one of the more abstract factors in strategic level, transformational HR and yet is one of the more needed elements at times of new challenges, uncertainty and fresh opportunities. HR's reputation as policing low-level 'incidents' and misdemeanours may not help it's cause but it has been somewhat thrust into this situation with managers who have instantly stepped away at the first sign of what feels like a breach of something legal. And yet, HR is also then considered culpable with corporate scandals (executive pay or bonuses, biased recruitment practices, unfair avoidance of taxes and employment rights, poor treatment of employees).

It does feel like this is the time for *just organizations* – to build more trust in organizations, to connect leaders to more ethical consequences of choices and treatment of people; and to improve how employees consider their working terms and not abuse benefits and supportive ways of working. I'd be happy to never hear of a 'Christmas party policy' reminder ever being sent. And I'd be happy to hear that workplace theft, abuse of overtime and fiddling expenses were on the decline because people and their employers had a more trusting and purposeful collaboration and understanding.

The key elements for me, in this aspect of a more strategic view of transformational HR, is *wellness*. Stress at work, overwork, emotional fatigue, whatever you want to call it, is causing many of us to become ill and prematurely retire or even worse pass away too early.

Already there are signs that many corporate organizations and even smaller enterprises are giving well-being the *employee engagement* like tick in the box.

Fresh fruit and a negotiated discount with the gym nearby? That'll do.

Well, it would if you didn't under-price your jobs, force people to work for way more hours than is healthy to bring the job in on time and budget. And repeat this so you burn them out, cast them aside and recruit someone else willing to put up with oppressive management routines.

Wellness or well-being is complex area as it is about the complex thing that is the human being. We saw, in Chapter 9, that Widen and Menlo Innovations in particular went to noticeable lengths to have well-being as part of their way. It is hard, because there is an heroic feel for some in long-hours culture, to the guilt associated with missing your children's bedtime stories, to giving up weekends and perhaps to skipping holidays and jeopardizing your health. Commitment to the cause is an oft-cited way to show a high achiever. But at what cost?

I am perhaps fortunate in loving what I do. I am alive with the work I do and so I rarely have moments of stress. Three times in my career I did experience the pain of disillusionment. They were times that were devoid of the love of what I was doing and more about over-committing, others not understanding me and me just plain rebelling. You let people down, you let yourself down. You cause damage and are damaged. No-one wins when well-being is sacrificed or compromised.

So at those times, my state of well-being suffered badly and I needed help, support and hope. So increasingly, HR's role could and perhaps should be more of a *crucible-like* guardian of people's well-being at work alongside four other critical elements in this dimension.

The power of purpose This is a hot headline right now. Having seen the power in purposes like Menlo Innovations '*To end human suffering as it relates to technology*' and the famous Google line '*to manage the world's information*' represent much sought after word-based *elixirs* that lure the brightest talent and investors to your enterprise. This cannot be faked though – a cleverly crafted strapline to define your purpose cannot mask a toxic culture, poor leadership or profit at-any-price methods for ever.

There is no denying that nobility of cause is a thing, witnessed by the explosion of interest in Simon Sinek's TEDx talk – the Golden Circle – and his book, *Start With Why* (2011). It has become something people now pay much more attention to – why does this company exist and what *why* in the world, is it serving? To many people, this is the reason to feel pride in your place of work, to rise to challenges and to have a sense of calm and focus on a Sunday evening (before heading to work for another Monday – something far too many people dread).

HR's role in this is often part of the cultural identity, the employer brand even and it is given such prominence of role, that Singularity University's Salim Ismail and Yuri Van Geest called this out in their book looking at fast-growth start-ups *Exponential Organizations* (2014). In their work they looked at the DNA of super-quick challengers to new markets and existing arenas, and identified they all had something in their purpose – a *massive transformative purpose*. In their interviews and research they found this to be like a *force majeure* in bringing people together; identifying a precision view of the destination and a chance to differentiate them in the marketplace. Uber's *evolve the way the world moves* is a grand sounding and truly massive concept. Yet a recent turn of events there have proven that this is not enough to avoid toxicity of culture and fairer treatment of people working under the brand. So it isn't something to *hide* behind, but it can be something to *get* behind.

Transformational HR professionals could do well to scrutinize, craft and relaunch the purpose of a company if it is found lacking in its *force majeure* qualities. By including people who are employees, alumni, investors, partners, consumers and non-consumers, the view of the organization's reason for being can be given a sense check and given words that truly means something to people. Using this purpose to help craft something that gives the sense of heritage, intention, reason and beliefs. If all there is 'make more money' I'd suggest the entire company philosophy needs a health check because it's my view that this is no longer desired or even good enough to sustain success (unless you work for the Royal Mint of course).

Conscious leadership This is our next area of just organizations. Oh, we've had all sorts of prefixes to leadership over the last 20+ years so I won't even list them. Yet I've added one – conscious. Why conscious? This is a deliberate prod at the conscience and the awareness elements that conjure up in our minds when we use this word. Awareness of the impacts of leadership on people to the point that you either help them out-perform or you suppress them into reluctant compliance or even subterfuge rebellion. Awareness that you can tune into people's needs or you are oblivious to the small gestures that make a huge difference to people. Awareness that you should stand and fight for your people or that you cave in to corporate demands and be complicit in some form of oppressive subjugation.

And the conscience to act ethically, morally and in a just way. Corporate scandals and the wrong-doing we find organizations engaged in, are as a result of people acting in this way: either through some left-with-little-choice direction and insistence of others, or by themselves. In being a conscious leader you are aware of the knowing and doing of just, right and fair things and allow that conscience to guide you. Where perhaps the conscience is more easily swayed towards unethical or questionable actions, leaders need some help to stay on track. This is where a transformational HR professional can help. As a moral compass, a coach, a confidante and someone to provide safety and surety mixed with stoically holding firm on key principles.

HR professionals engaged in conversational practice with leaders around consciousness, partnership working on tricky issues and more alliances generally, can all help this cause.

We are sometimes unknowing of our impairing acts and sometimes deliberate and inconsiderate, justifying some higher need. Transforming this view of the world would go a long way to self-regulation and the morality of purpose would override any shortcuts that damage reputation, trust and impair lasting success.

Participatory activism Participatory activism is the widest possible way to describe the inclusion and crowd-sourcing inside organizations. We see so much willingness untapped, so much diversity of thought unknown and so much creativity underused that we should be looking to design our working systems that not only engage our people, they activate them. That people from all parts of the organization want to join in with new product research activities, potential acquisition identification and customer-led innovation to keep the market share healthy.

In the decline of union influence and the reputation for adversarial dialogue have been the hallmarks of workplace activists until now. Yet I sense we're in need of a new model of dialogue between people at various levels in an organizational structure.

So by participatory activism, I mean productive, collaborative and influential acts that are in the name of corporate and human good. One of the most frustrating things people describe about why they leave a company isn't that it's their relationship with their manager, *it's their inability to influence things for what they feel or believe is better*. Better prospects, better working lives and better ways to be led are all about influence being void. More activism and shaping things for the better of all would lead to more satisfaction, more innovation and more harmony at work.

Which leads me back to what I mentioned in Chapter 3 as part of the one skill to rule them all.

The elimination of interference Interference is not something we necessarily talk about much at work and yet is at the heart of well meant, or poorly delivered ways of working and leading others. We sometimes create forms, and bureaucracy, policies and directives which we must believe are fair, helpful or necessary and are often at the heart of unproductive made-up, work about work. Having to key in the same data by two or three different people is an example. We're now so used to self-serving automated routines in e-commerce that we take it for granted that we're doing the work, for a service or something we need.

HR being at it's most guilty has created a lot of interference. In the convulsive (and sometimes over) reaction to something minor, HR creates a ton of friction and often interference to people doing productive and useful work. Much of this – I have to be fair to my profession – is an epidemic of the loss of personal responsibility and accountability.

This is where HR needs a balance of an engineer's mindset with that of an artist. Understanding the paradox that is routines and human creativity. The balance of prescription versus self-derived accountability. It's where many workplaces feel like an extension of parent–child and not adult to adult.

We could say 'If employees stopped acting like spoiled children we wouldn't have to be parental' versus the paradox to that which is 'if we treated people like adults, they might show up and behave like them needing no parental advisory controls'.

Douglas McGregor called this out in the 1960s with his Theory X and Theory Y of management (McGregor, 2006). And tragically, in around those

50 years since this theory, we've barely moved on. Of course, the companies I used as case studies have all made some progress towards a more Theory Y-model and it has worked well for them. Why not others?

Theory X, perhaps controversially, perhaps not, is my choice to retire to management Room 101. It's the cause of so much friction and interference in my past career and in speaking to the many thousands of people I've come across in my 20+ years of business, the vast majority of them too. And yet, Theory X has not been expunged from our way of managing people.

Whatever transformational HR can do to eliminate and eradicate this great friction creator (Theory X) would be a modern-day triumph akin to the overthrowing of a dictator. A spectre in our midst that prevents people truly reaching their full potential. A ghost in the machine that is the haunting of workplaces in the pursuit of good work for all.

A just leader in a real world setting

I've come across a young and powerful force for leadership in a major retail store in the East of England who is the *embodiment* of progressive leadership. In this, one young woman is all that good leadership is and all that good people development is.

HR has had some small part to play in shaping this leader but it's been down to a range of factors that – were HR to bottle this and create some magic potion – would result in a total reinvention of what we mean when we say 'they're a great manager'. Frictionless, interference free, dialogue friendly and purposeful about everything her people do, this example is like a beacon of hope for removing all the interference at play, in the workplace. It can be done. One inspiring leader and one team with her, at a time.

A leader who creates a true sense of belonging in her people and who experience what fulfilling work is all about, daily.

Reference

Ismail, Salim, Van Geest, Yuri and Malone, Michael (2014) *Exponential Organisations*, Diversion Books, New York

McGregor, D (2006) *The human side of enterprise, annotated edition*, McGraw Hill Education, London

Merchant, Nilofer (2012) *11 Rules for creating value in the #SocialEra*, Harvard Business Review Press, Brighton MA

Sinek, Simon (2011) *Start with why*, Penguin, London

Transformational HR 12

A new model at play

Introduction

In this section we look deliberately at how we can make the shifts and bring together the personal T-HR model, the four-zone framework (from Chapter 7) and the three development levels (introduced in Chapter 11) of transformational HR. With a lot of new thinking, it may be somewhat daunting for those enthused enough about this to put things into play. So let's begin with the T-HR model.

Becoming a transformational HR practitioner

A little like this book's structure, it helps if you know the heritage of the profession you're in. Understanding why and how HR is like it is, is a useful start. Much of this will come from teaching programmes and yet not everyone arrives into HR via a taught programme. So in some respects, this book now serves as the foundation to this element of understanding.

This will allow professionals in the 'people at work game' to get all of the horizontal elements of the T model to a level of understanding that is sufficient enough to not overlook established practices, theories and models. It will help us to utilize the established practices as a sense-check to guide any innovative ways we might be looking to transform how people are recruited, join, developed, advanced, deployed, rewarded, guided, led, protected and exited.

The fun really starts with the thick, vertical trunk of this T-HR model. Many 'ologies' are listed in Chapter 7 along with a (not exhaustive) list of other sciences, competences and academic topics. It is my belief that through more depth of knowledge and application of these areas, a transformational HR professional can operate with more rigour, confidence and credibility.

Key considerations for the T-HR model

1 Identify the sciences, academic areas and skills and competences that interest you the most and would have most use in your role as a transformational HR practitioner. Draw up a list and map the outcomes they would achieve in line with your personal, professional and situational goals and needs.

2 Knowing your preferred learning and study format, you can then locate the right people, content and programmes that will service your need. If it's a qualification you'd welcome (because you're vocationally oriented), then perhaps you can do a certified MOOC or another formal programme. If qualifications aren't as important, you can take a playlist approach to your lifelong learning programme and include a range of sourcing and storing methods.

3 Having a learning partner could help you stay on track whatever the type of programme you decide on and bring you closer to others in your professional field or a different professional field. Identifying the areas and asking in your network could lead you to a fruitful and shared endeavour to build your skills and identify opportunities that will build your vertical in the T-HR model.

Working in the four zones of transformational HR

Alongside the T-HR model I introduced the four-zone model. In order to change both the way work is done by HR people and partners, and to influence a shift in how people operate, this model will service both personal and professional transformation.

About the four-zone model

As with all models, this is meant as a *framework*, a set of *principles* and guiding *philosophies*. It isn't intended to be a blanket, totalitarian implementation of something the same, everywhere.

It follows much of the great thinking and doing of others – all models are likely to be iterations and derivatives of others. Therefore if you think it looks a lot like Professor Ulrich's model, it does. Yet it's different.

Figure 12.1   Strategic skills and competencies for transformational HR professionals

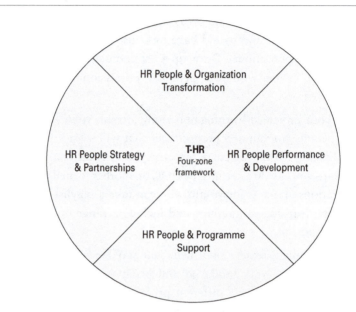

This model refreshes the language we've used in previous models as explained in Chapter 7 and also it looks at the dynamism that previous models have espoused to, but perhaps has been lacking in – especially when it comes to implementation of the model. This model is built with fluidity and not fixed in roles or mindset. This model isn't set as a *cookie-cutter* for allocation of resources or skills involved, nor is there some formula for regularity of movement.

So the following scenarios will bring this to more clarity through descriptions and narrative. And a reminder that through my research and understanding of the HR market, I don't know of anyone explicitly using this model, in this way.

Although of course it may not be a totally new concept – someone may recognize a lot of this as their own version of doing HR. If this is similar to others work, it is entirely random and unintended, yet somewhat comforting that this model may be in operation and others are coming to similar conclusions to me. I believe in open source as a methodology and Creative Commons as a recognition and reference framework. The reason for putting this book together is to activate and help people who care enough about their's – and other's – future, to turn that *now* into a transformed *new*.

Back to the four-zone model. In each of the zones, I will unpack and illustrate how I believe it could be used in an operationalized context. I will use four key elements and further narrative to provide that illustration:

1 The philosophy – what is the thinking and short defining purpose for this element?

2 The mission – what is the model intended to do in statement format to provide greater clarity?

3 The vision – how we might describe this model to others who aren't familiar with it?

4 The narrative – bringing the model further to life.

What this section will not do, is build the competency profile for practitioners operating in some or all of the zones. It won't set any timetables for how long it will take to implement the model and move people to different parts of the model as the needs of the work necessitates. That will all be down to you as enthusiasts and experts in the work you do.

Philosophy, mission, vision, narrative

Overall then, for the entire model (and then the four zones), I see it as the following:

Table 12.1 Description of the four-zone model

The philosophy	The four-zone model is a framework to continually metamorphosize the HR proposition to better help people in a transforming world of work.
The mission	The four-zone model will help HR and people professionals in all elements of engaging, utilizing, developing and inspiring the most impactful human endeavours, for all aspects of work now and in the emerging future, to help people live more purposeful, healthy and better lives through fulfilling work.
The vision	Using a next-stage thinking approach defined in the four-zone model, it will deploy the people of HR to make a transformative difference to the people and organizations they work with.
The narrative	All contained in the four zones that follow via the norm of HR professionals working in partnership situations.

HR People & Programme Support

The narrative

HR People & Programme Support (HRPPS) are responsible for *HR colleague experience* through providing governance and support for HR transformation programmes whilst also being the lead on organizational recruitment campaigns, learning and development logistics and the benefits/reward programmes.

HRPPS also support wider employer branding activities, is a part of the overall *employee experience* and helps the HR leadership team with projects, logistics and information management.

The flow of work to the HRPPS includes:

- responding to and answering individual queries;

- HR information systems (HRIS) maintenance and governance;

- pay and benefits systems management;

- casework, mediation, dispute resolution and specialist employee relations with union or staff council colleagues;

- recruitment campaign requests and management plus recruitment technology support; and

- acting as scrum master and coordinators for HR transformational programmes working with transformation teams on critical initiatives shaping the future of the organization.

Table 12.2 Description of HR People & Programme Support, the four-zone model

The philosophy	HRPPS exists to orchestrate harmony across people, the organization and processes.
The mission	HRPPS will deliver secure, swift and specialized support to recruitment, joining, development and leaving alongside support for transformational projects and initiatives.
The vision	HRPPS act as project 'scrum masters' and supercharged administrators for essential processes that power the HR proposition supporting the organization's strategic goals, and creating a superior colleague experience.

In a larger organization, this zone will have a decent-sized team and will be able to fully activate pair-working.

So instead of one person for L&D administration and one for recruitment campaigns, the two will join forces and share the workload. Also working together to plan in welcome days, early learning activities for the essential skills and knowledge learning (on and offline) and setting up mentors and access to the social learning network.

In smaller organizations, this may mean pairing more with (for example) the recruitment manager or with others in the HR team. Whilst some people might think the entering of recruitment campaign information into the system is now a job they left behind for something 'more strategic', for others it would be a welcome break from their usual work and gives a stronger sense of what's going on with all the work across the HR team. In essence the paired working is intending to give stronger appreciation of all the aspects of the HR workflow and allow people to learn from each other as a natural part of that process.

There are regularized continuing improvement benefits to working in pairs. So a recruitment manager who DOES enter data into the system more regularly, may spot a design flaw in the user experience and commission the supplier to create a bespoke element that suits the organization better.

In summary, HRPPS is a lot more than a relabelled shared service centre. It is a mixture of essential functions that power the organization through its people, and essential administration and the support needed to manage the transformational HR programmes. When automation and chatbots come into play here (the HR AI – artificial intelligence evolution), a more adept and multi-skilled HR people and programme support professional will not only be engaged in that transformation programme, they will be better equipped to move to new and alternative areas of HR work. Far from being an admin centre waiting to be digitized, this zone is powering much of the transformational activity to come for HR and the organization.

HR People Strategy & Partnerships

Narrative

Something never really inspired me about the term 'HR business partner' (HRBP). Yes, I've used partnerships in this rebooted, reimagined version of a near-equivalent of this role, but being a 'partner' to the 'business' created more distance in my mind than it ever meant to. I even heard some people say 'but we're a part of this business, not a partner to it'.

Table 12.3   Description of HR People Strategy & Partnerships, the four-zone model

The philosophy	HRPSP exists to build relationships *with* people and intelligence *about* people.
The mission	HRPSP will work closely with people at all levels across the organization, developing a greater understanding of their work and needs. Through collaborative working and the gathering of intelligence on what matters to people, provide insight on how HR can make ever greater differences to personal fulfilment and collective success.
The vision	HRPSP will use their relationship strength and insight-led approaches to inform the most acutely tuned strategy for the betterment of people and the organization.

So the HR People Strategy & Partnerships (HRPSP) role is about strategy. And intelligence. It isn't the *only* place where the strategy itself is crafted but it is the place where the strategy 'rubber hits the road'. Meaning, this is where the intent of the people strategy is delivered through the relationships and the dialogue HR practitioners working in this zone will deliver, and where the strategy can be influenced and adapted through intelligence gathered from deployment, experience and creativity.

Many learning programmes, new initiatives and platforms are launched on the business and they fail to gain the traction they should. Many new legislative requirements are put into place and a confusing array of forms, responsibilities and protocols now have to be followed.

Much of the data, information and intelligence we seek to validate and shape HR propositions is lacking and difficult to extract from people across the organization.

This is where this (HRPSP) role becomes an intelligence conduit. Intelligence *shared and given* to the organization's people through advocacy, dialogue, forums and board meetings. Intelligence gathered *from* people through conversation, study, surveys and workshops.

And intelligence also means insight, useful information, new initiatives and why we have those initiatives, joining in with people and organization development programmes. Instead of just rolling out programmes, HR can involve a wider group of people more in the intelligence behind those programmes and gathering intelligence to shape those programmes. Building intelligence about the success of programmes and initiatives and gathering compelling data that proves the impact of HR work on organization and individual success and what's being learned at an organizational level.

So it's more than business partnering, order-taking and elbowing your way into strategic meeting rooms. It's being with, part of and trusted in business situations and building supercharged relationships full of belief, challenge and convergence on what's right and needed for the people.

It *isn't* getting deeply involved in casework or building recruitment campaigns. It's consulting with their internal client, gathering intelligence and then commissioning the right colleague from HRPPS Where each commissioned piece of work is treated as a specific project with a backlog of tasks, milestones, roles, an agreed outcome and managed in pairs with an experienced HR professional and a supportive HR colleague.

Again, in larger organizations, the HRPSP professionals will work in pairs. Even in the situation where one colleague looks after the entire North of the UK and another the South, they will work collaboratively at all times using technology to close any physical distance.

We've already seen the design of the HRBP model introduce more layers of management (with the introduction of a senior HRBP). Whilst this is no doubt well-intended development – to act as coordinating point and escalation point – it has added to unnecessary bureaucracy, reporting and somewhat added to the view that people in HR are busy being busy.

Working in pairs negates this need. Where escalation is needed there is the most senior representative in the HR function (HRD/CHRO) and yet between the two HRPSP professionals working together, there should be sufficient expertise and management of each other to negate the need for a more senior colleague simply to report to and direct their work.

Working across more HR disciplines (having a greater understanding of learning programmes; organizational design through internal HR pair working) gives this role deeper insight through not stopping at order-taking and requirement-passing that appears to be a feature of the HR Business Partner Model.

The HRBPs of now appear to get very involved in casework, disputes and mediation routines, making up recruitment panels and advising on maternity leave options. In the four-zone model, these are all delivered through the HRPPS zone. This removal of the HRBP features will allow the HRPSP professional to spend more time coaching with their clients, designing solutions with their HR colleagues and obtaining and using the intelligence they gather through a higher-plains view of their client's world.

HRBPs – in the current model and being supremely generic and not at all meaning to offend anyone – are involved in *too much* symptomatic work (lots of low level problem fixes) and not enough strategic work (looking at a *longer-tail* cause/effect to eradicate the cause of the low-level problems).

For example, getting involved in 10 grievances in one division is demanding work. Something's not right here but working out some mediated response to restore some harmony takes a lot of graft. Yet taking a more systems-led and zoomed-out view reveals that there is an inflexible and ambiguous approach being taken by a director which is being poorly implemented by line managers and causing friction with a particular group of people adversely affected by the inflexible directive (and amplified by its clumsy implementation).

So gather intelligence, review with the director, clarify the aspiration, engage people most impacted, create a compromised but clearly understood position, issue revised operating guidelines and bottom out the friction. However, if the Director has no strength of relationship with the HR professional and has little belief in their approach, they may dogmatically refuse to budge and 10 grievances becomes 20, and two go to an Employment Tribunal and three managers leave because of stress and sick absence becomes unmanageable and then the local newspaper headlines.

That is the sad and all too familiar tale of HRBPs caught in the vortex. We need to remove this trap, and building stronger relationships is our starting point. HRPSP professionals build relationships first; to gain belief and trust. Then use that strengthened relationship to gather and deliver intelligence, to better advise their business clients and inform and adapt the people strategy with their HR colleagues.

When at the top of their game, HRPSP professionals should be creating more but also less:

- There should be less disputes to refer to employment law specialists.

- There should be less sick absence losses to calculate.

- There should be less hamster-wheel recruitment campaigns due to high turnover.

- There should be less negative publicity to field, damaging the organization's reputation.

In summary HRPSP is more than a reworking of the HRBP role. It's a reinvention and a transformation to this role. It should never be the same again once given the right strategic and intelligence sourcing elements.

Relationships, autonomy, sense of value, variety, challenge – all stimulating elements of work – are present in this role. Which cannot be said so confidently about the (sometimes) poorly defined descriptors of what an HRBP actually IS. Bringing a sense of clarity and therefore professional pride and belonging to the reboot of this role will help transformational activities more likely to take hold and succeed.

So when people say 'what do you do in HR?' and you say 'I'm an HR business partner: working strategically with an area of the business' the response is often 'What does that even mean?'

In the transformed model of the future the answer may be 'I'm in HR and I bring our people strategy to life to create more meaning in the work people do'.

HR People Performance & Development

Narrative

Moving towards a distinct *connection* between development and performance, this zone brings the best in human and organizational sciences together with applied practice in professional and personal development. Rather than a centre of excellence, this is a dispersed force for good.

There are a group of specialists and a series of generalists that operate in this zone ranging from learning technologists and organization design consultants through to coaches, business analysts and master facilitators.

Understanding the flow of work and the application of human skill and adaptability is ever more critical in a *post-lean, part-automated* world of work.

Working in harmony with their HRPPS and HRPSP colleagues, this is a very delivery-focused team of activists and thinkers, designers and makers,

Table 12.4 Description of HR People Performance & Development, the four-zone model

The philosophy	HR People Performance & Development (HRPPD) exists to create the circumstances for people to do their best work.
The mission	HRPPD will work closely with people at all levels across the organization, understanding the best ways to help people do great work that is individually fulfilling and effective for the organization, whilst providing critical development pathways and sense of personal and professional growth.
The vision	HRPPD bring science, art and energy to the continuing advancement of people's skills, behaviours and their applied endeavours at work.

innovators and energizers. In Nathan Ott's GC Index® terms, we have *implementers, playmakers* and *polishers* building high quality conversations, interventions and programmes creating the *learner experience* organizations truly need to power them into the future.

With their HRPSP colleagues gathering intelligence and insight, design becomes a pair-working situation to design and then deliver high impact activities to show the value HR is adding through intelligent, advanced application of people and work methodologies. The HR People Performance & Development (HRPPD) teams then work with their HRPSP colleagues to gather intelligence on the impact of their work and use this insight to help iterate on further design as well as report to the most senior levels about the successes and learning from their work. Talent, leadership and reward are all driven by more insight and applied sciences with experimental and scenario modelling methods, will help HR overcome the challenge of expensive and extensive programmes of learning and behavioural shift with questionable results and impact.

One example to bring to mind here is we have rarely seen people who constantly help other colleagues develop given reward specifically for that. Yet we see people with sales target successes who are self-centred, obstructive to colleagues and difficult to be around, achieve bonuses based on the achievement of sales targets. We have a miscalibrated reward system and this zone should address this in conjunction with their HR teams and business colleagues. We also need more sophisticated performance measuring systems that take into account the value that is created specifically through developed people and not just through sales, calls taken, lack of complaints and the usual surface level indicators. Customer loyalty, strength of supplier relationships, efficiency, innovation, supporting colleagues, external reputation, community partnerships and more.

We need more meaningful reward systems and identification of the value created by the likes of our good corporate citizens rather than the boom and bust approaches that deliver faux successes via those people now labelled as 'high performance jerks'.

In summary, HRPPD has similarities to the existing centre of excellence aspect and is also more than an OD/L&D leg of HR. It's a deeper focus and more hard-edged approach to developing people linked more explicitly to the elements of business outcomes and organizational success.

The people in this zone will rely on partnership working with their HR colleagues to deliver business intelligence and need and then work in partnership with them and with others in their zone to be expert analysts designers, builders and facilitators. Conversations and dialogue are their key tools supported by the sciences and models of people and organizational life fit for the 21st century.

No longer restricted to saying 'a trainer' in response to people's obvious question of 'What do you do?', The HR performance and development professional is now a designer *and* engineer: of energized and fulfilling performance enhancement in people.

HR People & Organization Transformation

Narrative

This is the additional element lacking in most HR models – a permanent transformative force. Except in this model this section of the model *isn't permanent*. It is transitional, it's flexible, it is the opposite of permanent. It is *not* a team or a leaders it is a space. It's *special ops* – mobilized when needed.

Transformational activities may be the priority at a given time for an organization, and this is when this zone becomes activated. Filled with people from parts of the HR model *and* their colleagues from other parts of the organization. And then, when the major transformational activities are embedded, the team disassembles until some reformation (normally with other people) for the next transformational programme or project.

It is an important distinction to the normal model for HR – where the three elements are operating both business as usual *and* transformational activities.

Table 12.5 Description of HR People & Organization Transformation, the four-zone model

The philosophy	HR People & Organization Transformation (HRPOT) is a space to create the future for people and the work they do.
The mission	HRPOT work through a series of projects that create fundamental shifts in the nature of work processes and structures, whilst building supporting and enabling activities that help people through business transformation.
The vision	HRPOT is the go-to place for innovative thinking and doing that designs systems and processes to transform ways of working for future organizational and individual success.

This isn't some attempt to over staff HR: it's to differentiate from hugely powerful, much-needed transformation and day-to-day activities. To create more agility, fluidity and focus to transformational activities and bring the likelihood of success with such critical factors with much needed creativity and energy.

Using the agile project management methodology as its signature of operating, it will require an upskilling for many in HR and brings the best features of business change, digital development and product management theories and practices into the mix for HR to give a much needed 21st-century upgrade to HR.

Agile 101 for transformational HR

In this scenario, we take a fictitious scenario for a medium sized engineering company. They are moving from car parts to making motors for drones. A programme of transformation is scoped and developed by the Executive Board and it is clear that this requires a transformation programme – vital to create a new shape to the organization, to create the new set of products and services for a new customer base.

A team of product designers, business analysts and systems architects are working on the business venture and with there being significant people implications, the HR director is given the people and organization design transformation mandate.

The major aspect of this is to form a small team – or scrum – from the other three zones of the HR team, to scope the nature of the impact of the transformation and produce what is known in agile as the 'backlog' – a series of tasks to do as a first wave of anticipated activity.

First though, is the story. The transformation programme is envisioned as a story – what will the programme do and how will it affect people. From this, a series of impacts are assessed and tasks created to manage those impacts.

A series of deliverables are created – deliverables are products for example:

- paper to the management board on salary implications;
- a presentation the motors team on what the new venture will need from existing skills and resources; and
- a review of the recruitment protocols to attract engineers who are experienced in creating micro-motors.

There will be one or more backlogs of tasks that are needed to produce the papers – to manage the review of the recruitment processes and the creation and delivery of the presentation to the motors team. Once the team have identified as much of the tasks backlogs as they can, and have their story, they set out a series of *sprints* – time-bound stages of design and build activity to move through the process of development. Normally sprints are around one week or up to four weeks depending on complexity and prioritization. In the midst of sprints are sprint meetings: active tests of functions and products with (in this case) the new ventures programme lead and the HR director.

Each backlog is recorded by the lead from HRPPS, a project governance board set up in the office space shared by the HR People and Organization Transformation (HRPOT) scrum and work begins. The HRSP lead on the scrum team is sent off to share the nature of what the work is to update people and gather intelligence and input to test and assure products and deliverables that come from the HRPOT scrum team. Knowing the tasks and the nature of skills needed to complete this task means some additional support is needed.

The HRPPS lead acts as scrum master coordinating efforts and securing the additional resources. They are also responsible for bringing together a communications plan and drafting communication updates to go out to all people across the company. It is then agreed to bolster the team with a colleague who is a business analyst, on loan from the new ventures team, a specialist engineer on secondment to HR and an external consultant in HR but with a technology company background. HRPPS secure this resource and the timetable is set based on their joining HRPOT.

It is an important part of an agile approach that people allocate themselves towards activities in the backlog and apportion a duration to the activity. This allows for the creation of what is called the 'burndown chart' (a three way plan of hours, tasks and timetable). In the methodology I'm advocating for our future-state HR team, we are also working in pairs to achieve focus, creativity and accountability without overbearing management overheads. People are paired up and the work begins on deliverables from the task backlog.

Once the sprint planning is done, a *daily sprint* meeting keeps a track on progress of the activities on the backlog. The scrum master from HRPPS may be using a project management application to track progress and allocation on top of this dialogue. During the sprints the team can react to any shifts in the requirement and need, so this has the advantage of being focused but not totally fixed. Sprints are adapted and burndown charts adjusted. The sprints continue until all the backlog is clear and the products and deliverables are built and tested as fit for purpose.

Figure 12.2   Generic agile approach to transformational project work

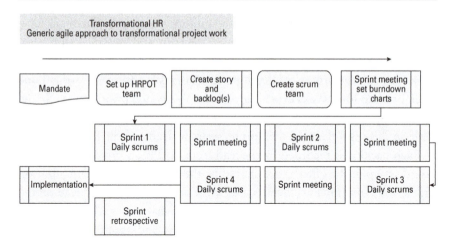

Eventually when the programme is fully delivered, there will be a retrospective scrum to see what can be learned for future projects and the team is then disbanded. Figure 12.2 summarizes the agile approach.

Conclusion

HR People & Organization Transformation is the major change to this model and is a fluid, non-static element of this model aimed at episodic and flexible approaches to delivering on peak transformational activities. It is anticipated that whilst not staffed permanently, the rate of change in the world of work means there is likely to be some activity in this zone at any given time but there may be times of no transformation in favour of some operational consolidation.

There are undoubtedly many questions racing through your mind about the nature of this zone and how easy it could be to not devote time, focus and people to this in favour of immediate short-term demands. Yet there are likely to be peak periods of transformation where the people involved in this work are likely to benefit from an increased intensity to this work and the removal of interference by other work and day-to-day tasks.

Of course in some sized companies or smaller scale transformation programmes, there may not be a total immersion in this zone for weeks or months at a time, it may be that for three days per week someone is working on transformation programme and the other two they are working as a reward specialist or facilitating a learning programme. The important element to this would be that they are still 'allocated' to transformation specifically for some of their time. Whether this is a physical shift to a different part of the office space or simply that they work with others for three out of the five days, there will be a specific set of circumstances that denote working on transformation programmes.

Transformation focus is the important feature of this remodelling of HR. How you do it will depend on your circumstances but making a deliberate show of marking this work out from other normalized activities is intended to create a helpful distinction for people and the nature of the work.

It is only a part of transformational HR as we've seen throughout this chapter but nonetheless it symbolizes strongly that this is a different HR model, and will never be the same as it was before there it has transformed itself.

Much of the influence for this shift comes from the digital technology world. Where we have seen a huge transformation from waterfall, trickle-down projects which seem to eat resources and take a long time to produce (and even then, failed to deliver projects that were fully operational) to the faster, more nimble iterative approaches with agile built from more energizing approaches to product and project development and delivery.

So I'm not advocating that HR becomes a digital force, but that HR learns from another industry and adopts a digital technological methodology to the world of people at work.

The end but a new beginning

Congratulations for getting this far. You and this book have covered a lot of ground. We have looked at:

- Chapter 1: The world around us and the changes we're seeing in all realms of life on the planet;

- Chapter 2: A brief look at a personal journey of working lives through the recent ages;

- Chapter 3: A look at how the HR profession has arrived to this point in time;

- Chapter 4: A reminder of what we have in the HR profession and where we can build from;

- Chapter 5: Defining transformational HR – what do we mean by it? How can we be transformational?;

- Chapter 6: Models that give us shape, clarity and dialogue for past, present and future of work;
- Chapter 7: A model specific to HR – the Ulrich model and how it can be transformed;
- Chapter 8: Tales of transformation – narratives from people working and aspiring to transform;
- Chapter 9: Stories of the future – examples of organizations who have and are transforming work;
- Chapter 10: Our playbook – for how HR might transform itself to create a better future of work;
- Chapter 11: Strategic HR – strategic-level shifts to have a transformative effect;
- Chapter 12: Transformational HR – a new model at play.

The intent of this book is to time travel somewhat, dream a little, realize a lot but mostly to spark. Spark HR and people professionals into a desire to transform. Yes change if you like, but it feels like transformation is a better word to look back or down less and look ahead and up more.

So if you're tired of working in, and with, HR and being frustrated by a lack of transformative impact, then I hope this book has fuelled your desires, equipped your strategies and sparked your imagination into overdrive.

HR and all of us need you. We need you to think, be and do transformational things. If you think that you're just one person and there's a grand schema to impact upon then you're right. And so are tens of thousands of others. If somehow, we can bring the energy, artistry and graft of those tens of thousands of people we might just make the differences we all believe we need and deserve.

So if you're a little let down that I have only covered 'knowledge workers' and I haven't covered an example of a company where people are working on manual stuff with their hands, and are being transformational, then please tell me and the world about it when you find one. Or if you set one up.

You don't have to be a hero to create a noble company, work well with others and do good for a lot of people – to create that story of good and just and fair. You might need an act of heroism to tell the world about it. Because many people will say it's naive, soft or ideological. And they do so out of fear. Because they're frightened you might be onto something. That HR isn't going to always be the one to criticize. *They* might be in for some criticism.

Bravery, guile, commitment. We all need to show up a little more to *be* transformative and yet if we're not, then we have to accept that what we have is what we deserve. We are born into situations with gifts – our spirit and our imagination – and what we do with them will help us determine what we get out of life – be that our working lives, or our life's work.

We need each other – of course – to transform. Solo transformation at scale is a tough task and reserved for the likes of William Shakespeare, Mahatma Gandhi, Nelson Mandela, Marie Curie and Dr Martin Luther King Junior. Individual acts of transformation are powerful when linked to others and a movement created. A movement to transform. Am I advocating a movement to transform HR and therefore work? I am. I am also sensing the the conditions are prevailing that is not simply a desired state of mind, but a necessity. Whilst the world is transforming around us, we can use this to catalyse ourselves to transform HR, work and what people do that defines their craft and way of earning a living.

Hopes

In closing I suppose I have hopes to leave you with. Hopes that as a reader connected to HR, you have enjoyed the story of HR *to now,* and want to be part of the HR *to be.* Whether you're in total concordance with the ways I've described the future possibilities or only some of them. I'd love to feel you're joining me in that movement. Hopes that if you don't agree that at least this has sparked something in you to create your version of this. I'd prefer it that, rather than argue against my propositions and view of the world, you simply go and create your own and prove it is better than my account of things. Healthy discourse and challenge are fine and I'm not professing to have carte blanche on the future of HR and the world of work. Go for it I'd say, with pleasure. Use your energy to do something with purpose is always a good use of energy. Hopes that if you're not necessarily close to HR, yet have been previously activated by any of the things covered in this book, you are even more so and want to do your thing with added energy, insight and application. It might even want you to get closer to HR and help us out a little more. We need it and would welcome it I'm sure. Hope that this does something for the world.

I suppose whenever you write a book it's a little bit of you that you're giving the world the chance to see and experience. I suspect every author wants that 'tipping point' of change to happen with their book. That though, dear readers, HR professionals, change agents, entrepreneurs, leaders, artists, academics and people at work, is down to you.

Closing words 13

Just as we started, we close – the world of work in a state of flux. In producing a closing to this book , it will not be *just* a reflective end to things – more a bridge to where it all gets going.

I've deliberately invited you, as readers to look at individual, self-transformation alongside those of transformation at a collective level – be that in the team, partnership, community or cohort environments you work in. And of course alongside that of the strategic, macro, professional level in need of transformation.

We are in a world where, in what appears to be a short period of time, things we believed in have been upturned and are being repealed. So transformation is happening, but it is my assertion that this sort of transformation is sometimes happening with a backwards glance and perspective. *The butterfly does not de-metamorphosize back into a chrysalis.*

The transformation we need at work and for HR – that we may be aspiring to – could be a reboot of traditional elements we have lost through previous changes. It will also be a transformed, newer and more relevant version of a new way. So no backwards glance but a forward looking, upgraded version of a vision for work we need as our sanctuary of meaning, belonging and esteem. Re-discovery not de-discovery.

So we keep looking around us – for the asymmetries of the future helping us sense and explore our way to a new dawn – and looking within us. Within us to genuinely find what we need. What is it about our need that we need work to service? As author Greg McKeown found, essentialism is what we should seek not even existentialism (McKeown, 2014).

I have found some essentialism in my work with Traci Fenton and WorldBlu. Not just another company but a philosophy of freedom at work, of democratic principles in the workplace and of inclusion, fairness, belief, dignity and most of all humanity. There are lots of others doing great things but that three of my case studies here are WorldBlu certified companies is no fluke. I am astounded by the stories that come from WorldBlu companies and by what Traci and the small team have created. The most big-hearted, successful and humane companies I've had the pleasure of working with. Traci's vision – and the almost super-human nature of the people who operate in WorldBlu certified companies – gives me hope and inspiration that the better way for work has already been codified. In looking ahead, I hope the next five years sees WorldBlu's philosophy become a more powerful thing for HR, leaders and people at work to know about and aspire to.

In looking forward (a rather flipped way of writing closing words) we also need to find out what needs of *ours* we are servicing through the lens of transforming our work. If we find that need and transform our work as a result of it, we can help the HR profession transform. Given the role that HR has – of looking out for the people of the workplace – that could be a noble cause.

Human resources may not be a phrase we like, but let's lift ourselves above workplace definitions and transform the professional field in spite of any clumsiness of naming conventions. We are human. We are resourceful. We acquire and utilize resources of all descriptions.

Let's do all we can together to bring about that HR metamorphosis for a transforming world of work.

For in our grasp lies better work, for us all. For our world. For our future.

Reference

McKeown, G (2014) *Essentialism: the disciplined pursuit of less*, Random House Publishing, London.

INDEX

Note: Page locators in *italics* refer to figures or tables.